# RIDING

# GOD'S

# RAINBOW

by Kim Spranger

*This book is dedicated to families everywhere:*

*Never let a day go by without appreciating each other and the story you are writing together.*

*A special thank you:*

*... to God, for deeming us worthy of such a life story!*

> *... to my husband, Todd, for being my kindred spirit and the wind beneath my wings:*

>> *... to my children, for teaching me so much and making my life so abundant;*

>>> *... and to all the people who were God's hands and feet to help us through this storm. We are forever grateful!*

CREDITS:
Cover art by Lauren Spranger
Interior background image by Mathias P.R. Reding (Pexels)

# Introduction

*I am giving you a sign of my covenant with you and with all living creatures, for all generations to come. I have placed my rainbow in the clouds.*

*Genesis 9:13.*

I sat staring out the hospital window overlooking Lake Superior; this vast body of water that seemed to go on forever. It had started as a beautiful day but now a storm was rolling in. I watched the dark clouds quickly overtake the horizon. As I watched, the Spirit whispered to me:

Do you see that sky, it is like your life right now. ...blue with puffy clouds until the storm of cancer rolled in. As I pondered the analogy the Spirit said "Do you want to know how to get through this storm and beat this cancer?" Before I could even answer, a beautiful rainbow emerged from the clouds and the Spirit said "You get on my rainbow and you ride it!"

This is the story of our journey through a family's crisis and Noah's story. It is a collection of my journal entries seeking to understand the covenant God made with Noah and what it means to ride God's rainbow. I wrote this book as a reminder of all the ways that I saw God work during that season of my life; may I never forget what I experienced. I also wrote it to encourage others in the midst of a storm, to trust God and listen closely for His voice. Finally, I wrote it for unbelievers that need evidence that God is present today. Our story, I pray, will help them see God through the eyes of faith.

To all whose hands this book may fall into, allow it to speak to you as God intends. Be open to the way God did and can work; and let the story inspire you to "Ride God's Rainbow".

# Table of Contents

# Chapter One:

# *Faith, Our Foundation*

*Therefore everyone who comes to me, who learns these teachings*
*of mine and obeys them; I will show you what he is like: He is like*
*a prudent man building his house, who dug and went down deep,*
*and laid a foundation on the rock; and the rain descended and the*
*floods came and the winds blew, and they lashed against the house*
*but could not shake it. It did not fall for it was founded on the rock."*

*Matthew 7:24-27 and Luke 6:47-49*

Before our "storm" hit, we were a somewhat typical American family: two preschool kids, a mortgage on our little home in the woods outside of town, two incomes and a church we regularly attended. We were simple people, very content raising our family and enjoying an active outdoor life in a northern climate. We had spiritual roots that were planted in good soil. My husband, Todd and I had both accepted Jesus Christ as our Savior and we strived to build a foundation of faith within our home.

This foundation sustained us, gave us hope, and directed our actions and decisions once the storm enveloped us. We experienced our spiritual roots growing deeper as we went through each aspect of the storm.

♥

My walk with God and my tests of faith began when I was young. My father was diagnosed with leukemia when I was four years old. He was a devout Christian, and it was very important to him that all of his children knew about God. My mother was not brought up in the same religion as he was, but, she agreed with the basic premise of his religion and hence allowed her children to be raised in it. It was her efforts which got all six of us to religion class every week.

Looking back, my spiritual upbringing taught me about God and how to formally interact with Him through memorized prayer. It failed, however to teach me that God wanted to have a personal relationship with ME through his son Jesus Christ; and that my primary goal in life should be to pursue that relationship. It also failed to teach me how to rely on God and trust Him when trials arise.

When I was twelve, my father lost his battle with Leukemia. He left a wife and six kids under the age of nineteen. He died at home with all of us at his bedside. I recall how he opened his eyes and stared in amazement as he took his last breath. Watching him die convinced me that there was a heaven and that my dad was there. However, his passing brought many questions about God and His mercy. God had not answered our prayers and healed my dad. I wondered if God would take care of us now that my dad was gone.

Over the next five years, my understanding of God changed dramatically. My mom started taking us to a neighborhood nondenominational Christian Church. God was alive in that place!!!! I got involved with the high school youth group called "The Enthusiastics". I learned through this group that Jesus wanted to have a personal relationship with me and that I needed to make Him a priority in my life. I had to seek Him in order to find Him.

The summer I turned seventeen, I accepted Jesus as my personal Savior at a youth retreat. When I left the retreat I was on fire for God and this new relationship with Jesus, however, once I returned to my "world", it quickly began to smolder. I would think about my faith, but I did not act on it. I didn't really want to make God a priority in my life at that point, and I just wanted to be a normal teenager.

God knew my feelings but He also knew the future and that soon I would need to rely on and trust Him more than ever before. Six months later, my fifteen-year-old brother, John, was diagnosed with Lymphoma. John's doctors were pretty optimistic. He would only need chemotherapy which he should tolerate it easily and there was an 85% chance that would cure him. In reality John suffered significantly through the chemotherapy and relapsed almost immediately after he finished. Our entire family struggled watching him endure this.

I thought that God would answer my prayers this time. But, retrospectively, my prayers were like a wish list and not a real trust in God. I didn't listen for God's still silent voice or accept His will; I just told Him what I wanted. I was an immature teenager, and I was angry. I was angry with cancer. It had dominated my childhood, and now it was stealing away my life as a high school senior and stealing away my brother... my best friend... my running partner.

God's love and compassion carried our entire family through that trial. He kept our general attitude positive and hopeful. He held our family together, especially my mom, through some very difficult days. But our prayers for healing were not answered. John died nine months after his diagnosis; one week after I began my freshmen year in college.

Before he died, John asked for private time with each of his siblings. As I sat at his bedside, he shared with me how the Spirit had inspired him the previous week as he lay in a coma. He said "Kim, keep believing in the Lord... don't be angry and don't feel sorry for me. God has a big assignment for me. He's taking me so young because He has something really important for me to do."

John's words and his example of faith and trust in God's will permanently impacted my perspective and focus. It prepared me for days ahead.

♥

Todd and I met my first day of college. I was there early for a sports camp and couldn't get into the locked field house. Todd had just finished up football practice and he politely let me in the door as he was leaving. Ironically, that was the only time that John was ever at Coe College, a small liberal arts private college in Iowa. He was waiting in the car with my mom and didn't get to meet or see Todd. Who would have ever thought that this polite young man who opened the door for me was my future mate and best friend for life and that he had this one chance to meet my brother, my current best friend. Unfortunately, that meeting never took place, and John died two weeks later.

Todd and I started to date in January of my freshman year. On our first date, he took me to the movie *Terms of Endearment*. Neither of us knew what it was about before we walked into the theater. I sobbed as I watched the young mother die of breast cancer and relived all the emotional hardships this places on a family. Todd was right there handing me Kleenexes. He had no idea about my family's experience with cancer or the recent death of my brother. As we ate pizza after the movie, I filled Todd in on why the movie had such an impact on me. At first I'm sure he thought "great first date this was", but actually it created a bond between us that has never been broken. Our relationship has never been based on the guarantee of an easy life, but rather on experiencing all of life together.

Over the next six years, we did just that, EXPERIENCED LIFE! We both had a love for the outdoors and tasting all that life had to offer. We finished school, got married, moved to the Upper Peninsula of Michigan and started a family. We spent our spare time camping, canoeing, kayaking, mountain biking and hiking. God showered us with many blessings: a great marriage, happy healthy children, good jobs and a great place to live. We both knew that our life was too easy, too perfect and had intuition separately that a trial was coming.

The foundation of our relationship was not our faith. It was good communication, flexibility, mutual respect, and true love for one another. There was never any doubt in my mind that God intended us to be together; but God wasn't our common thread. I knew He needed and wanted to be. My Grandma Pearl wrote me a letter before our wedding. In it she said:

*"Kimmie, don't ever forget a good marriage is like a tight braid. The strands that make up this braid must be you, Todd and God. If these strands are woven together very tightly, the braid will be very flexible yet strong and durable."*

In our first years of marriage, my faith was actually a point of contention between us. I wanted Todd to be as interested in his faith and being involved with a church as I was. I tried to push Todd into it and instead I actually pushed him away. I should have known God had a plan. I should have prayed instead of pushed; and waited patiently for God's timing. That day did come as Todd watched our daughter Lauren come into this world. Seeing the miracle of new life opened his spiritual eyes and in the months that followed he started to read the bible and seek a relationship with Jesus.

As Lauren grew and Tucker was born, Todd and I began to share with one another our personal beliefs about God and Jesus as we decided what we wanted to teach our children. Once the kids began to talk, they began to teach us as much about faith and God as we taught them. Their simple, humble perspective on life helped us to see God's kingdom more clearly.

A great example of this occurred on Mother's Day when Tucker was three. I was cuddling him before bedtime. Suddenly he looked up at me and said: "Mom, do you believe in God?" I assured him that I did. He then replied, "Mom, do you know if you don't believe in God, you just shrivel up and die!" I thought about that for a moment and then agreed. Tucker then added, "Mom, I love you so much I'm going to die when you die."

♥

The week that our storm hit, God blessed us with two reminders of His love and faithfulness. The first reminder came at church Sunday morning.

Todd had become an Elder at the church and was sitting one row ahead of us because he was helping with the service. While the kids were up front at the children's sermon I started doodling. I wrote on a large, yellow sticky note: "GOD LOVES YOU, TUCKER" in big, bold, colorful letters. When Tucker returned to our seat, he noticed the sign right away and asked if he could have it. I gave it to him, and he proceeded to play with it all through the sermon. After Todd finished serving communion and sat down, Tucker stuck the sign on Todd's back. I thought it was cute and didn't think that Todd had to get up again, so I left it on. Suddenly, our minister asked all the Elders to come up front. I tried to grab the sign as Todd walked past, but I missed. So Todd stood in front of the entire congregation with that sign on. It was very obvious because the Elders had their backs to us. Everyone giggled and patted Todd on the back, but no one removed the sign! It was only after church that Todd found out about it. He removed it from his back and hung it on the dash of our car, something he has never done before. That faded tattered sign hung there for the next year as a constant reminder of God's Love for our little boy.

God's second reminder was a birthday present. My birthday was that week and Todd wanted to find me a book. The kids went birthday shopping with him at the Christian bookstore. He didn't have any particular title or author in mind; he hoped something would jump off the shelf at him. Shopping for an adult book with two preschoolers proved to be challenging, so after ten to fifteen minutes, Todd settled on a book on history of women in the church. He was walking to the checkout when another book caught his eye. The author was Anne Graham Lotz. Todd knew that I had just finished the book *Living beyond the Limits* by Franklin Graham. I had commented after reading about Anne in Franklin's book, "What a neat Christian she must to be." Todd stopped and looked at Anne's book, *God's Story*. It was about God's message to us in the Book of Genesis. Todd wasn't sure why but felted nudged to get me Anne's book. The nudge definitely was a godsend. In the introduction Anne stated that not only is God sovereign and has a plan to make something good out of all evil but He also wants to use our trials for His glory. She pointed us to Noah's story and the first ever rainbow as an example of this.

# Chapter Two:

# *The Storm*

*All the foundations of the great deep were broken up, and the windows of heaven were opened, and the rain was on the earth forty days and forty nights.*

*Genesis 7: 11-12*

Our storm began abruptly on June 10, 1999. The warning sign was a simple stomachache. For a month prior to this one, Tucker had been waking up occasionally at night complaining that he was hungry or had a stomachache. Initially Todd and I thought it was because he was a picky eater. We started to offer him more food throughout the day. Despite our efforts, the stomachaches continued.

I started to get concerned and called our family doctor. He suggested that we try adding more fiber to his diet. We were in the process of seeing if this helped when Tucker had two really bad stomachaches in one day; one during his nap and the other during the night. I sat up with him all through the night rubbing his tummy. I called the emergency room at two am to rule out appendicitis. The nurse said his symptoms really weren't consistent with appendicitis, but that I could bring him in if I was that concerned about it. After I hung up the phone, Tucker looked at me and said: "Mom, I think I need to go to the doctor!" I took his little hand to comfort him, and I noticed that his hand was quite warm. Suddenly I started to get anxious... night pain and a fever... I knew from my medical training that these are both signs of cancer. As I took his temperature I tried to stay calm, but my mind rushed back to the storms of my past. I remembered my mom telling me that she always knew that John was sick because his hands were always so warm. The beep of the thermometer startled me back to the present. Tucker's temperature was 100.1.

The rest of the night was agonizing. I kept telling myself that I was over-reacting, but deep down I knew. I had thought about this possibility long before I had ever conceived Tucker. I was afraid of having a boy. The cancer in my family has all been in the male gender and my sisters have all female children, eight girls' total. After Tucker was born, I tried to bury this fear; but that night it resurfaced and haunted me like never before. I laid there in the darkness caressing Tucker's head. I tried to extinguish those horrible thoughts and prayed I was wrong.

The next morning, Tucker woke up feeling fine, but I was adamant the he was going to see a doctor that day. After getting a morning appointment, we all went into town. As we pulled out of the driveway, Todd looked at me and said: "Gosh, Kim you look worried, what do you think it is?" I hesitated and then answered "You know what I think it is..." Todd did know. He knew I had always been concerned about cancer in our children. It was a very quiet thir-ty-minute ride into the medical center.

As I had hoped, Dr. Skenzel listened to and acted on my concerns even though Tucker's physical exam was normal. He ordered blood work and an abdominal x-ray. We went to radiology immediately, and had the x-ray in hand ready for Dr. Skenzel by noon.

Dr. Skenzel's face as he walked back in the room after reading the x-ray told it all. With a stunned look he said: "Kim, you were right, there is some-thing there." As he showed us the shadow over Tucker's liver on the x-ray I felt my world crashing down on me! I couldn't comprehend what Dr. Skendzel was saying; all I could hear was my soul crying, "I don't want to be right! I want it to be something else! I know cancer; I have lost to it two times before! I can't beat this, not CANCER!!!"

Dr. Skenzel interrupted my thoughts when he started to tell us about what we needed to do next. He sent us over to the hospital to get a CT scan done immediately. That test would more clearly define what the shadow was.

Todd and I both tried to hold it together as we made the short drive to the hospital. We parked in the ramp. Todd turned off the car, and we all just sat there. I managed to break the silence and ask if someone could say a prayer before we went in. Neither Todd nor I were able to vocalize anything. Tucker's beautiful crystal voice announced from the back seat that he would say it. He proceeded to say the Lord's Prayer with more passion and feeling than I had ever heard before. He ended it with a boisterous, resonating "For THINE is the KINGDOM and the POWER and the GLORY FOREVER! AMEN."

As I listened, a peace came over me. God was already coming to our rescue...through whom? Through our child! That is God's way. I hid the moment in my heart.

Once Tucker was admitted, things happened very fast. The CT was done by three o'clock, and the physicians were back at our room by four o'clock to discuss the results.

The CT showed that Tucker had a large abdominal mass, which appeared to originate on his right kidney. They said a specialist from Michigan State University (MSU) had looked at it and thought it was either a Wilm's tumor or Neuroblastoma. In either case, it was not something they could treat in Marquette. They recommended that we go to Sparrow Hospital in Lansing Michigan for work-up and treatment.

We both were at a loss; we had no family or friends within six hours of Lansing. We asked about the possibility of going to Madison or the Mayo Clinic where would have some local support. Our physicians were open to sending us to these other facilities. However, they explained the relationship they already had with MSU for treatment of this sort of patient. We decided that we would follow their recommendation. Retrospectively, it was the right decision.

Before the physicians left the room; I muttered, "Is there any hope?" Dr.Bohnsak answered "There is always hope." Although his answer did not make me feel better at the time, I now know the truth in his words. No matter what the medical world quotes as survival rates, with God, the chance of healing is one hundred percent, if it is His will. Time or space does not bind God. He says He is a healing God, and He can heal if it is His will.

Once the room cleared out and we were left alone, Todd and I held each other as we stared out the window. We both knew our lives would never be the same. We were in shock from the events of the day, and completely consumed by the fear of what tomorrow would bring. The kids, on the other hand, were oblivious to anything that had happened all day. They sat on the bed playing with the controls that made it move and giggled. They were living for the day and not worrying about tomorrow. They were living how God tells us to live: trusting Him and finding joy in the moment.

As I stood there in Todd's arms watching the kids, I contemplated the irony of the day. Weeks before I had signed up to participate in "The Relay for Life", a fundraiser for the American Cancer Society. I had signed up to run my leg at four o'clock. So at the very moment I thought I would be running to raise money for cancer research and pay tribute to those who had fought the battle of cancer, I was instead starting a new race against it.

Later, Todd and I discussed the timing of everything that day; it was so perfect. The specialist Dr. Gehra from MSU who read Tucker's CT and diagnosed his disease was in Marquette that day only for a pediatric oncology clinic. That clinic is held once every two months. She looked at Tucker's CT and gave her impression at four o'clock after the clinic was finished. Her plane left for Lansing at five o'clock. Had Dr. Skendzel delayed things until Monday or the CT scanner not been available that afternoon, our experience might have been very different. Retrospectively, God was very gentle with us that day. We did not have to wait agonizing weeks to determine what was wrong with Tucker. We did not have to put up with the deaf ear of a physician or missed diagnosis. We found out in three hours the cruel reality of the trial we now faced.

♥

We were discharged from the hospital by that evening with a follow-up appointment on Sunday at Sparrow Hospital in Lansing. Once home, we tried to keep the mood light as we ate dinner and talked about how we were going to celebrate my birthday the next day. Todd and I both did a pretty good job masking our devastation from the kids. It was only after they were in bed and we had to call our families that we became overwhelmed.

It was especially hard for me to call my mom. She has gone through this battle so many times already: her dad, her husband, her son, and now her only grandson. I wanted to protect her from reliving this horror. She tried to be positive and strong, but I could tell that I was breaking her heart with my news.

Todd's family, on the other hand, had never known this disease. They had so many questions that Todd had no answer for. He had to keep saying, "We just don't know yet." When we hung up the phone for the last time, we were both emotionally and physically exhausted

We went to bed well after midnight, but neither of us slept. We would drift off for a few minutes, just long enough to wake up and hope that this was all a nightmare that would be over in the morning. My feelings were of sadness and guilt. I loved my life and family so much, I didn't want life to change. I recalled talking with Todd only months before about how perfect our life together was. Both of us knew that someday we would have a trial. But this... why God, why this??? What part of Your big plan is this and why?? The guilt was devouring me!! I knew Tucker had inherited the susceptibility for cancer from me. I had brought this terrible curse to my family!!! After my dad and grandpa had died and times were tough, I had wondered what life would have been like if I had been born into a family who wasn't plagued by cancer? Now my kids would also wonder that. Because of me, my husband and kids would suffer through this hellish trial. It was almost more than I could bear as I lay there in the dark wondering what the future held for us. I prayed for peace and strength until dawn.

Saturday, my birthday, was a gift from God. I can honestly say that I will never forget that day; our last day at home before everything changed. Every moment was cherished and frozen in time like a dream. Both kids were in extraordinary moods. We had our traditional waffle breakfast complete with wild blueberries that we had picked from our woods. All morning we played our favorite games: "jumping monkeys", marbles, and "Don't Tip the Waiter". Right before lunch we all went hiking through our woods; exploring under rocks, listening to the birds, enjoying the warm sun.

After lunch, we went to town to pick up Tucker's charts from the hospital and for the kids to do some last-minute birthday shopping. On our drive in, Todd and I both felt the nudge to share our news with Marc and Lynn Vanwelsenears. Lynn was Todd's boss and hence she would take care of things at his office, but more importantly they were good friends and devoted Christians that we knew would be there to support us. We acted on the nudge and stopped at their home when we first arrived in town. Marc and Lynn were both home. In fact, they had a whole house full of family because their second child, Alexandra, had been born earlier that week. After they recovered from the initial shock of the news, they immediately looked for ways that they could help. Marc's family visiting from the Lansing volunteered to escort us down to Sparrow Hospital the next day. Over the next two weeks, they adopted us and made our initial stay away from home so much easier. We will be forever grateful for their generosity and hospitality.

Our decision to stop at Lynn and Marc's house, I think, was very significant. This was the first door that God opened to help us where we had to choose whether or not we wanted to go through it. We both could have disregarded the nudge we felt to stop, especially after we saw that all of Marc's family was there, but something told us to stop. I believe that it was God working through the Holy Spirit that lives within each of us.

After we left Marc and Lynn's, we went to the department store so the kids could do their birthday shopping. Tucker marched right in and picked out my present as if he had been thinking about it for days. It was a watch. Todd and Lauren tried to talk him out of it. I already had a nice sports watch. Tucker was insistent, "This is the watch for my mom!" and he bought it. Lauren picked out a birthstone pinkie ring.

When we returned home in the late afternoon, we took a couple of hours to prepare our home for an anticipated lengthy time away. As I worked in the yard and watched our children play, I appreciated who they really were. I loved the boy in Tucker: how he was so brave that he would pick up a grass snake with his bare hands. I loved the girl in Lauren: being so caring about life that she would pick the buttercups in the yard before we mowed them over.

That night they gave me their gifts, each was so appropriate for the moment. Todd's gift: the book *God's Story*. My mom's gift: a cross pendent with a pearl in the center, signifying my Savior and my grandmother, Pearl. Lauren's gift: a friendship ring symbolizing my birth. Most importantly, Tucker's gift: the gift of time, the one thing he may not be able to give me.

We ended our day with a slumber party in the living room around the fireplace. We all shared our favorite thing about the day before we fell asleep. I remember drifting off snuggled up with Tucker, watching the light from the fire flicker across his beautiful face.

♥

Sunday morning we packed our bags and prepared ourselves to start this trial. Todd and I both needed some private time with God before we left. Running down our dirt road with the woods close around us, being in touch with His creation; we each heard God that morning. The lack of human noise made God's quiet voice so easy to hear. When I asked "Why", God answered, "This time it is different, Kim, this time it is about teaching people that faith works." That was just what I needed to hear to get myself in the car and bravely face the unknown. As I ran, I adopted the motto: "My faith will not falter." I chanted it over and over again as I asked Jesus to walk with us and God to guide us through this storm.

As Todd ran down the same road after I had finished, he let all his repressed emotions out. He cried for his son and his family, he cried in fear of the future, and for the loss of our carefree simple life. When he reached the stream he screamed as long and loud as he could. As he stood screaming and watching the sunbeam through the morning fog he saw a big doe jump out of the tall grass nearby and into the stream. They stared at each other for a very long time. As Todd watched her bound off into the woods, he felt the Spirit whispering to him, "It is strength and grace that will get you through this trial. You must put away your fear and pity and be strong for your family. I will take care of you". All the way home, Todd focused on this thought. He had heard God and, he, too was ready to begin this trial.

We left our house mid-morning. As we pulled out of the drive we said goodbye to our world... our home, our dogs and our perfect little life. I knew the next time I saw this place; I would be a very different person with a different perspective on life.

The drive downstate gave us time to prepare for what we would have to face in the following days. The drive itself was uneventful, thanks to Marc's family. Todd followed their black pick-up for eight hours while I read *"God's Story"* out loud to him, and the kids played in the back seat. We stopped for lunch at a park that overlooked the Mackinac Bridge, one of the largest suspension bridge in the world. This bridge spans the 5-mile Mackinac Strait and joins the Upper and Lower Peninsulas of Michigan. The kids had never seen the Mackinac Bridge before and were thrilled when they found out we were going to drive over it. Again they were living for the day, enjoying the new adventure and never questioning where we were going.

Todd and I learned much that day about God's perspective and power. *God's Story* gave us example after example of how God takes care of those who love Him. It explained how God is timeless and space less and through Him all things are possible. We learned that the key is to listen and see the doors that He opens. It also is to accept humbly when He provides and not to let pride get in the way.

At lunch Marc's Mom, Joanne, gave us a card. We opened it in the car as we drove out of the park. I cried as I tried to read out loud the note inside. Enclosed was 100 dollars. Todd immediately said, "We have to give that money back!" I hesitated for a minute and then replied, "Todd, have you been listening to this book? God is providing for us through people like Joanne. The social worker at Marquette General advised us to allow others to help. This is a trial we can't overcome on our own."

Todd contemplated my words as we drove over the Mackinac Bridge. Minutes later, he said "You're right Kim; we are going to need help. I guess I need to humbly accept this gift." After a long pause he added, "I just hope someday I can be there for someone else."

Crossing that "pride" bridge as a couple was as significant as crossing the Mackinac Bridge. Just as that bridge joins two bodies of land, this decision (to put away our pride and allow people to help) joined us with our supports. It made us a team with all whom wanted to help us and eased the burden of this trial.

We arrived in Lansing by late afternoon. Marc's family showed us where the hospital was and helped us find a hotel before saying good bye. After we checked into the hotel and had dinner, we made our way to the hospital. We walked into Sparrow Hospital with mixed emotions. On one hand, we wanted to find out what was wrong, and on the other, we just wanted to run away from it all. Tucker looked so healthy and full of energy as he raced his sister down the hall that it was hard to believe that a tumor could really be growing in his body. I prayed that it was all a mistake. I knew, however, deep inside this was no mistake. This was the journey we were meant to take.

Tucker was admitted under the care of Dr. Jobie Scott, a delightful African-American man with a laugh and smile that lit up the entire room. He was there when we arrived at the nurse's desk and immediately came to our room and started Tucker's workup. After he had chance to review the CT and X-ray that we brought with us from Marquette, he returned to our room to discuss the situation with us.

Dr. Scott told us that he thought Tucker had neuroblastoma, a relatively common cancer found in children under five. Tucker's tumor was very large; so large that it crossed midline. This meant that he already had either stage III or IV disease. Dr.Scott went on to explain the battery of tests that Tucker would have over the next several days to determine the true nature and extent of this cancer.

As he talked, I noticed the cross that hung around his neck. When he finished, I followed him out into the hallway. There, I told him my fears about chemotherapy and how I envisioned my son spending his last few months of life just like my brother suffering the effects of chemotherapy. With much compassion, He assured me that the side effects of the chemotherapy would be less painful and debilitating than the disease would be if we did nothing. Before we parted, I told Dr. Scott that we had put this situation in God's hand and that it meant a lot to see the cross around his neck. He responded: "I'm just an instrument of His hands." Then he embraced me and we cried together.

♥

I stayed at the hospital with Tucker that first night. The real "fun" didn't begin until after Lauren and Todd left for the hotel. They took Tucker into a treatment room and inserted both a catheter and an IV. I held him down and tried to comfort him through both of these painful procedures. It was one a.m. before he finally fell asleep. I never did sleep; I laid awake all night in the recliner next to his bed. Sometimes I read my bible and prayed, and other times I contemplated the day and seriousness of the situation and wept. Finally, I became completely overwhelmed, in desperation, I asked God for a sign that He was there watching over us. I laid very still waiting for His reply. Slowly, silently, I was filled with an inner peace, a peace beyond human understanding. I smiled... Jesus was there beside me and the Spirit was within me.

The next morning the medical team wasted no time getting started. Dr. Harmon, the surgeon, arrived at Tucker's room at seven. Blurry-eyed and still in my pajamas, I listened to him say that after looking at Tucker's CT he didn't think that the tumor was operable. He went on to explain that it was so large that it involved the right renal artery and the aorta. He recommended shrinking the tumor with chemotherapy first and then removing it.

After he left, I sat there somewhat stunned. This was the first bit of news I had to hear without Todd at my side. I had prayed last night that God would provide an easy path. Dr. Harmon's news did not make it sound like this was going to be easy. I tried not to let my mind wander. Instead, I tried to stay in the moment and enjoy Tucker when he woke up. We started our day with the "Rudolph the Red-nose Reindeer" videotape and Legos. I was so relieved when Todd and Lauren arrived. I needed Todd's reassuring smile and the love of his arms.

Later that morning, we met Dr. Scott's associates, Dr. Kulkarni and Leslie Hoover, a pediatric nurse specialist. I liked both of these women immediately. Dr. Kulkarni was bright, enthusiastic and optimistic. Leslie was organized, compassionate and friendly. They eased my mind and gave me confidence that we had made the right decision coming to Sparrow Hospital for treatment.

The tests also started that day: bone marrow biopsy, bone scan, bone survey, renal flow scan, MRI and urine catecholamine measurement. Each test was like a piece of a puzzle, helping to define the extent of Tucker's disease. During each one, I prayed for a clean result; that God would have mercy on us. Retrospectively, I know that isn't how God works. He doesn't answer prayers when we tell Him what it is we want. He answers prayers when we surrender our situation to Him, trust Him and allow Him to work through our situation in His way. We make it too hard, telling Him how to bring healing when he is the Great Healer. He will carry us if we let Him.

♥

Tucker really struggled through these days. They wouldn't allow him to eat because of the tests. He had never been in the hospital before, and he hated the parade of nurses, residents, care aide etc., which poked and prodded him each day. Helplessly, I watched as the twinkle left Tucker's eye and the joy left his voice. Lauren was named "the doctor of smiles and giggles", and she tried her best to engage him in play with only minimal success. As Tucker became more withdrawn and clung to us, my spirit cried out for him. I wanted to make this nightmare over for my little guy, but I couldn't. As I watched him, I carefully considered whether we should treat him or just go home and let him enjoy what life he had left.

Tucker had his last test, the MRI, on Wednesday morning. Todd accompanied him down to the MRI. While they were gone I met with Kathy Cooke, our social worker. Kathy and I started our conversation at the nurse's station. She told me that our insurance company had denied Tucker's admission. Immediately, I started to fall apart. I couldn't believe it! How could they deny admission for something like this? Kathy tried to explain that as soon as there was a definitive diagnosis they would reconsider, but I wasn't listening.

I was losing hope! The stress was getting to me. Kathy sensed where I was at and took me away from the nurse's desk and down the hall to the family lounge. I sat down at the table and sobbed. I was ready to jump off a bridge. I said that to Kathy and then immediately took it back. I knew that God had a plan for me and it did not include jumping off a bridge. I didn't want Kathy to think I was really suicidal. Kathy did not over-react to my comment she listened with a compassionate heart as I told her all of my concerns. I needed a friend, and she became that friend.

After our conversation, Kathy went and found Dr. Kulkarni and Leslie. They came in and talked to me briefly. They had the preliminary results of the tests and were ready to discuss them. I didn't want to hear them without Todd, so we all went down to the MRI to find him.

When we arrived, we could see Todd through the window, sitting very quietly next to Tucker with his eyes closed. Leslie commented," I think he is sleeping." I knew better. He was praying. When he came out he grabbed my hand reassuringly. He whispered in my ear, "I just had a great conversation with God. Don't worry; it's going to be okay!!" I tried to hold that thought as Dr. Kulkarni told us that Tucker's bone marrow and bone scan were positive. This meant that the cancer had spread into the bone marrow and to many other parts of his body such as the shoulders, skull and legs.

Dr. Kulkarni was honest with this information, but not pessimistic. She still felt that we should try treatment. Leslie volunteered to carry out my request of a team meeting that afternoon with all the physicians involved so that we could discuss possible treatment options.

Todd and I thanked them for their honesty and hopefulness and then asked them if we could have a few minutes alone. After they left, we held each other and cried. We cried for what we feared... for what we now knew we must endure... for what our children would have to endure. Then we prayed. We knew that God loved us, and we knew that God could make a way, even when there seemed to be no way. We had to trust Him.

Todd's Dad arrived from Iowa while we were in the MRI. When we got back to the room, he, Todd's mom and his sister, Libby, were anxious to hear what the doctors had told us. For obvious reasons, Todd did not want to discuss the test results in front of Tucker and Lauren. He took them down to the family lounge at the other end of the floor. He walked in front of them all the way down the long corridor. He was numb. The hall seemed to last forever. Once in the family conference room, Todd explained to them that Tucker had advanced neuroblastoma that had spread into other parts of his body including his bone marrow. He told them that Dr. Kulkarni had recommended treatment but certainly wasn't guaranteeing that it was curable.

Everyone was very quiet and teary. Their hearts were breaking. They had never been through this before and had no idea what to expect. They all sat there for a long while in shock and disbelief that this was really happening. They hid the burden of the news in their hearts when they returned to Tucker's room.

After Tucker woke up from the anesthesia he had been given for the MRI, we took him to Potter's Park to get away from the hospital for a while. Retrospectively, this was a bad decision. Tucker was too sick to enjoy it. He didn't want to run or even walk. He was pale, thin and listless. I took him down to look at the ducks. As I sat in the sunshine with my little boy on my lap, the memories of my brother John and all that he endured flooded my mind.

Later as I walked through the park with Ken, my father-in-law, I mourned for my little boy and what I knew he would have to face... days and days of nausea and vomiting, lethargy and weakness. I felt so cheated! Why did I have to watch this happen again, why couldn't it be me this time! I cried on Ken's shoulder as we walked through the park. Ken didn't know what to say. He had never had a challenge like this before. He had endured many trials, but he couldn't imagine what this felt like. I watched his heart break as he watched his little buddy that afternoon in the park.

When we got back to the hospital, Todd and I went running while Ken watched the kids. We needed this time alone before we met with the physicians. As we ran, we talked about what God had impressed upon us this week. Todd knew that God would take care of us. He told me, "God has a plan. No matter what we hear this afternoon, remember that!" As we ran back up Pennsylvania Ave., my wavering hope was restored. I knew that Todd was right. I just had to hang on and let Jesus carry me through this day. Retrospectively, I believe that Jesus was watching from Heaven and cheering at Todd's words. There was a plan and it was soon going to start unveiling itself.

We finished our run and got onto elevator heading for our hospital home on the fifth floor. When we stepped in, the elevator was empty and no one got in with us. The doors shut and then just before it left the floor, the doors reopened and a couple got in. The lady looked at me and said, "I can't believe that we are on the elevator with you two. As we drove up Pennsylvania Ave., we were stopped at every red light and each time you ran past us. I commented to my husband how dedicated you must be to run on this hot of a day!" She paused for a moment and then added, "Is this how you always visit your friends in the hospital or do you work here?"

Just as the elevator stopped on the third floor, their destination, I briefly responded to her question. I said that we were from the Upper Peninsula and that our three-year old son was in the hospital. As they got off the elevator, I touched this lady's arm and I said, "His name is Tucker, would you please keep him in your prayers." Without reservation, they both said they would. Then they disappeared as the elevator doors shut.

Once back at Tucker's room, we got ready for our meeting with the physicians. Before we went into the conference room, I asked God for just one negative test as reassurance that we were to go ahead with treatment.

Dr. Kulkarni and Dr. Harmon began the meeting by going through all the test results. It was difficult to look at the MRI and CT films, which showed the size of the tumor and how it was pushing on all his other abdominal organs. No wonder he had terrible stomachaches. It was also difficult to look at the bone scan. There were so many areas that lit up. Each of these were areas where the cancer had already spread.

I kept holding out for that one negative test. Finally, they went through the results of the bone survey, which showed no sign that the bones were beginning to break down because of the cancer and the MRI, which showed no sign that the tumor had penetrated the liver.

I smiled as the physicians finished their presentation. God had answered my prayer. He had given me two negative tests. Now I was to be obedient and boldly begin focusing on Tucker's treatment.

Dr. Kulkarni began to tell us what the odds were that Tucker would survive this disease. Before she could quote us the percentage, Todd interrupted and said, "If we are going to treat this, then don't tell me any percentages because I don't want to lose hope if the chance is slim, and I don't want to slack off if it is good." The physicians respected Todd's wishes, and, together, we agreed on a treatment regimen that included a tumor biopsy the next morning and chemotherapy as soon as he recovered from the biopsy.

After the meeting was over, we stayed and chatted with Leslie about the details of the next two weeks, including where we were going to stay. Leslie was going on vacation the next week, and she offered us her home so we could get out of the hotel. We gratefully accepted and marveled at the love that exuded from this newfound friend.

That was not the end of God's provision for us that day. After that meeting, we went to dinner in the cafeteria. While I was wandering around trying to find something to eat, I noticed the lady we had talked to on the elevator. She appeared to be looking for someone. We caught each other's eye and then she approached me and asked, "Do you mind if my husband and I have a prayer with you?" "Do I mind?" I replied, "I have asked everyone I see to pray for us! Of course, I don't mind, I would love to pray with you!"

This lady also found Todd and we all met at a large round table in the front of the cafeteria. They introduced themselves as Mike and Susie O'Berski, and then Mike offered to say a prayer. We joined hands and listened to Mike asked God for healing and strength through this trial.

After the prayer, Mike told us that he was a minister at a local church and asked if there was anything that they could do to help. I felt the nudge of the Holy Spirit. We had prayed that God would help us with our housing problem. God knew we had no place to stay in the area and that a hotel would be a real financial strain over time. Were these people God's answers to our prayers?

I responded to the nudge. I told Mike and Susie about our housing problems and asked if they would mention it at church on Sunday and perhaps someone might have a low cost apartment we could rent. Without hesitation Mike said, "You can stay with us!" Susie went on to explain that one of their sons was gone for the summer and his bedroom in the basement was available.

Somewhat surprised, we thanked them for their generosity and made plans with them to have dinner next week to get to know one another.

After Mike and Susie left the cafeteria, Todd's Dad looked at us and said, "I think I might stay around a week and see what else God is going to provide for you four." We all laughed, and I agreed that our situation had definitely improved over the last three hours. God was using His angels here on earth to make our journey easier.

♥

Susie and Mike's persistence to find and help us that afternoon was a modern day example of the Good Samaritan. Susie felt the nudge to help us as soon as the elevator door shut. She didn't say anything to Mike right away, but later as they were getting ready to leave the hospital, she told him she wanted to try to find Tucker's family and at least pray with them.

Mike agreed, and they began their search. All they knew about us was that we were on the fifth floor and our son's name was Tucker. They inquired at the nurse's station, where they were given our room number, and informed that we were down in the cafeteria. Susie did not dismiss the nudge and decide it was "too inconvenient or not meant to be because we were not in the room". She felt the nudge from the Holy Spirit, and she did not take that lightly. She was overjoyed when she caught my eye near the salad bar.

Mike and Susie and their five boys set an incredible example of what God intended the family to be. They adopted us and became pillars of strength in our lives. Through printed verses framed on their walls, conversations around their dinner table, prayer circles at bedtime etc., we came to know and understand God so much better. Talking over ice cream and/or popcorn about God and how He works in our world became a favorite part of my days.

As a young working mom, it was especially eye opening for me to spend time with Susie. Her number one priority has always been to raise her kids to be faithful Christians who know Jesus Christ as their personal savior. Susie doesn't belong to a hundred organizations, and she will never be citizen of the year because her priority is not to impress the world. It is to walk with God. Susie never misses an opportunity God puts in front of her. After getting to know her, I know why God sent her to help us. He knew she would hear His call; she wouldn't be too busy or too embarrassed. She would do her Father's work. He also knew I needed her example in my life.

♥

After we finished dinner in the cafeteria, we said goodbye to the O'Berskis and Todd's dad. We were back to just the four of us. Todd stayed with Tucker that night. As I drove to the hotel with Lauren, I thought about the meeting with the physicians. Even though they had not given us percentages at Todd's request, I could tell by their words and body language that Tucker's chances of surviving this disease were not very good. I sat at a stoplight and started to cry. I questioned why I was so confident that this time was going to be different. I let Satan slip in and fill me with doubt. He told me to be realistic; Tucker's chances of surviving were much less than Dad's or John's.

The Spirit quickly intervened in this battle for my peace. I felt nudged to look around; there was something there I needed to read. Across the street from the stoplight was a church, and on their sign it announced the title of that week's sermon. It said: **Whose report do you believe?** I had to read it twice to make sure that was what it said. I knew instantly that God was asking me: *Who do you believe… Me and what I told you while you were running before you left for Lansing, or humans and their percentages?*

♥

Tucker's biopsy was just after noon the next day. I went with him down to the holding area, and then, with Dr. Harmon's permission, I carried Tucker into the operating room. He was asleep in my arms as I carried him down the hall. I gazed at his perfect little face and prayed that God would stay with my little boy and guide the surgeon's hand. I laid him down on the hard, stiff table and kissed his beautiful lips. My tears fell on his cheek. These were tears of pure love. They remained as I was escorted to the waiting room.

My companion for the next two hours while I waited was *God's Story*. Instead of reading the chapters in order, I decided to look at the table of contents and see what "spoke" to me. Chapter eight was titled *He Calms Your Fearfulness*. That seemed very appropriate. I knew that God had a plan and was providing for us, but I was still afraid. I had seen too much in my thirty-three years to believe that bad things don't happen to those who love God.

I settled down into a chair and read about Noah, his trial and the promises that God gave him (and me). The chapter immediately got my attention as it described the frightening experiences that Noah was exposed to and his reaction to them: "Noah was totally helpless to change his situation" it said. "*So am I*", I wrote in the margin. "There was nothing Noah could do except to stay on the ark and tend to the needs of his family and of the animals until God in some way brought deliverance. He had to keep his faith in God while waiting out the silence that followed the storm." *"So do we!!!"* I again wrote in the margin.

As I wrote this, I knew that these parallels with Noah were no coincidence and that I needed to look at Noah's story a little more closely. I turned to the eighth chapter of Genesis and read about the events of Noah's trial. It rained for forty days and nights. They drifted at sea for one hundred and fifty one days. The ark landed on the mountaintop on the first week of the tenth month. Noah sent out the dove and the raven for enlightenment and encouragement on the first day of the first month. Finally, Noah and his family left the ark and observed the first rainbow as a sign of God's love and reassurance that their trial was over on the twenty-seventh day of the second month.

I highlighted these events and dates in my Bible and wondered what would happen to us on those dates. I had a funny feeling about them that I hid away in my heart. I then went back and finished reading the chapter in *God's Story* on calming your fearfulness.

The chapter reassured me that God had not forgotten Noah nor had He forgotten us. "In His own time and way, God began to change Noah's circumstances... on His own initiative, which required nothing of Noah except patient waiting, God sent a wind to evaporate the waters and dry up the earth."

These sentences put a twinkle in my eye. I needed to do nothing but trust God and wait patiently. I recalled what God had told me while I was running, *"This time it is different Kim. This time it is about showing people that faith works!"* God wanted to work through this trial. All I needed to do was to watch His handiwork and respond to His nudges. The chapter went on to explain how each of these events in Noah's trial strengthened Noah's faith in God. Each had to happen to get Noah and his family ready for what was going to happen next. "God can change our circumstances, but sometimes He waits for us to show real desire for change as well as faith in him." As I read these words I understood more clearly the challenge before me. I was to wait patiently for God to help me through each day and look for the teaching He was providing. Most importantly, I had to trust Him unconditionally, to keep focused on Him and allow Him to guide every decision.

I had just finished the chapter and said a prayer of thanks for this book when Dr. Harmon came in the waiting room. As he escorted me to a consultation room, I prayed for strength to accept God's will and for peace. God granted me both of these as I listened to Dr. Harmon's operative findings.

Dr. Harmon told me that the tumor was very gelatinous, and hence it was difficult to get a good piece of it to study. As expected, it was not encapsulated, but rather had many tentacles invading other areas of Tucker's abdomen. Fortunately, it had not invaded the liver. He could find a definite plane between the two. Dr. Harmon went on to reassure me that Tucker had tolerated the entire procedure very well and that soon I could join him in the recovery room.

An hour later, the recovery room nurses allowed me to see Tucker. As I walked up to his crib, I noticed the two nurses near him looked as if they had been crying. I sat down on the stool next to his crib and took his little hand. His face was flush and little beads of sweat dotted his brow. As I stroked his head, I asked Cheryl, his nurse, how he was doing. As she turned to talk to me, I could see tears welling in her eyes and her bottom lip trembling slightly. I hesitated, and then asked, "Are those tears for my son?" Ellie, the other nurse joined Cheryl at that point and they explained their tears. Both had four-year-old sons. They had read Tucker's chart and knew his diagnosis. They couldn't imagine the pain in my heart. It overwhelmed them to tears.

I was moved by their compassion. As a healthcare professional, I know it is easy to get callous to another person's situation. God warns us of this possibility. He commands us to love our neighbor as ourselves and to have true compassion and love for each other. Ellie and Cheryl had mastered God's command. For the next hour, as Tucker woke up, the three of us talked about God, trials, and the precious gift of children.

Ellie had a special softness for Tucker for she, too, had battled against cancer as a child. At sixteen, she was diagnosed with Hodgkin's Lymphoma. She shared her insight into the challenges that Tucker faced. Both she and Cheryl promised they would pray for us.

As we left the recovery room that afternoon, I smiled and thanked God for allowing our paths to cross just for a brief time. I would never forget the tears of these strangers. Cheryl and Ellie also didn't forget this encounter. Five days later, Ellie came by Tucker's room and brought him a book about God's love and a stuffed animal. Two months later, Tucker received a certificate booklet from Ellie's church. When he opened the booklet, his eyes sparkled and he exclaimed, "Jesus!" Sure enough a picture of Jesus reaching out to Tucker filled the inside cover.

Tucker renamed this certificate his "Jesus Picture". It became his prized possession. He requested it at all of his medical tests and difficult procedures. He focused on Jesus's face instead of on the things being done to him. I believe the picture reminded Tucker of the one who gives strength and is always faithful. And to think that this gift came from a young mother... a fellow healthcare provider... a cancer survivor... a believer who responded to the nudge of the Holy Spirit.

♥

My sister, Pam, came from North Dakota to spend the weekend with us. Her cheerful face was a welcome site. When she walked into the room she immediately came over and hugged me. Our embrace was long. It was a "hello, sister"..."I'm sorry this is happening to your family"... "I love you"... and "It will be OK"... all wrapped up into one hug. I didn't think that anyone else in the world could understand how I felt to be going down this path again, but as I hugged my sister, I knew she did.

That weekend visit with Pam revived my soul. We had not spent much time together since she had moved to North Dakota and I had married and started a family. It was so nice to spend time together, even if it was in a hospital room.

On Friday afternoon, we were allowed to escape from the hospital for a few hours and take the kids downtown to the "Riverwalk". Lynn, Marc and their kids drove down from Marquette and joined us there. I never imagined walking in the sunshine pushing my son in a wheelchair would feel so good. As we walked past a scuba class being taught on the river's edge and through the annual chili cook-off, I was reminded that life goes on for others even when one is in the midst of a storm.

Initially, Tucker was very quiet and lethargic. He didn't even want to try to walk. He just sat in the wheelchair taking it all in. We found a playground and a little sidewalk café for lunch. As we ate spinach quiche and drank strawberry soda, we giggled at Lauren and Andrew (Lynn and Marc's two year old) on the jungle gym. Tucker watched them play but made no attempt to join in.

As the afternoon passed, Tucker's disposition improved. He began smiling (especially at Pam) and even said a few words. He saw ducks at the river's edge and asked us to push him closer. Firmly, but with encouragement, we told him that he would have to walk over there if he wanted to see them. After much hesitation, he got out of the wheelchair and walked over to the river's edge to see the baby ducks. Lauren and Andrew joined him and soon all three were interacting. We enjoyed the rest of the afternoon, listening to and watching the kids play.

Later that evening, Pam and I went for a run along the same river. As we ran, we reminisced about our time together during my early college years. I had gone away to college in Iowa. She had moved to that same area a year before me and was my only family within five hours. We had been each other's support after John died. Now eighteen years later, we were facing the same disease, but we both had life experiences behind us which colored our attitude toward it. We reflected on how God had been present and a source of strength in all our trials. The sooner we gave control to Him, the sooner a solution appeared. The key was to trust and wait patiently.

On our way back to the hospital, we stopped and prayed at the dock that stretched out into the river. After that run, this dock, this tiny peaceful oasis within this big, busy, city; became a sacred place where I stopped and prayed every time I went running.

Pam flew home on Sunday. Tucker kept her busy playing games and Legos until the very last minute. After she left with Todd and Lauren for the airport, Tucker asked me to take him up to the eighth floor so he could watch her airplane take off. It was a crystal clear day and the sun warmed us through the large windows as we sat and looked out over the city of Lansing. In the horizon we searched for an airplane heading west. After a while I began to nod off. Not Tucker, he kept a careful watch for a half an hour before saw a large jet heading the right direction. "There it is!" he shouted and woke me up. Then he softened his tone and said, "Bye, bye Auntie Pam. Thanks for coming," as he waved out the window. As we got on the elevator to go back to our room, Tucker looked up at me and said, "Boy, I'm going to miss her!" Tears filled my eyes, "Me too, Tucker, Me too!"

♥

That week and throughout the entire storm, we became keenly aware of the bond and the support within our extended families. Every member was there for us. Encouraging us and using their gifts to lessen our burden and improve our perspective.

Todd's brother, Jeff sent us a gift which spoke to our hearts and encouraged us beyond measure. It was a daily devotional titled, *God Calling*. It came with the following letter:

*Dear Todd and Kim,*

*I needed to write down what has been going through my head the last few days. This is what I know and feel in my heart. I want so badly to be there and make this better for you. I love both of you so much! When I think of you two, I think of one unit. I am absolutely sure that Tucker getting sick is a vehicle for something good.. You are two of the strongest people I know and together you are invincible. God never gives us challenges we cannot handle. I do not pretend to know what that purpose is. We will discover that in the days to come. I do know that the two of you were chosen to help Tucker in his first years of life. This task was given to you because you can handle it better than anyone else.*

*Know that you are not alone! You have two families that are strong. Please let us know how we can help. My nephews and nieces are the closest thing I have to my own kids. By far, this lays heaviest on you, but it affects all of us. I want to do my part!*

*I know you will make it through this test. Someday we will know why it had to happen. For now my thoughts and prayers are with you.*

*Love Jeff*

After Todd and I read this letter, we picked up *God Calling* to get a taste of its content. The page it "fell" open to was April 21st. The words we read seemed as if they were straight from God:

### *"You Will Conquer"*

*You will conquer. Do not fear changes. You can never fear changes when I, your Lord, change not. Jesus Christ, the same yesterday, today, and forever. I am beside you. Steadfastness, unchangingness, come to you too, as you dwell with Me. Rest in Me.*

*As breathing rightly, from being a matter of careful practice, becomes a habit, unconsciously, yet rightly performed, so if you regularly practice this getting back into My presence, when the slightest feeling of unrest disturbs your perfect calm and harmony, so this, too, will become habit, and you will grow to live in that perfect consciousness of My presence and perfect calm and harmony will be yours.*

*Life is a training school. Remember only the pupil giving great promise for future good work would be so singled out by the Master for strenuous and unwearied discipline, teaching and training.*

*I am asking both of you to be not as hundreds of My followers, nay as many, many thousands, but to be even as those who reflect Me in all they say and do and are. So, my dear children, take this training, not as harsh, but as the tender loving answer to your petition.*

*Life can never be the same again for either of you. Once you have drunk of the wine of my giving, the life eternal, all earth's attempts to quench your thirst will fail.*

This reading contained a unique message for us. Something we had not considered until now. It encouraged us to think of ourselves as being chosen for this rigorous training. That God was calling us into a closer relationship with Him and the only way He could get our attention was through adversity. We stored that message in our hearts. Reading this book together every day became our new normal.

♥

Tucker was scheduled to begin chemotherapy that weekend. Prior to the first infusion, Leslie had gone through with Todd and I the drug regimen and possible side effects. Tucker would receive four different drugs via an IV over a six-day period. The possible side effects of these drugs collectively included permanent hearing loss, hair loss, mouth sores, kidney failure, heart and bladder damage, low blood counts, nausea and vomiting.

As I stood in the shower one morning, I tried to prepare myself for what it would be like to help a three year old through the side effects of chemotherapy. Thoughts of John vomiting in the car and in "Denny's Restaurant" flooded my mind. I prayed, "God, please give me those side effects, I would gladly bear them for Tucker." God heard my prayer!!! Tucker tolerated all the drugs beautifully. He had very little nausea or vomiting that first infusion, and I on the other hand was plagued by mouth sores and nausea all week. Physically I felt lousy, but spiritually I was humbled and amazed .

♥

During the next week, as Tucker went through chemotherapy, we began to find a new normalcy in our lives. The thunder and lightning of the diagnosis had passed, but it was still raining. Like Noah, we were getting used to the sound of the rain and were settling into a routine to care for our family and get through this storm. Like Noah, we put our trust in God.

Every evening after dinner, we would treat the kids to movie and popcorn. After the movie, the kids would fall asleep and we would stay up late talking. Around midnight one of us would pick up our sleeping Lauren and head back to Leslie's house for the night.

In the morning, Tucker was always awake and ready to go. He was out of his pajamas and into play clothes before his breakfast tray arrived at eight a.m. We dressed him every day to promote normalcy and wellness in his life. We didn't want him to think of himself as being sick. Lauren, on the other hand, liked to sleep in at Leslie's house and stay in her pajamas while she ate breakfast on the porch and played with the neighborhood cat. By late morning we all met up in the playroom for an afternoon of painting, games or special activities planned by the Child Life Specialists.

As we repeated this routine each day, we developed a fondness for many of the special staff at Sparrow. We had no idea that God was using us to plant seeds among these people. Looking back, I felt like the needy one, the one who received so much from them. Later, I would realize that it was mutual. They were growing emotionally and spiritually with us each month when we returned.

♥

One of the staff who was very helpful early on was Judy Brady the child psychologist. She helped us understand how family's cope and what parents could do to minimize the impact on both the patient and siblings. One day she asked if we would like to meet another family who had gone through this experience. We replied with a definite yes. She contacted a local family, Doug and Romani Schrem, and set it up for an evening right in Tucker's hospital room.

Doug and Romani seemed a bit tentative and reserved when they first arrived. I could tell that they weren't sure how well we were coping with Tucker's disease yet and wanted to be careful what they said. It didn't take long, however, for them to get a sense of where our hearts were and where we put our trust. Then they opened up and really began connecting with us. They told us all about their daughter, Karsha, and her battle against neuroblastoma. Karsha was now eight and in remission.

When Judy had first asked us if we would be interested in meeting the Schrem's, I was afraid to ask if their child was still alive. I was relieved when Judy volunteered that Karsha was now eight years old and doing well. Romani and Doug did not share Karsha's entire story that day, and I am grateful for that. Months later, when we learned Karsha's story in it's entirely, I was overwhelmed by the length and tragedy of it. Had Doug and Romani initially shared all that they had gone through, I believe it would have crushed my hope and ignited my fears.

Instead, the Schrem's visit was just what Todd and I needed at that point. Prior to their visit, we had many visitors and family supporting us, but no one who had ever really gone through this kind of trial with such a young child. We had many questions about parenting young children through such an enormous life change. We were doing what "felt" right, but we really needed some guidance from parents who had traveled this road.

The positive energy we felt from Doug and Romani that evening was a gift from God. These strangers became our instant soul mates. Much of the insight they gave us that evening and in future phone conversations molded our attitude toward beating this disease. Doug said, "I'm so relieved that you are already Christians and that you are looking to God for strength. I don't know how we would have made it through all of this without God." They both encouraged us to take life day by day; not to look too far ahead because it was too overwhelming.

Romani shared her story about Karsha's first night in the hospital. They were in this very room. She sat in the chair next to Karsha's bed with her bible and begged God for enlightenment and mercy. As I listened to her story, I saw many similarities in our souls. I knew that we would become comrades in this fight and that our families would grow close.

Before Doug and Romani left, we stood in a circle, held hands and prayed. We asked God to care for our children, and, if it was His will, to make our children examples of how faith can move mountains. Little did we know then how closely God was listening. In the upcoming months, He would move mountains for both Tucker and Karsha.

♥

Tucker's ability to handle the chemotherapy so well prompted us to think about discharge. It seemed like months since we had left our home in the Upper Peninsula. We were not the same people who left there two weeks ago. We were no longer an "All-American Family" living a storybook life. Now we had a big storm looming over us. People would be watching us and most likely pitying us. How would we handle that? What would our attitude be like? Would we glorify God and show how He is working through this or would we struggle and focus on all that is hard and bad about this crisis we found ourselves in?

We also began to consider the financial burden this trial would place on us. One morning, Todd and I had an opportunity to discuss this over breakfast. We had already decided that Todd would take a leave of absence from work. We knew that without his income, keeping the eight dogs that make up our dogsled team would be an unnecessary financial strain. However, the thought of giving away all of our dogs was really disturbing to both of us. We love winter. That was why we moved up north. The dogs provide winter adventure. There is nothing like gliding across the snow with these beautiful animals pulling you on skis or a sled. Now we had to face the reality that we weren't going to have neither the time nor the money for them.

As Todd and I talked about the dogs and our finances, I was nudged by the Holy Spirit to say something that had been on my heart for a year regarding tithing to our church. We have never tithed. Every year we tried to increase our giving by twenty or thirty dollars every month, but we had never given the ten percent that the bible refers to.

The previous summer, I had a very insightful conversation about tithing with my sister, DeeAnn, and her husband, Ron. I was at their house in Orange, California. We were taking an evening walk through their neighborhood. Everyone had manicured lawns and in-ground swimming pools. We talked about how hard it is to live in a place like that and not get wrapped up in materialism. Ron, my brother-in law, said, "Nice things are fine, but they can't be your priority. Your priority has to be God and your relationship with him. Material things will never make you happy. Fill the spiritual needs that you have and then you will be truly happy. Tithing is one component of making God your first priority." My heart knew that Ron's words were God-inspired and that we were being called to tithe; but, my head couldn't make the numbers add up. We couldn't afford to give that much to our church and still live our current lifestyle. I was honest and told this to Ron. He replied: "That's God! He asks us to take a leap of faith, to dive in, even regarding money. Be faithful to His request, and He will provide."

When I returned from California, I shared this conversation with Todd, but neither of us was ready to make that commitment. Now a year later, as we sat eating breakfast, I reminded Todd of that conversation I had with Ron and DeeAnn. I added, "If we are really relying on God to carry us through this trial, to heal our son, we have to do what He asks of us. If God's word speaks of the blessing of tithing then we need to do it; even if that means giving up our sled dog team and/or making other life style modifications."

Todd whole-heartedly agreed with me and immediately began to problem solve out loud about how we could disband the dog team. As Todd was throwing out possible options, I interrupted: "Let's pray about it. If God wants us to keep all these dogs, He will provide a way." So we stopped and prayed that God would direct us regarding these dogs. We vowed to God and each other that we would start tithing and that we would listen for God's will regarding the dogs.

❤

By the end of the week were packing for home and what a job that was. Tucker had received so many packages from family and friends that we could barely fit all of them in the hospital room much less in our little Subaru. Todd had practiced "car packing wizardry" on previous occasions (Christmas at Grandma's), but this was the ultimate challenge.

Even in this seemingly insignificant detail, God provided. After Todd had attempted and failed to get everything in the car, we had an unexpected visit from Dennis West, a friend from church back home. He had driven down for a work-related conference. After visiting with us for a while he asked "Hey, I've got an empty van, can I take anything back to the Upper Peninsula for you?" Up to this point in the conversation, Todd hadn't mentioned our packing dilemma. Todd and I could hardly believe his question! We replied with a thankful laugh and then let Dennis in on how he was an answer to prayer.

❤

Tucker finished his chemotherapy at 11 pm.. He was so anxious to leave the hospital, that we were allowed to be discharge at midnight and we all got to spend the night at Leslie's. It felt so good to be together as a family somewhere other than a hospital. As we settled the kids in bed, we reflected on the past when we tucked them into bed taking their health for granted. This night we took extra time just to watch them sleep and notice the beauty of their slumbering faces. Todd and I then slid into bed and held one another. We had almost forgotten what it was like to sleep together. It felt so good to fall asleep in Todd's reassuring, loving arms.

Before leaving Leslie's the next morning, we made a big banner which said: **Jesus is Smiling Down on You!!!** and hung it in their garage. We used ladders and soccer goals to stretch the banner across both car stalls so they wouldn't miss it when they got home. Leslie told us later that her girls loved it and now hoped for a banner after every vacation!

On our drive home we stopped in Mackinac City for a break. It is a beautiful little resort town at the tip of the Lower Peninsula. As we walked along Lake Huron and enjoyed the sun and the sound of carefree life all around us, I felt so different. Everyone appeared so focused on worldly things: buying treasures at the local shops... getting tickets for boat cruises... eating the world famous fudge, etc. We had just spent two weeks making decisions about our son's life and conversing with God on an hourly basis. I wondered, "Will we ever live a 'worldly life' again... a life that is "self-centered" instead of "God-centered?"

By early evening we made it home. We stopped at the end of the road to wake Tucker so he could enjoy the moment with us. We called his name and shook him gently. We couldn't arouse him! Panicking a little, we both got out of the car and got him out of his car seat. He was breathing, but he wouldn't wake up. I couldn't believe that this was happening one minute from our home!!! I looked at Todd and said, "We better go right to the emergency room." At that Tucker opened his eyes and said, "No, I want to go home!!!"

Todd and I both let out a sigh of relief. "Let's go home," we both responded in unison. With Tucker on my lap, we drove down our road and into our drive.

Our little house in the woods was everything I remembered it to be. The smell of the woods and the sound of the hermit thrush were so welcome. The kids quickly informed me that toad village and the fishpond were still inhabited. The dogs howled a "Hello".

As we walked around the yard it was apparent that our friends and neighbors were already supporting us and helping however they could. The grass had been mowed and two new apple trees had been planted in the front yard; on their branches hung pink, yellow and blue ribbons. The ribbons were inscribed with messages of hope and love from the people with whom I work. I tried to keep my composure as I read each message to the kids. The love and compassion relayed through these ribbons was so overwhelming that eventually the tears won out, and I had to quit reading.

Inside the house we were greeted by our dog, Copain, and our cat Polk-e-dots and a counter full of mail. The kids ran directly to their rooms to get reacquainted with all of their favorite toys. I opened the refrigerator to put away the few groceries we had picked up on the way home. Much to my surprise, there was a complete beef stew dinner waiting for us inside. On the counter, I found a welcome home note from my friend Jeannie. She was responsible for the apple trees and the dinner. As I read the card, I reflected on the gift of a good friend.

♥

The next month was a readjustment time for everyone, much like it must have been for crew aboard the ark. Just as they had to find a routine to care for all the animals; we had to develop a routine to care for Tucker. He had a central line that had to be flushed with heparin daily; and the dressing around it had to be changed twice weekly. For ten days after each round of chemotherapy, we had to drive thirty miles to the clinic daily for a Neupogen shot to boost Tucker's white blood cell recovery. We also had to give Tucker several medicines daily.

Making all of these changes was an entire family commitment. Initially, Tucker did not cooperate. He threw up his medicine, fussed during his dressing changes and screamed during his Neupogen shots. It was only through Todd's consistent, calm, patient manner that these tasks became a routine that Tucker came to accept as part of his day.

Lauren also helped Tucker with this adjustment. She reminded him to wash after he used the bathroom and before meals. She entertained him in the back seat during the trips to the clinic. She even tried to make central line dressing changes fun for him. She would pretend that her doll had a central line, and she would change the doll's "patch" while I was doing Tucker's. After Tucker's dressing was finished, Lauren would help Tucker change the "patch" on Truckie (his model four-wheeler).

In addition to taking care of Tucker, Todd and I had to readjust to our new vocational challenges. Todd's challenge was to adapt to being a full-time, stay-home dad. He now worked in a child's world and lived by their schedule. He no longer had any adult to interact with on a regular basis besides me. This was especially the case during the days when Tucker was neutropenic (very susceptible to infection because of low neutrophil counts). During these times, the doctors recommended that Tucker stay out of all public places and that visitor be kept to a minimum.

My challenge was to figure out what God's will was for me as a physical therapist. At first, it was just a challenge to find a way to be the "new me" in this old environment that I had left so abruptly. It was also a challenge to trust God with Tucker's life and to not be so overwhelmed with our situation that I could not have compassion for the patients I worked with. I learned to look for God in everything and for His will in every interaction. When He opened a door, whether it was regarding Tucker's treatment or something else, I learned to go through it with courage.

I took one of those major steps just a few days after we arrived home. One of our pastors, Dave Maire, called and invited us to a prayer service for our family. I was humbled and a bit overwhelmed by this gesture. As we talked I began to share with him all the crazy cool ways God was working during this storm. Dave asked if I would want to share a few words at the service. I did not even hesitate in answering yes. I knew God wanted this trial to glorify him. He was giving me an opportunity.

♥

The following Tuesday was the prayer service and my first day back to work. I got up early that morning and spent a lot of time in prayer before heading off to work. I asked God for strength and peace in a day that I knew would be a challenge. God answered my prayers. Throughout my entire workday, Jesus helped me keep my head high and my smile close by as I interacted with my colleagues and tried to serve other people as a physical therapist. The love and concern that I received from the staff at the hospital was overwhelming.

The first thing I did that morning as the acute care physical therapy supervisor was have a staff meeting. At that meeting, I filled in my staff on Tucker's illness including our tentative schedule for the next year. I volunteered to step down from my position as their supervisor. I knew that I would have to rely heavily on all of them to keep our department running well. If collectively, their preference was to have someone else appointed to my position, I certainly would have understood.

They chose instead to divide up my responsibilities and work together to overcome the challenges ahead. Their reaction to me that morning helped more than any of them could ever know. Their words and action told me, "We have confidence in you. You can do this and we are going to help you!" Like angels, they lifted me up and made me smile!

Looking back, they were not just giving me "lip service" that day. They did a phenomenal job over the next year working together to provide excellent care. I was told many times by patients and other staff that these people went above and beyond the call. Three of them were named employee of the month over that year; an honor that was well deserved.

♥

Our experience at the prayer service that evening was equally as encouraging. There were about a hundred people in the sanctuary when Lauren and I walked in. Most didn't know we were coming so we caught them off guard. We found seats near the front, and before sitting down, I thanked them all for coming. I also told them that Todd and Tucker would be joining the service but they would not be able to stay or interact with anyone after the service because Tucker's risk for infection was too high. Moments later, Todd and Tucker walked in and the service began.

Once again, I was again overwhelmed by the love and compassion I felt in this room from coworkers, church acquaintances, and people of this community that I hardly knew. However, the mood was so sad and hopeless that I felt like I was at Tucker's funeral. As I listened to people sniffle out prayers for healing, coping and strength, I reconsidered saying anything up front. Was this really the time or place? God nudged me... "Yes it is"! So when the prayers came to a conclusion, I stood up and shared what I felt God had prompted me to say.

I started by telling them why I was up there talking tonight. "The Bible says 'Do not be overcome by evil, but overcome evil with good!' As soon as Dave told me about this service I knew that God was giving me an opportunity to do good; to share our story so that others would be encouraged to look for how God wanted to work in the adversity in their life."

I initiated my story by describing my family's previous battles with cancer. I shared the details of watching John and my dad take their last breaths at our family home. Then I described my relationship with God before Tucker was diagnosed: Jesus was my Savior but not as close personal friend as He wanted to be. I did pray and thank God for my blessings daily, but I didn't really look for God's will and align myself with it. We had never tithed to our church. We always had an excuse why it wasn't in the budget. I could talk about my faith with fellow Christians but I wasn't comfortable evangelizing to non-Christians. I felt inadequate, and unprepared for such a task. I had a spark of compassion for others, yet I didn't recognize this as the Holy Spirit trying to work through me.

I then switched gears and shared the details of June 10th through the 13th. I described the agony and disbelief we felt as the doctors told us that Tucker had cancer. I described the precious moments of my birthday. Finally, I shared what God had said to me during my Sunday morning run: "This time it is different Kim. This time it is about showing people the power of faith!" I then described some of the ways that God had provided in Lansing. I told of the incredible peace Todd and I had regarding Tucker's illness, a peace beyond understanding.

I closed by challenging them to make God a priority in their lives and to look to where God was working and move toward it. I left them with some words from the Christian writer, Max Lucado: "God is God. When you can't trace His hand, you must trust His heart." I asked for continued prayers that we do just that as we continued through this storm.

Their reaction to my words was amazing. The burden of grief that was present when the service began was now gone, Afterward, people approached me not with tears and pity but with empowerment and encouragement. As each one shook my hand, they promised they would pray for us. I knew that was what we needed most of all.

♥

The next afternoon Tucker had his first doctor's appointment and blood draw in Marquette. Dr. Chen, the local oncologist we had chosen, was out of town, so we saw Dr. Skendzel, the family practice doctor who diagnosed Tucker. It was very nice to see and personally thank this doctor who had listened and reacted to my concerns, not dismissed me as an overreacting mother. He is not only a good doctor, but also a devout Believer. He told us that he and his wife had been praying for us daily.

The results of Tucker's blood test were frightening. His ANC had dropped to from 7000 to 10. This was an expected side effect on the chemotherapy, which made him very susceptible to infection. Dr. Skendzel encouraged us to go home and adopt all the neutropenic precautions Leslie had discussed with us. This included eating no fresh vegetables or fruits, staying away from anyone other than immediate family members, washing hands before all meals and after using the bathroom, etc... He also encouraged us to check Tucker's temperature often. If he ran a fever over 100.5, we needed to call Dr.Chen or go to the emergency room.

As we left the office and drove home, Todd and I both felt uneasy. I wanted to clean every inch of our home with a toothbrush to protect my little guy from any germ that might be looming! Later that evening Todd and I discussed our need to find a balance between being protective enough to keep Tucker healthy and permissive enough to keep Tucker's enthusiasm for life alive. We prayed that God would watch over Tucker and that He would help us make good decisions regarding Tucker's care. Again God heard our prayers. Not only did Tucker remain free of fever and infection after the first round of chemotherapy but after every subsequent round as well!

♥

Along with Tucker's blood counts went his hair. It started to fall out about a week after we got home. We tried to reduce the impact of this on Tucker by shaving his hair really short earlier in the week. Todd shaved his own head as well so Tucker would think it was just a neat guy thing to do in the summer. Our strategy worked well. Tucker's hair was so short neither of the kids really noticed when it fell out. I noticed that it was falling out as I sat rocking him in our bedroom stroking his head. The tiny blonde hairs in my hand brought tears to my eyes.

Up to that day, I was hoping that God would choose for Tucker not to lose his hair. Retrospectively, I believe that God allowed Tucker's hair to fall out for a reason. He wanted to teach me a lesson about true beauty; about judging others by their physical appearance. This lesson had to be learned by being the victim. Once Tucker was bald, I could no longer hide the fact that he had cancer. We were no longer the All-American family in the eyes of a stranger, but rather a family to pity. My son was no longer adorable, but different.

Being bald didn't bother Tucker at all. It didn't bother him to wear a hat. His army-green fishing hat had been a part of his daily dress for the past two years because of his fair complexion. On the other hand, he did not demand to wear a hat. He was not self-conscious about his head or the lack of hair on it. He did not worry about what other people thought. He did not hide, but rather charmed all he met with his sweet, loving, personality.

As I watched Tucker, I adopted his attitude. I stopped worrying about what others thought and instead used the attention brought to Tucker's bald head to tell our story and how God was caring for us. What a slap in the face this must have been to Satan. What he intended to use to destroy me (and my pride), God helped me make into a tool to further His Kingdom.

By the 4th of July, Tucker's counts had recovered and we were anticipating a visit from my Mom. She hadn't seen Tucker since May and memories of my Brother John's frail young body while he was going through treatment haunted her. She was pleasantly surprised to find Tucker looking so well. Instead of having to encourage a sickly boy lying on the sofa to play, she was able to assist with our Fourth of July party with a few of the neighborhood kids. All afternoon we hit water baseballs off of a tee in the backyard, broke a piñata, made huge bubble creatures with soap and played with our pet turtle, Speedy. Throughout all of this fun, my mom kept saying: "I can't believe how good Tucker looks."

At the end of Mom's weekend visit, we all drove to Mackinac City and Island for a short vacation before we headed back downstate for more treatment. It was a perfect end to her visit. The kids slept in the back seat as we traveled, giving mom and I some uninterrupted time to discuss priorities, faith and trials. The drive along Lake Michigan was breath taking. I was awed by how the blue of the lake matched the hues of the sky so perfectly. The beauty and infiniteness of the view reminded me of the God I was getting to know so much better.

That evening we got another chance to experience the beauty of the lake. We took the evening vesper cruise under the Mackinac Bridge and into the sunset, singing hymns of God's love and sovereignty. As we sang and listened to the message, I reflected on the day. It was our twelfth wedding anniversary. It was a beautiful day with my Mom, my husband and my kids. I never would have dreamed a month ago that anything positive could come from Tucker's disease, but here I was enjoying life like never before. I was appreciating people for who they were, not judging them for what I expected them to be. I was living for the day and taking opportunities when they presented themselves.

I also reflected on my relationship with Todd. Would I have ever guessed twelve years ago when I said: "I do" and "in sickness and health" that this was part of God's plan for us? Why were we being called to such a difficult training so early in our married life? Should we consider it a privilege to experience God so intimately as a couple so early in our relationship together?

At the end of the cruise the minister asked people who were having a birthday or anniversary to raise their hands. He then went around and introduced every one with their hands raised so the entire audience could congratulate them. After he asked me a few questions, he commented "What a beautiful family!" At this, tears welled up in my eyes as I thanked him. He saw only our blessings, not our burdens. As the boat turned around and headed toward shore, I reflected on all of my blessings: a strong faith and relationship with

God, a great marriage, two wonderful kids, a loving, supportive extended family, a job where I can make a living...and a difference, and a home in a place where everything is a reminder of God's power and beauty. As I left the boat I smiled, and thanked God for an awesome evening!

♥

The next morning we took an early boat to Mackinac Island. Our boat was named "Cadillac". Tucker would definitely agree with the name. He picked this type of boat because it sprayed water twenty feet out from the back of the boat like a rooster tail. Tucker was impressed by the boat's power. It was the highlight of the day for him; an experience he would remember. Every subsequent trip through Mackinac City we looked for "Cadillac" billboards and searched for "our boat" on the lake as we crossed the Mackinac Bridge.

Our day on the island was delightful. It had its exciting moments, (when the two teams of draft horses broke away from their drivers and ran down the crowded main street) but mostly it was a peaceful step back in time. There are no automobiles on this island so the only way to see it is either on bikes or by horse. We chose the horse drawn buggy. Our driver had grown up on the island so as he drove us around he told us much of the island's history including his own stories. Our horses, Barney and Todd, trotted us past the majestic Grand Hotel, Fort Mackinac, and the beautiful vistas overlooking the Mackinaw Straits.

As we played in the park that afternoon, I noticed how much my entire family's perspective had changed. After our last month, none of us really cared what we did that day. We didn't race to catch every attraction that this place offered. Much of the day was spent swinging and enjoying the sunshine and each other. I watched other families rush their kids around trying to fit it all in. They really didn't look like they were enjoying themselves. I felt we had jumped off the treadmill of life and were now running life at our own pace.

A pace I now savored. (Just like the fresh island fudge we had for a bedtime snack!)

♥

The next morning after breakfast we had to say good bye to Grandma Phyllis. She headed back to Wisconsin, and we headed south to the University of Michigan for some additional testing before starting the next round of chemotherapy at Sparrow.

As we drove south, it slowly sunk in with all of us that it was time for more hospital stuff. Tucker asked lots of questions about the test. Would it hurt? How long would it take? Would we be at the same hospital we were last time?

Todd and I were ill equipped to answer many of his questions. We had never been to Ann Arbor or the University of Michigan (U of M) and we had no idea what to expect. To ease all of our minds and regain the right focus, we spent the morning drive reminding each other of all the ways that God had cared for us over the last month. We knew He was walking with us and we knew He would get us through this day.

We arrived at U of M in the early afternoon. As we drove up, we were all overwhelmed by the size of the place. It was so much bigger than Sparrow Hospital or Marquette General. We quickly learned that U of M is a complex of seven hospitals plus clinics. It has over 700 beds. Despite its size, however, we quickly experienced that staff stilled cared. Tucker wasn't just another kid with cancer.

We met two women that week at U of M who displayed incredible spirits of love and compassion. They made that visit and each subsequent visit there tolerable and even something to which we looked forward.

We met the first woman, Lahti, at the Pediatric Nuclear Medicine office; the place where Tucker would have this test called an MIBG scan. Lahti, a petite blonde with a short "nineties" haircut and sharp features, at first didn't look like someone with whom I would strike any common ground. However, she quickly volunteered that she was originally from the Upper Peninsula (U.P.). We spent the next half hour discussing the U.P. and its unique people. She was from Ontanogon, a little town three hours west of us. I knew many people from there because of my job. We had some mutual acquaintances and a common love for the Upper Peninsula, which we discussed casually.

From that day on, Lahti took us under her wing as if it was her duty as a one-time "Yooper". She gave us lots of information about how to get around Ann Arbor and where to go to get away from the city. She took her time with Tucker and always made sure the *Power Rangers* videotape was available for him to watch during his test. She had a great "prize box" that she let him pick many treasures out of after he completed the scan or an injection.

Many times, Lahti would see me or Todd sitting in the waiting room reading our Bible. After a while, she started to volunteer more about her faith. She belonged to a bible-based Charismatic Church. She loved to discuss morality and spiritual issues. During one visit, she gave Todd a book entitled *The Message* which translated the New Testament into contemporary language. Later she gave us a copy of *The Prayer of Jabez* by Bruce Wilkerson.

Lahti's care for us I am sure made Jesus smile. She befriended us and helped us in a very practical way early on. Later, when she knew where we stood spiritually, she nurtured our souls with seeds that had been planted by other Christians in her life.

♥

The other woman, Betsy, worked as a nurse right next door to Lahti in outpatient surgery. This tall slender woman with twinkling eyes and beautiful smile completed Tucker's admission for testing that first afternoon. She immediately became our self-appointed advocate at the U of M; interacting with all of us, calming our fears and easing us into this new healthcare system.

Each time we returned to outpatient surgery, Betsy was watching out for us. She helped us find our way around the hospital and around Ann Arbor. With each interaction I had with Betsy, I liked her more. Just like with Lahti, early on our conservations were about practical and logistical things related to Tucker's care. Over time however, our conversations focused more on God and how He was working through this trial. She relayed stories of other families and how faith really seemed to be the "deciding factor" on how they coped with their situation. It did not guarantee a positive outcome, God never promised that; but it did guarantee a more positive outlook regardless of the outcome.

Betsy helped us all understand the test that Tucker was at the U of M to have. It was called a MIBG scan and it would define the location and extent of the cancer throughout his body. It involved injecting a small dose of radiation attached to MIBG nucleotides into the arm and then doing a scan twelve and thirty two hours later. Tucker would be sedated for the scans so that he would stay absolutely still for the entire forty-five minutes it took to perform it.

Tucker understood and did very well through the entire process. He finished the second scan early on Thursday morning and we were not due to start his chemotherapy at Sparrow until that evening. Lahti recommended a visit to this great wildlife preserve in the area. We took her advice and headed to the preserve for a picnic. We ate our lunch (with the Canadian Geese) and spent the afternoon playing "hurricane a-coming" on the jungle gym and flying kites. By the time we arrived at Sparrow that evening we felt rejuvenated from our day in the sunshine.

The second round of treatment at Sparrow began with a repeat bone marrow biopsy to see what impact the chemotherapy had on Tucker's cancer. Once again, I sat in on the biopsy. A pediatric resident performed the biopsy under Dr.Scott's direction. I cringed inside as Dr. Scott explained the technique to obtain a clear core biopsy. The resident pushed the large needle into Tucker's hip as Doctor Scott had instructed. Unfortunately, he was not successful in getting a clean biopsy and had to repeat the procedure on the other hip. This time while he was pushing the needle into the bone, Dr. Scott advised him to push harder, "This kid isn't feeling it!" The resident followed Dr. Scott's direction and pushed with more vigor.

The room was very quiet as the resident worked. After what seemed like an eternity, Dr. Guertin, the intensivist, said "There is only one person in this room who is feeling this and she will never forget it!" Immediately my face flushed as I felt all eyes turn to me. He was so right! Watching your three-year-old go through this hell is torture. A parent's instinct is to protect your child from pain and suffering. Instead we were signing consents and observing while pain was being inflicted upon our son in the hopes of beating this very crafty enemy. As I stood there watching them finish up, I reflected on how many times I had wished it was me instead of Tucker. Then I remembered what I learned about God's will. It was no mistake that Tucker was the one with cancer. God has a plan, and He promises that it is good.

Tucker did not tolerate the anesthesia or the chemotherapy very well that day. He slept all afternoon, waking only long enough to vomit. He was very pale and his eyes were almost swollen shut. I could hardly believe this was the same little boy who ran and played at the park less then twenty-four hours before.

Midafternoon I went out for a run. Running had become so therapeutic for me. It was my time to escape reality and spend time with Jesus. During this particular run, I did more crying than running. I was crying because I felt so inadequate. I couldn't make this trial go away for my son. I couldn't even handle watching him on the first day that he had really struggled with his treatment.

I wondered why Tucker was so sick this time. Were people forgetting to pray for him? Was God punishing me? As I ran, I vented, I cried and then I started to feel better. It was as if Jesus listened to my questions and my whining and then filled me with a peace as He told me, "No, this is not a punishment. The suffering is the part of the experience that draws you closer to Me. I hear the prayers. I am faithful. You must just be patient."

When I returned from my run, Tucker was awake and looking much better. He ate a little dinner, and then we all enjoyed an evening watching *Jungle Book* and eating ice cream. The rest of the week of chemotherapy went much better. Tucker felt good and enjoyed playing with Kaleb, his roommate. Early each morning, Kaleb and Tucker would get on the BIG WHEELS and race down the halls with their Dads in-tow pushing the IV poles.

I drove back to Ann Arbor to meet with one of the bone marrow transplant physicians at the end of the week. Todd and I had decided that I would go alone since I understood medicine more and he would stay with the kids in Lansing. The goal was to find out more about MIBG therapy, an experimental treatment that Lahti had mentioned to us. I met with Dr. Hutchinson, a very soft-spoken physician who was direct yet gentle. He told me all about MIBG. It was first discovered at U of M nineteen years prior. It is a nucleotide that binds predominantly to neuroblastoma cells. Because it only has an affinity for these types of cancer cells, it is very useful in diagnosing and treating this disease.

To treat neuroblastoma with MIBG radiation, a high dose of radiation is attached to the nucleotide. It is then infused in through a central line while the patient is in strict contact isolation for 24 to 72 hours while the radiation passes through his system. The cancer cells absorb the high dose radiation and then die. The rest of the body does not absorb the MIBG, so it is relatively unaffected.

U of M had been using this type MIBG therapy with neuroblastoma patients for at least ten years, but unfortunately it was not curing the disease. It just slowed it down for a while. Dr. Hutchinson went on to explain the investigational study they were currently conducting which combined MIBG therapy and a stem cell rescue (bone marrow transplant) in the hopes of curing this disease. They had used the proposed protocol on two children already, both of which were still in remission six months post-transplant.

As I listened to what Dr. Hutchinson said, I had a hard time imagining Tucker being in strict isolation for up to 72 hours. How would he get through it? He was only three years old. I knew however, that I must not disregard a very promising treatment option just because it was logistically difficult. I contemplated these difficulties while Dr. Hutchinson went and got the results from the MIBG scan they had done on Tucker earlier that week. Before he returned I had decided that we at least needed to get the opinions of other bone marrow transplant specialists around the country about the use MIBG therapy in conjunction with a stem cell rescue.

The results of Tucker's MIBG scan were not good. It showed extensive metastatic disease in multiple areas of Tucker's bone marrow. I felt sick to my stomach as I read about all the areas of neuroblastoma in my little boy. Dr. Hutchinson was very up front with me. He said "With this advanced disease, I would really consider MIBG therapy if I were you." I listened as tears ran down my face. It was all I could do to thank him for his time and get myself to my car before I fell apart.

The drive back to Lansing is just a blur in my mind. I was crying so hard, I could barely see the road. I stopped trusting God with Tucker's life. The result from Tucker's scan stole away my hope. I thought this trial must be even too big for God to handle. I let Satan sneak in and he attempted to destroy me!!!!! By the time I got back to Sparrow, I had the worst headache I had ever experienced.

God says in James 1:6, *"But when he asks, he must believe and not doubt, because he who doubts is like a wave of the sea blown and tossed by the wind."* That afternoon driving back to Sparrow, I doubted, and I got tossed and blown by the wind in a big way. It was the worst feeling of hopelessness I had ever experienced. It was the deepest valley I ever dropped into during this entire trial. I knew before I got out of the car, I had to find my hope or I would not survive the rest of this trial.

We were discharged from Sparrow the next morning but not before Tucker and Kaleb had one last race on their big wheels. This time they were both free of their IV poles! It was neck and neck all the way. Kaleb won by inches!!!!

The drive home changed my attitude. The kids were in great moods, and from the first mile, they chatted and giggled in their own imaginary world. As I listened to them I asked myself, "Who is feeling sick today, You or Tucker? ...ME. Who just received chemotherapy for the last six days? ...Tucker. Then why is he so happy and you feel so crappy? ...because I am not trusting God and living for the day, I'm worrying about the future, and that is wrecking the present!"

Right then one of my memory verses popped into my head: *"If you want to know how to live, watch a child".* I closed my eyes and prayed "Father, I hear the message You're sending me. Help me to be as a child, full of hope and enthusiasm, and trusting You in every detail of my life."

That was the final lesson I had to learn over the first forty days of our trial. It was quite a storm. Many times, I felt like Noah as he experienced his first lightning strike or thunder crash. Retrospectively, however, I am humbled and awed at the mercy that God showed my family and the tools He provided us to overcome each obstacle.

One such tool was a book entitled *Me and My Big Mouth* by Joyce Myers, that was in the mail when we first returned home from Lansing. The book had been sent by my book club" because I failed to return the "NO, I DO NOT WANT THE BOOK OF THE MONTH" card. As I dug through the mail our first weekend home, I opened the package and pulled out the book. The title caught my eye, so I put the book on my nightstand for bedtime reading.

Joyce's words spoke right to my heart. The opening line was a question, "Do you have a mountain to move?" Yes, I answered to myself. She continued, "The way to move a mountain is through your mouth." She went on to explain that you must truly believe that God can move your mountain and you must speak that with confidence daily. You also must surround yourself with God, His people and His Word. If you do these things, you will move your mountain, no matter how big it is!

I shared Joyce's words with Todd. We both found them very interesting because neither of us had any desire to watch television, listen to the radio nor read the paper since Tucker's diagnosis. Our only desire was to surround ourselves with God, His Word and His people. It was there that we had hope and could see meaning. After reading Joyce's book, I began keeping a journal of affirming pieces of scripture. I would recite them out loud and meditate daily on them until they were ingrained into my mind and I believed them with all of my being. They gave me a focus and helped me begin living my reality through the truths of the Bible.

## Chapter Three:

# *Drifting at Sea*

*And the waters prevailed on the earth one hundred and fifty days. Then God remembered Noah and every living thing, and all the animals that were with him in the ark. And God made a wind to pass over the earth and the waters subsided...At the end of one hundred and fifty days the waters decreased.*

*Genesis 7:24-8:3*

After the thunder and lightning of Tucker's initial diagnosis was over, we (like Noah and his family) drifted at sea for months through six rounds of chemotherapy. We tried our best to be obedient as we waited with hope for God's plan to be played out. God however was more interested in our journey than in the end, for He already knew the ending. He used this time to teach us many lessons about being true disciples.

I became bolder about my faith and more transparent about how God was working through this storm with my coworkers and patients. Each day, before I walked into the hospital, I prayed for discernment to be God's hands and feet in a bold yet humble way. God heard my prayers and started to use me. The more He used me, the closer our relationship grew and the more I enjoyed my job. I felt like I had two reasons for seeing every patient: to restore their physical self and to plant a seed within their spiritual self.

Two patients in particular touched by heart that summer. Ironically, both were named John. The first man was in his mid-fifties and was dying from lung cancer. He was in room 418, the same room that Tucker would eventually have each time he was admitted for blood transfusions. When I met John, his cancer had metastasized into his spine and had left his legs very weak and painful. The doctor had ordered physical therapy in combination with radiation therapy to restore John's strength enough for him to return home to enjoy his last few months.

As soon as I entered John's room the first time, I knew that he would be a physical and spiritual challenge. He did not even look at me as I introduced myself and explained what my role was. Anger and resistance were written all over his face.

His wife Shelly was there and we immediately connected. She willingly shared much about their life with me that day. She worked as a nurse for Lake Superior Hospice. John was a Vietnam Veteran who had many different jobs over the years. Shelly and John had been married for only five years. Before that, both of them had struggled through several rocky relationships. When they met, it was true love and has continued to be that way to this day. They lived in a small two-story house nearby. They loved doing anything together, especially riding their Harley along Lake Superior.

Shelly made it very clear that she was well aware of John's prognosis and probable limited time left here on earth; She was committed to taking him home and caring for him no matter how difficult. That included getting him up the very steep stairs into the house. She knew it would be long shot, but her dream was for them to ride their Harley to the beach for one last picnic.

I could really relate to Shelly. Like me, she was a healthcare professional who suddenly found herself on the other side of the system. After I had shared with her a little of my story, she told me, "So many times, I have prayed for God's will to be done so that my suffering patients could end their struggle. But now that it is my family member, I don't want God's will. I want my will!!!! I just found John, after so many bad relationships, why would God take him from me now?"

I heard Shelly's question, but I knew that no one could answer that question for her. She needed to ask that question in her prayers and wait for God's still quiet voice. John had an answer for Shelly's question. He said "Cuz that is the way God works. He just lets you get on your feet from something like

Vietnam, and then He kicks you in the ass again!" Those were the only words that John uttered that afternoon.

I completed my evaluation of John's strength and function and afterward told them what I thought we could do so that John could get home. We agreed that I would come back in the morning and we would work on transfers and climbing stairs.

Later, as I sat documenting at the nurse's station, Shelly came out to talk with me. She apologized for John's demeanor and thanked me for sharing my situation and my thoughts about God. She admitted that she was questioning God, and it helped to hear about the struggles of others and how faith is pulling them through.

I thought about Shelly and John all the way home. The Spirit nudged me to put together a care package for them. In it I enclosed my copy of *Me and My Big Mouth*, *God Calling*, some of my favorite Christian music and a letter encouraging them to develop a close personal relationship together with Jesus Christ before it was too late. I reminded them how limited cancer was; it cannot destroy the eternity that God has prepared, unless we let it.

The next morning, John, Shelly and I worked for an hour on transfers and negotiating the stairs. John was much more receptive to me this day. He had a mission (to get home), and he knew that I was the key to reaching that goal. To recreate the stairs at their home, we used the very steep back stairs to oncology. John laughed, perspired, cried and swore as he worked with Shelly and me on maneuvering his weak body up those stairs. As they worked together, they talked about days gone past and their dreams for the future.

John and Shelly reached their goal that day. He was discharged that afternoon with my care package in hand. I heard later that John lived for two more months and that Shelly cared for him at home until the end. I only hope and pray that they used that time to find Jesus Christ and develop a personal relationship with Him and that John today is riding his Harley in Heaven.

♥

The second John who touched my heart was very appropriately nicknamed "Sunny". I'm not quite sure of the origin of this nickname, but I would guess it was related to his unwavering optimism even in bleak circumstances. Sunny showed me how to look death right in the face and win!

Sunny was in the hospital because he had developed a Staph infection in a cut on his leg and unfortunately this infection had vegetated throughout his body including his heart valve and spine. Almost immediately after being admitted, he was moved to intensive care unit and put on a ventilator. His physicians had twice told his wife that they did not expect that he would live through the night. Sunny surprised them and kept on fighting.

Physical therapy was ordered for Sunny to increase leg strength once he was out of intensive care and off the ventilator. The infection was getting better, but it had done irreversible damage to his spine and heart. He was virtually paralyzed from the waist down and one of his heart valves was leaking so badly that it would have to be replaced if he was to recover. His physicians were not optimistic about his prognosis.

When I met Sunny, I immediately sensed a difference in him. I came to learn that Sunny was a man of faith and that he trusted God completely. He had a peace that I had rarely observed in people in his situation. I worked with Sunny and his wife twice a day. During that time we talked much about our trials and how God was strengthening us through adversity. They were very interested in my trial and asked me about my family daily. We became comrades in our fight against the evil that was attempting to destroy our families.

Sunny's physicians eventually decided that they would attempt to replace his valve. They did not specify in the chart when that surgery would take place, but it sounded like it would be soon. Sunny and I discussed the risks and implication of that surgery. Sunny was not afraid to die. Before I left him each day, we prayed together for strength and courage for both of our families and for healing for Sunny if that was God's will.

One morning when I came to see Sunny, he had just been taken to surgery to replace his heart valve. I immediately found a quiet corner and said a prayer for my friend. That was the Friday before Labor Day weekend, so I had to wait until the following Tuesday to see how Sunny had faired. I told my family about him and we all kept him in our prayers that weekend.

I was encouraged when I looked at the hospital census on Tuesday morning and saw that Sunny was already out of the intensive care unit. I was floored when I walked past his room later that day and heard him yell, "Hey Blondie! Get in here and get me moving!" When I peaked in and saw his radiant smile and sparkling eyes, I rejoiced and thanked God for answered prayer!

I obliged Sunny and started his therapy that very instant. We started with leg exercises and transfers into a chair. His legs were still very weak and I was concerned about the amount of pressure he put through his arms in order to stand. Usually after open heart surgery, patients are not allowed to use their arms at all to get up in the fear that they would split their sternum that has just been wired together.

After we finished our session, I found the heart surgeon's assistant, Bill, and asked if they had per chance put more wire around Sunny's sternum than usual because of his pre-existing lower extremity weakness. Bill laughed in reply and then said: "Are you kidding? Do you think that we thought for one minute that this guy would ever even make it off the table or the vent? I can't figure it out. Do you know we never even gave him any medication to control his blood pressure post op! That is almost unheard of."

Before Bill and I parted he cautioned me: "This guy has got a bag for a heart. Don't push him too hard, he still is not out of trouble." As I walked away I smiled and thought, "You don't know who is on his side!!!"

Sunny worked at his therapy each day and remained optimistic, but he was also very homesick. At the end of every therapy session he would ask "When can I go home...I just want to go home!!" I explained to him that he wasn't strong enough to go home because his wife couldn't care for him yet. I told him about the rehab transfer that I recommended. I explained that rehab was a step toward home. It was an opportunity for him and his wife to work on transfers, walking, dressing, and bathing in a home-like setting before they were on their own.

Sunny was receptive to the rehab transfer but was saddened that he still wouldn't be home. To cheer him up, I offered to take him over to rehab on a tour. He loved the idea of getting off the unit and checking out this new place.

I really didn't have time that morning to take Sunny to rehab, but I was nudged by th Spirit to do it, so I did. Little did I know what God had planned! As I was showing Sunny and his wife the dining room on the rehab unit, I heard some commotion at the end of the hall. I look down to see what was going on and there stood Todd, Lauren and Tucker. They were just going into my office to leave me a note. I motioned them over and told Sunny and his wife that this was my family. Tucker sauntered down the hall in his cowboy outfit complete with his big black hat, boots, and a leather vest and chaps. He gave me a big hug and then shook Sunny's hand. It was a magical moment; miracle meeting miracle. All who witnessed the interaction and conversation had tears welling in their eyes. It was a "God Moment"...God inspired and planned. No one else has that kind of timing.

The next day Sunny was transferred to rehab and two weeks later Sunny beat the odds and reached his goal: he WALKED with his wife out to their car and went home.

Sunny 's story reminded me to never stop believing. Never discount the "God factor". It reminded me to never lose my hope, faith and optimism no matter how tough the trial; his example was my "sun" shine" during many cloudy days over the following months.

♥

I wrote the following entry in my journal just before we left for Tucker's third round of chemotherapy:

*We are now two months into curing Tucker's cancer. We are in the middle, a very dangerous place. As Joyce states in Me and My Big Mouth: "The middle is often the testing place of faith. The initial shock and unlimited support of the beginning are gone. Friends and family are still supportive and concerned, but life goes on and our trial has become yesterday's news." It is now that our faith will have to carry us though. No doubt, our faith will be tested. Can we ride out the storm with grace or will we jump overboard?*

*Joyce states that faith is like a muscle; it is strengthened by using it, not by talking about it. Each storm we go through equips us to handle the next one better. I need to remember this as we journey through the middle.*

The next few days really did test my faith and taught me to trust the Holy Spirit's voice above all else and be obedient to its nudging. I felt very anxious all afternoon at work the day before we were to leave for Lansing; as if I had forgotten to do something. I called Sparrow Hospital to confirm that they were expecting us and asked if they wanted me to fax them Tucker's blood counts from three days ago. The nurse replied "Is that the most current blood draw you have?" Hesitantly, I answered "Yes." She warned me that Tucker's ANC had to be above 1000 to start chemotherapy. I knew that, but it had been 1900 and rising when last checked. After I hung up, that little voice told me to have another blood draw done.

I tried to get in touch with Todd, but I was not successful. So, instead, I went and found two of the oncologists at the hospital and got their opinion on checking Tucker's counts before leaving for Lansing. Both agreed based on the previous blood work that the chance of his ANC now being under 1000 was very small. They told me not to worry about it. This made me feel a little better, but that small voice saying "Get those counts checked" wouldn't go away.

Late in the afternoon, Todd called me at work. I told him about my conversation with the nurse at Sparrow and the oncologists at the hospital. He immediately said: "Well I can try to get there, but we are about thirty miles away and Tucker just fell asleep." Both of us were then silent for a long uncomfortable moment. Finally, I decided that I was just being paranoid and I dismissed that inner voice. I replied to Todd, "OK, let's just skip it. I'll see you at home."

All the way down to Lansing the next day, I had an empty feeling inside. I couldn't feel the Holy Spirit's presence. I wondered had I offended God...not followed His will? Was God asleep, or was He stepping back and allowing me to try my own wings?

We checked into Sparrow on Saturday morning. They were waiting for us, and everything got going like clockwork. By noon they had finished hydrating Tucker with IV fluids and were ready to start chemotherapy. We were already in the playroom set for an afternoon of building a fort when our nurse, Pam, came in and said, "We have a little problem. We checked Tucker's blood counts and his ANC is only 700."

Her words caught me completely off guard. I had quit worrying about his counts and everything seemed "right" this morning. My heart sank and I cursed myself, "That voice... why didn't you listen to that voice!" I recalled the sign I had read on the church marquee during our first trip to Lansing, Who's Report Do You Believe? I questioned myself: "Who do you believe... two doctors who aren't even involved in the case or the Great Physician?" I had dismissed the Holy Spirit's voice, and now we all had to face the consequences.

The consequences were that we stayed overnight and rechecked his counts in the morning. His ANC had only risen to 769 so by noon we had repacked all of our stuff and were back in the car headed north.

I pouted as I packed. I was sorry for not listening, but why did my kids also have to suffer the consequences (sixteen more hours in the car that week).

God cemented the lesson's importance through that morning's reading in *God Calling*:

### NOT PUNISHMENT

*I will guide your efforts. You are not being punished for past sins. Take my words, revealed to you each day from the beginning, and do in all things as I say. I have been showing you the way. You have not obeyed me in this.*

*I have a plan that can only in this way be revealed. So rarely do I find two souls in union who want only My will, and only to serve me. The union is miracle-working.*

*I have told you that I am longing to use you. Long ago My world would have been brought to Me, had I been served by many such two souls.*

*It was always "two and two".*

God was telling me, "I see your striving, not your perfection. I want to help you and use you, but you must listen. Do not despair, keep trusting Me!"

On our way home I copied the following prayer from Joyce Meyers (with my modifications) regarding listening to the Holy Spirit in my journal.

*Lord, I pray that You will help me to develop sensitivity to the Holy Spirit concerning all of my manner of conversation and my decisions regarding Tucker's care. I do not want to be stubborn like a horse or mule that will not obey without a bridle or bit. I want to move in your direction with only a gentle nudge from You.*

*During the storms of life, while I am crossing over to the other side; I ask for Your help. I always need Your help, Lord, but these times are special times of temptations. Place a guard over my lips and let all the words of my mouth be acceptable in Your sight O Lord my strength and Redeemer. In Jesus' name, I pray. Amen.*

God did carry us through that week of waiting. The kids did not mind the trip home. They recorded silly stories and noises on Lauren's tape recorder for most of the drive. Once home we had a campfire dinner complete with pizza pudgy pies and marshmallows. We sang songs around the fire long after dark. The rest of the week was equally as enjoyable. We made no plans; instead we took what God gave us each day. By Friday, Tucker's ANC was high enough to begin treatment.

As we drove downstate Saturday morning, I was more aware than usual of the beauty of God's creation: The white sand beaches of Lake Michigan that go on for endless miles; the breathtaking view of river gorges and the smell of pristine pine forests. I thought about how everything that God created is in balance and has an eternal circle of life. This is in contrast to what man has created. Our dwellings, automobiles, roads and bridges take significant energy to maintain and they slowly rust, crack and become an eyesore until somebody puts them in a landfill. I was awed by God's ability to create a world with eternal life.

♥

This time Tucker's week of chemotherapy went perfectly. In fact, he tolerated the treatment better than he had during either of the two previous months. The morning after he received Cytoxin (the toughest drug to tolerate), he was jumping around the playroom to the music of the "Kangaroo Hop". His doctors walked in during his performance and shook their heads and laughed.

Tucker was doing so well that Todd and I actually needed to find something we could do at the hospital to help pass the time. Konda, our nurse told Todd about Elderly Music, a favorite music store in Lansing. That sounded like something right up Todd's alley. I encouraged him to go for a break from the hospital. Todd went and stayed the entire afternoon!! He came back from the store with eyes–a-glowing. Music and that store were just what Todd needed. We decided before we left town that week to purchase a lap dulcimer for me, and a mandolin for Todd and the kids.

Retrospectively, I believe that bringing music into our lives and hospital room at that time was also part of God's plan to heal Tucker. Much of the reading I have done since that time on complementary medicine speaks of the healing force of music. In our situation, it kept the environment in our hospital room light and joyful. It was also a very intimate way for us to praise and worship God and stay focused.

♥

We knew that a stem cell transplant was the most aggressive treatment available to destroy any remaining the neuroblastoma cells within Tucker's body. It was highly recommended by our treatment team to be done after the induction chemotherapy and removal the tumor. Sparrow Hospital did not perform stem cell transplants, so we had to decide where we would go for this very long and dangerous treatment. Our Sparrow physicians recommended U of M Hospital but were receptive to us going elsewhere and encouraged us to investigate other programs.

Initially, we talked with several stem cell transplant centers to see if they were all the same. We found that they definitely were not. Some centers only transplant bone marrow while others could transplant stem cells harvested from the blood stream or bone marrow. We learned that the rate of relapse was lower with stem cell transplants than with bone marrow transplants. We also learned that L.A. Children's Hospital had a technique to purge cancer cells out of the stem cell harvest before they were frozen. The rate of relapse in children receiving these stem cells was even lower. This information made us very interested in going out to California for the transplant.

My sister, DeeAnn, who at time was a health care provider in L.A., talked with L.A. Children's transplant program chairman, Dr. Sieger, about the possibility of Tucker coming out there for his transplant. Dr. Seiger was receptive, and L.A. Children's Hospital became a very viable option. U of M Hospital became the other most viable option because of the MIBG therapy that could be done in combination with a stem cell transplant.

We waited to make our decision until God illuminated the path we should follow. We looked to other Christians to help us see that path. We asked Karsha's dad, Doug Shrem, about his thoughts on MIBG therapy. Doug sat and chatted with us for an hour about their experience with MIBG and U of M. He left us with some very strong words, "Don't be afraid of MIBG, be afraid of neuroblastoma!" These words stuck with both Todd and me. They helped us feel comfortable with choosing the most aggressive, hence riskiest, treatment option.

During that same week in Lansing, I contacted L.A. Children's Hospital to discuss their specific protocol. I talked with one of Dr.Seiger's colleagues. At the end of our discussion, I asked her opinion of MIBG therapy and if she would recommend MIBG therapy for Tucker if his MIBG scans did not pick up any cancer activity after his last round of induction chemotherapy? She hesitated for a moment and then said: "If that happens, call me back, because that would be a miracle!" As I hung up the phone, I knew that we needed to strongly consider doing the MIBG therapy, but I also knew what miracle I needed to start praying for: a clean MIBG scan before the transplant.

Todd was praying for a different miracle. After he heard what Doug had to say about beating this disease and what L.A. Children's had to say about their stem cell protocol, he couldn't understand why they wouldn't combine the two treatments and hence hit the cancer with every gun they had. He was praying that U of M and LA Children's Hospital would combine their protocols so that Tucker's stem cells would be purged and Tucker would get MIBG prior to his transplant. When Todd mentioned this possibility to our doctors in Lansing they didn't give him much hope that it would happen because of political and medical reasons. They explained that both of these institutions were doing controlled research on these treatment regimens for fighting neuroblastoma. If in one case they added a different uncontrolled variable it would make the data more difficult to interpret. Medically, they weren't even sure that it would be in Tucker's best interest to combine the treatments. It is a well-accepted fact that purging stem cells kills a significant number of them. It was questionable whether purged stem cells would engraft and grow in an environment where MIBG radiation has recently been. It was possible that residual radiation in Tucker's system would kill a share of the remaining stem cells and Tucker would be left in a situation in which his bone marrow would not grow back. Eventually he would die of some complication. The pessimism of the physicians did not dash Todd's hopes. He knew that God had a plan and he had a "feeling" about these treatment options. He prayed for this miracle and that God would be glorified through it.

Only time would tell if our prayers for a clean MIBG scan prior to transplant and cooperation between two major research hospitals would be answered. While we waited, we used both old and new forms of media to recruit Christians to pray for these miracles.

❤

Early in July, Todd's aunt sent us a card she had created with a picture of Tucker and a request for prayers next to the picture. I loved the idea. It was a simple way to remind people to pray for Tucker. I also loved the picture. It had been taken the previous summer at Todd's sister's wedding. The black tuxedo accented Tucker's fair features and his beautifully blue, innocent eyes. The only thing I didn't like was the tone of the prayer request. It made our situation seem so sad and desperate. I didn't want sympathy; I wanted to empower people to pray for us and believe that the prayers would be answered. So, I began designing my own card using the picture but with a different message. I searched for a Bible verse that voiced my feelings. I didn't tell anyone about the card or that I was looking for a verse that voiced how I felt about this trial. One day, my Mom called me and said a verse had really touched her heart regarding Tucker. It was John 11:4:

*This sickness is not unto death, but for the glory of God, that the Son of God may be glorified through it.*

As she read me the verse, I knew that it was what I had been searching for. From the first day of this trial, God had told me that this sickness would be for His glory and that He would care for Tucker as long as we trusted Him and put all into His hands. I thanked my mom and told her about the card. With the verse and picture and some help from Mike and Susie, I created a bookmark that was a thank you for prayers and request for continual prayer. It proclaimed Tucker's victory over cancer before it happened. It glorified God.

Over the next six months, fifteen hundred of these bookmarks were given out. Many of the people who received a bookmark, copied and distributed it, like a seed, to their field of Christians. I personally kept a few with me at work all the time and when God nudged me I would tell our story to my patient and at the end give them a bookmark and ask them to pray for Tucker. No one ever refused me.

That simple strip of paper with a picture, verse and "thank you" made our trial personal to all who saw it. Almost everyone has a soft spot for children, hence as soon as they saw Tucker's picture on the bookmark they became committed to pray for him. I started to draw strength from people inquiring about how Tucker was doing or telling me that they have his picture on their refrigerator and are praying for him every day.

At my work, it became a ministry tool. When I shared our trial with my patients and gave them a bookmark, it encouraged them to take their health burden to God. When they looked at the bookmark, not only did they pray for us, they started to talk with God about their own situation.

The other media source we used to spread our testimony and stay in touch with those praying for us was the Internet. Prior to this, neither Todd nor I knew anything about this media source. We didn't even own a computer. By

September, the bookmarks and word of mouth had increased our scope of spiritual support to a level where I was really struggling to keep everyone up to date of our situation. I didn't want to spend all of my family time on the phone yet I wanted people to know how to best pray. Then one morning as I was standing in the shower the idea of a website popped into my head. Once at work, I contacted J.J., a coworker of Todd's, who I knew was a "computer guru" and asked him what he thought of the idea. J.J. and his wife Bev, loved the idea and within a week had Tucker's website up and going. The site quickly drew readers from all over. They sent us words and prayers of encouragement and strength. Sunday school classes adopted Tucker as their prayer project and kept in touch with us through the site. It became bigger than just Tucker and cancer. It was about faith, prayer, tribulation and God. It allowed us to overcome evil with good on a much larger scale.

Mid-September, Tucker was scheduled for a bone marrow biopsy at Sparrow Hospital. This test would determine if Tucker's cells were "clean enough" for the stem cell harvest. We still did not know where we were going for the transplant but U of M and LA Children's Hospital had agreed that U of M would do the harvest.

A bone marrow biopsy is only a twenty-minute outpatient procedure. Hence, to save the kids' sixteen hours in the car over a two-day period we set up a flight to Lansing. The kids were very excited for they had never flown before. In making the arrangements for the flight; however, I kept reminding everyone that the entire trip was dependent upon Tucker's blood counts. The biopsy could not be done if his ANC was below 1500 because of the increased risk for infection. I had learned from the last month's challenge to not assume that Tucker's counts would be good and that all things would happen on God's time frame not mine.

On Tuesday morning as I read *God Calling* I cringed. It foretold of how my faith would fail me that day. It quoted Mark 9:24:

*Lord, we believe, help us with our unbelief.*

It went on to say that:

*"As the soul realizes Me and My power and knows Me as Helper and Savior, that the soul believes in Me more and more. I guarantee that your cry for more faith will be heard!!!"*

I tried not to fail. I had been warned and I tried not to get my hopes up about the flight. All morning I kept busy teaching a PT student the ins and outs of working in acute care. I tried to keep my focus on my work and serving my patients and my student. Just before lunch I called the oncology office to find out the results of Tucker's morning blood test. His ANC was only 500. I was crushed. I cried all noon hour as I ran down on the beach of Lake Superior. I asked God, "Why? Why? Can't my plan ever work? Haven't I tried to be patient? Haven't I prayed enough on this issue?" My faith in God's plan was failing just as predicted. I regained my composure after lunch, but inside I pouted all afternoon as I canceled all of the flight arrangements and called Todd.

On my way home I cried out of my soul, "Oh, God, I just need a sign that You really care and that You are leading our journey. Ten minutes later when I turned onto highway 94 and started heading straight east, the most brilliant rainbow that I had ever seen arched over the highway in front of me. I gasped as I gazed at its beauty and reflected on the timing of its appearance. I had just asked for a sign and here was the sign that God had given Noah as He said:

*"Rejoice: For I have set the rainbow in the clouds as a reminder of my everlasting love for you!"*

*Genesis 9:13*

Tears stream down my face as I marveled at God's incredible compassion for me. As I drove closer to the rainbow and home, I imagined that the rainbow arched over and ended right in our backyard. I hurried down the highway to see if I could witness what I imagined. However, just before I turned onto our gravel road the rainbow vanished.

With a tear-stricken face and joyous smile I bounded up the stairs and into the house to tell my family what I had just experienced. I didn't need to tell them. Todd and Lauren were waiting for me at the front door. The first words that Todd uttered were, "I'm not sure what all the tears are about, but I bet they have something to do with the rainbow that just ended under our apple tree!!"

♥

The next morning I decided to stay home with Tucker. I was already scheduled to be off, and I needed some one-on-one time with my little boy. After we took Lauren to school and sent Todd off to work (his first day back in four months), we sat down to Tucker's favorite breakfast, homemade waffles with wild blueberries! Just as I picked up my fork, the phone rang. It was Leslie Hoover from Sparrow. She called to inform us that L.A. Children's Hospital had called Sparrow yesterday afternoon after receiving Tucker's blood count values. They said that Tucker did not need the bone marrow biopsy to ensure the marrow was clean enough. They could tell by his counts that he was ready for the harvest. My heart started to race with this unexpected good news. Leslie then added: "We asked L.A. Children's to call U of M to discuss this opinion since U of M would be doing the actual harvest." She closed our conversation saying, "I will call you back later today and let you know U of M's response."

After I hung up the phone, I explained the situation the best I could to Tucker and then we joined hands and prayed. We prayed for wisdom, discernment and a spirit of cooperation amongst all of these physicians. Specifically, we prayed that they would forget about their research and protocols and instead work together and offer us the option that our Father knew would cure Tucker's disease.

Both of us immediately changed the subject as soon as we finished praying. With peace, I enjoyed my now very cold waffles as we made plans for our day together. Tucker described to me a waterfall that he wanted to take me to way back in the woods.

After breakfast, we did just that. We packed the 4-Runner with a picnic lunch and the maps of Hiawatha National Forest and went looking for Tucker's waterfall. We ended up on a two-track trail in a posted wilderness area. We had a blast "powering through the puddles" in our truck. Eventually we pulled off to the side of the road and started hiking down a trail that Tucker was sure would take us to his water fall. The trail was very rough. In fact at times we had to guess where the trail was. Eventually it led us to a grand overlook over the Rock River Valley, but never to the sought-after waterfall. We were not disappointed. We had a blast hiking through the waist-high ferns under the canopy of maple and pines. We soaked up the sun as we ate our lunch at what seemed like the top of the world

After lunch we found our way back to the 4-Runner and headed for home. Tucker fell asleep almost immediately. As I drove out of the woods with "Sunshine on my Shoulder" playing on the radio and the sunshine reflecting off the hues of greens and yellows all around me, I was filled with an inner peace beyond understanding. I bathed in this quiet assurance all the way home.

When we got home, Tucker was still sleeping so I left him in the truck and went inside to check the answering machine. There were three messages from Leslie; each telling of a different plan of how we would proceed from here. Finally on the last message she said, "Dr. Yanik will call you." As I was listening to this final message, the phone rang. It was Dr. Yanik. Before I let him tell me what he had discussed with L.A. Children's Hospital, I told him how Tucker and I had spent our day. He laughed with me and then said, "Kim, you might want to sit down before I tell what happened today." He then went on to tell me that Dr. Seiger, the department chair of L.A. Children's transplant team had agreed to work with U of M on Tucker's care. Specifically, he agreed to purge Tucker's stem cells and allow U of M to transplant them after the MIBG radiation if U of M would do the harvest now before another round of chemotherapy.

After I hung up the phone, I wept with happiness and humility as I recalled the events of the past twenty-four hours. I thought about how God must have laughed at me as I ran down the beach pleading with Him to let "my will" be done. Yet He had enough compassion for me that He blessed me with the rainbow of assurance on my drive home. Then today, how the Holy Spirit nudged me to stay home this morning and pray after our phone call with Leslie; our adventure and the peace it instilled in me, and finally the revelation of God's amazing plan for Tucker's cure.

I went back out to the car to check on Tucker. He was still sleeping so I climbed into the front seat and through my tears wrote this poem:

### MY RAINBOW

*The flight was set,*
*But the numbers were not met,*
*My faith was failing, my spirit ailing!*
*Oh God, I need a sign!!!!*
*What... what is that I see?*
*A rainbow shining down on me!*
*Actually,*
*I think as I drove in my car,*
*The rainbow is ending in my yard.*
*At home Todd and Lauren tell me*
*"The rainbow ended under our apple tree."*
*God's sign of His everlasting love for me!!*

♥

A week later we started the stem cell harvest at U of M. The harvest involved surgically inserting a very large catheter into Tucker's groin and drawing blood from that catheter into a machine for six to eight hours at a time. The machine separated the cells and plasma by density and in that way isolated the stem cells (which were just a little denser than the plasma). The coveted stem cells remained isolated in a bag above the machine while the rest of the plasma and cells returned to Tucker's blood stream.

Stem cells are the mother cells of all the different kinds of cells in the blood. Usually they are mostly within the bone marrow with only a relatively few being released into the bloodstream.

Prior to the harvest, Tucker was given a huge dose of a medication to increase the release of these stem cells. It worked, after four hours four million stem cells were collected. Tucker's physicians were very pleased. They came in at the end of the first day and said, "Great start! At this pace we should only need about two more days of collection."

Tucker was not encouraged with this news. The catheter was very uncomfortable and he was not even allowed to sit up with it in. He tried to be patient with it and enjoy our movie that night but I could tell it was agonizing for him to lie so still. I couldn't imagine him lying there for another two days.

Late in the afternoon of that second day, our physician still hadn't come in to tell us the count for that day. I needed a break so I left our room and went down to the business office to take care of some insurance issues. As I sat waiting in that office, I read a sign over the door that said:

*May the wisdom of your past*
*Give you strength and courage*
*for the present, and hope*
*and peace for the future.*

These words were just what I needed at that moment. They reminded me of how clearly God had led us over the past three months. They called me to use the strength and courage I had gained to handle this day with all its unknowns. They also gave me hope and peace about the upcoming surgery and stem cell transplant.

I returned to Tucker's room with a fresh smile and perspective. I knew with Jesus holding my hand, I could pull Tucker through one more day of laying still. When I walked in, Todd, Lauren and Tucker were all smiling. Tucker had BIG news! He grinned at me and said, "They got enough cells, I'm done!" I turned and looked at Todd for confirmation. He said they had collected nine million cells that day, for a grand total of thirteen million cells. The goal was to get twelve million. He added they were planning on discharging Tucker yet that night!

Later, as we drove to the hotel, we were all very quiet. We thought the kids were sleeping. Suddenly from the back seat a voice broke the silence with an announcement, "Daddy, you know I don't like the stuff they did to me in there." Todd replied, "Yes, Tucker, I know." After a long pause Tucker spoke again, "Daddy, you know I did it for you." Todd fought back tears as he replied, "Thank you Tucker." Again there was a long silence and then Tucker added, "Boy Daddy, I sure cranked out those stem cells, didn't I!"

♥

The next day was a free day. We had to stay in the area because it was time for Tucker to get his fourth round of chemotherapy; however, we had to wait a day for Tucker's blood counts to recover from the large doses of medication that he was given before his stem cell harvest. We took the opportunity to replenish our kid's souls with sunshine, fresh air and an adventure. I had no idea that it would also be a new kind of adventure for me.

This adventure took place in Brighton, a small town between Ann Arbor and Lansing. Larry Lane, the fire chief in Brighton, is the brother of our daycare provider in Marquette. Right after Tucker was diagnosed, Larry had offered to give us a tour of the fire station and a ride on a fire truck sometime when we were down in the area. I had contacted him earlier in the week and took him up on his offer. It was set for 11 am.

During my morning quiet time that day, I started reading the Book of Acts. Chapter 1 verse 7 spoke to me:

> And He said to them, "It is not for you to know times or seasons which the Father has put in His own authority. But you will receive power when the Holy Spirit has come upon you and you shall be witnesses to Me in Jerusalem, and in all Judea and Samaria, and to the end of the earth."

*Acts 1:7-8*

In the margins of this particular text, Max Lucado, the editor of the Bible I was using, questioned me, "Do you fear talking about your faith? Who is it that you fear?" I pondered that thought through breakfast and all the way to the fire station. I decided that I was very comfortable sharing my faith one-on-one with my patients and in "friendly fire", but I did not know if I would be comfortable sharing it publicly with an unknown audience. I thought about these questions all morning. As we pulled in to the fire station I quieted my heart's questioning by telling myself, "You have never had the chance to share your faith more publicly. I'm sure that you would if you had the chance."

Larry Lane was waiting for us. First he showed us the shiny new red and yellow engines and let the kids try all their bells and whistles. He also showed us the antique trucks which were pulled by horses or had a Model A engine. We proceeded into the fireman's quarters and got to slide down the pole and try on the fireman's jackets and helmets.

After we finished seeing everything inside, Larry took us out back where Stacey, a firewoman, was talking to a local newspaper photographer and maneuvering the aerial bucket of the biggest fire engine. Larry explained to us that Fire Prevention Week was coming up soon and that the photographer was taking some promotional photos for that week.

A few minutes later, Stacey waved us over and asked us if we would mind being in a few pictures up in the aerial. Tucker was not sure about going way up there, so Lauren and I went up to show Tucker that it was fun. Up we went seventy feet in the air! Below I could see Todd talking to the photographer. I felt a little surge in my soul as I recalled Max's question to me "How bold are you about your faith?" I wondered what God was up to. Was He going to let me off with "I have not had the chance" or was He going to give me the opportunity to see what I would do with it.

As soon as Stacey brought the aerial basket down, I found out just what God was up to. Todd asked me for a phone number at Sparrow where we could be reached the rest of the week. He added that he had filled the photographer in on why we were at the fire department. The photographer thought it might be a nice human-interest story. He wanted to go back to the office and suggest it to one of the reporters. If they liked the idea, they would contact us at the hospital.

I agreed to the idea and walked to the car with the photographer to get a number at Sparrow where we could be reached. As we walked, I shared a little about how God was providing for us each day. I was very bold about my faith with this stranger. Ten minutes later, he departed with the number, and I returned to our little tour group. They were now going back up in the aerial bucket, this time with Tucker. As I watched them, I reflected on my response to God's living word this morning. I felt a nearness to God, a peace because I had followed him blindly and witnessed to this stranger.

We then rode a big yellow fire engine across town to the other fire station. Tucker was in the back seat of the engine with Lauren and me. He was very quiet but very interested and awed with all the big equipment and engine's power.

Forty-five minutes later when we arrived back at the first fire station, there was a reporter waiting to talk with us. I smiled inside as I thought, "God really wants to see how bold I am about my faith." I spent the next half-hour sharing with this reporter our trial, our miracles and how God continued to provide for us.

The article was printed on the front page of the Brighton Gazette two weeks later. It was titled, "Brighton firefighters make Tucker's Day". How true that was. It was perfect adventure for a three -year old who loved everything about a trucks especially big, shiny firetrucks. It also was a perfect adventure for his mom.

# Chapter 4:

# *The Top of Our Mountain*

*And the waters decreased continually until the tenth month. In the tenth month, on the first day of the month, the tops of the mountains were seen.*

Genesis 8:5

When we arrived at Sparrow at the end of September for chemotherapy, Dr. Scott told us that they were going to repeat all the tests that Tucker had when he was first diagnosed to determine if the tumor was now small enough to remove. This news made me anxious yet somewhat excited. I had prayed for great results and now I needed to allow God's peace to flow and to accept His will no matter what.

One morning as Todd and Tucker sat on the bed playing Legos, Todd asked Tucker if he wanted to know what was going to happen that day. Tucker was scheduled for both a bone marrow biopsy and a CT scan. Tucker thought about it for a few minutes and then said, "Are you going to be with me Dad?" Todd responded "Of course". Tucker then replied: "Then I don't want to know. Just tell me when it's time to go and stay with me and hold my hand." Later, Todd and I discussed the incredible wisdom of Tucker's decision. That is just what God tells us we should do. He veils the future from us because it would overwhelm us. He commands us to trust Him and Jesus will hold our hand and carry us through.

I tried to adopt Tucker's attitude as we approached September 28th, the day that Dr. Scott had planned to go through the results of the tests with us. I found it very difficult. As the hour of the meeting approached, I became more and more anxious about what the results would show. I imagined both the best and worst-case scenarios. I wondered if my faith would pull me through.

My thoughts went back to those painful days in June when we first learned the extensiveness of Tucker's cancer.

The night before, I stayed awake praying and reading at Tucker's bedside long after Todd and Lauren left for the O'Berski's. I couldn't stand the anticipation of the next day; so much road of those results. They would change my whole life. I decided to read ahead in *God Calling* hoping that the words for September 28th would calm my fears and reassure me. Instead what I read gravely concerned me. Matthew 3:15 was the scripture quoted. It said: *"Suffer it to be so now; for thus it becometh us to fulfill all righteousness."* The associated devotional writing was equally as concerning. It said:

> *"Much that you both must accept in life is not to be accepted as being necessary for you personally, but accepted, as I accepted it, to set an example, to share in the sufferings and difficulties of mankind.*
>
> *In this "to share" means "to save". And there too, for you both...the same must be true as was so true of Me. "He saved others. Himself He cannot save."*
>
> *Beloved you are called to save and share in a very special way. The way of sorrows if walked with Me, the Man of Sorrows, is a path kept sacred and secret for My nearest and dearest, those whose one desire is to do all for Me, to sacrifice all for me, to count as My servant Paul did, 'all things but loss so that they might gain Me.' "*

I knew that these were words were true. I knew that God had chosen us to share in a very special way. I knew that this path we were on was very sacred and secret, and I enjoyed doing His work. Yet it was difficult to accept that I could not save Tucker, no matter how many people I share my faith with or how many seeds I plant. I feared that I was being called to suffer just as my Savior had. I cried myself to sleep.

The next morning, Todd's Dad called early even before Tucker was awake. I shared with him my anxiety about the reading in *God Calling* and the test results. Ken had also read *God Calling* that morning. The words had a very different meaning to him. He said, "Can't you see, Kimmy, how this trial is bringing people to Christ? You are planting seeds that will have eternal consequences! But heed the warning, don't get too righteous, only by grace can you be saved. Plant seeds because you love God and want to do His will not to earn a trip to heaven or to save Tucker. Keep trusting God no matter what." Ken ended the conversation with a few more words of encouragement, "Your journey would seem dreary to most, yet I know you see all that God is doing and are excited about how He is working. Don't lose that! Just watch and see, Kimmy, God's plan for Tucker is good."

A few minutes after I hung up the phone, Kelly, the child-life specialist, came and asked if our family would like to paint a mural on the playroom windows. Tucker loved the idea and sold Lauren on it as soon as she walked in with Todd fifteen minutes later. I decided it would be a great distracter for me until Dr. Scott came with the test results, so we all headed down to the playroom to paint.

Tucker and I painted a picture of our September adventure including the rainbow, waterfall and trail through the wilderness. Lauren and Todd painted a fall scene including an apple tree loaded with red ripe apples and a pumpkin patch.

Halfway into this project, Dr. Scott came in to examine Tucker and talk with us. I held my breath as he looked over Tucker and listened to his heart and lungs. I prepared myself for the results. When he finished examining Tucker, Dr Scott said, "I don't have all the results yet, so would it be okay if we went over them tomorrow?" I sighed a breath of relief. I was more than okay with that. I just wasn't ready to hear them yet. After Dr. Scott left, we returned to our painting. As I painted, I reflected on how gracious God was to hold the result from me today. I stayed in the day, ALL DAY, and enjoyed my family. I reflected on my blessings and did not worry about what tomorrow would bring. Just like today, I knew tomorrow would take care of itself.

By the next morning, I was much more mentally and spiritually ready to hear the test results. Dr. Scott and Leslie came in mid-morning and went over the results with us. All of the tests showed a significant improvement in Tucker's condition! Dr. Scott was very pleased and thought that the tumor was now small enough to remove. He would consult the surgeons and get their opinion sometime within the next week.

That night after Tucker finished his last chemotherapy infusion we celebrated! We had completed the stem cell harvest, the fourth round of chemotherapy and had some tangible evidence that our prayers for a cure were being answered. We thank God for his mercy and help; and enjoyed popcorn and root beer with our movie!

On October 1st, Leslie called us at home to say that Dr. Harmon, one of the pediatric surgeons, had looked at Tucker's test results and agreed that the tumor was now small enough to be removed. As I listened to Leslie, I marveled at the timing of her call as it related to the scripture in Genesis. Just like Noah, on the first day of the tenth month we saw the top of our mountain.

♥

October 1st was not only a day in which we watched our hopes become our reality; it was also a day in which we saw a glimpse from which the power came to make these hopes into reality.

That morning at work, Matt Flynn, a fellow believer and colleague of mine to whom I had given a stack of Tucker's bookmarks, approached me at my desk. He relayed to me what his dad had experienced the day before in church. Months prior to this, Matt had given his parents one of Tucker's bookmarks. They had photocopied it and shared our story and need for prayers with their community of Gulliver, a small town about two hours from us.

The previous morning Matt's parents went to church in Manistique, a slightly larger town nearby. They were brought to tears by the children's service. The priest talked about the power of prayer and miracles. At the end of his sermon he said: "Now, who are we lifting up in prayer this week?" In response all the kids stood and held up their copy of Tucker's bookmark and yelled "TUCKER!!!!!!"

As I listened to Matt's story, tears rolled down my cheeks. These were not only tears of gratefulness for all those prayers; they were also tears of awesome wonder. I was experiencing what God had told me during my run, "Kimmy, this time it's different. This time this battle is about showing you and others the power of faith. After Matt left me, I sat at my desk and prayed: "Father, Thank you for all those like Matt's family; for being fertile ground in which to plant our seed of need...for being our messengers to the world. Father, thank you for having mercy on our family, for loving us and caring for us. I am humbled that you have chosen us to expand and strengthen Your Kingdom. Help us to stay focused and close to You, to follow only Your will and to live each day to the fullest."

♥

By October 8th, Tucker's blood counts had hit an all-time low. Leslie had warned us that Tucker's hematologic recovery from the chemotherapy would get increasingly more difficult with each successive round. On this date, his hemoglobin was down to 6.6 and his platelet count was at 38,000. Dr. Chen called Todd with these results and recommended that Tucker be admitted overnight for a blood and platelet transfusion.

Todd could hardly believe that Tucker's counts were so low because he had been playing hard all day with no signs of fatigue. In fact, as Todd was speaking with Dr. Chen, Tucker was running around the yard playing cowboy. Despite that, Todd agreed to bring him into the hospital for a blood transfusion.

Todd and the kids arrived at the hospital in late afternoon as I was finishing up work. As I was walking over to oncology, I remembered that Lauren had asked for a movie night when we discussed our weekend plans that morning. In response, I stopped by the hospital education department to see what videos they had available. They had about twenty kid's movies, and one of them just happened to be *Casper, The Friendly Ghost*. Lauren had specifically requested that movie. My heart leaped when I saw the title and I smiled and said a quick prayer of thanks in this seemingly insignificant detail in my day. Little did I know that God His own reason for a making *Casper* available.

Tucker tolerated the blood transfusion beautifully (thanks to the Benadryl and Tylenol that they gave him prior to the transfusion). He woke up by six o'clock Saturday morning ready to go. No time to sit in a hospital and watch a movie! They discharged us by eight am telling us to take *Casper* home with us and have a Saturday movie night.

We wasted no time once discharged making the most of this beautiful fall day. We loaded up the canoe and headed for the Big Island Canoe Area. It was amazing. The trees were fully dressed in their scarlet and gold colors. The sky was a brilliant blue and the sun was just warm enough to chase away the fall chill in the air. We spent the day exploring new portage trails, lakes and campsites. The kids and I climbed on a beaver's house and pretended we were part of his family as Todd harvested birch bark from a tree the beaver's had recently cut. The kids even attempted to tight-rope walk down a tree trunk that had fallen into the water. They escaped that adventure with only damp shoes!

Tucker was especially funny that afternoon. The blood transfusion gave him amazing energy! He scurried up portage trails singing his own little songs and looking for little treasures. When in the boat, he paddled furiously with his little paddle. We watched in disbelief: is that the kid whose hemoglobin was six yesterday and just finished chemotherapy a week ago? We joked that next time we were going to ask for some of that blood too!

We ended that perfect day with *Casper* and popcorn. The movie was not what I expected. It was actually pretty unnerving. As the plot played out I wondered why I had been "blessed" with it. I kept hoping it would get better but it never really did. It was about a young boy who died at around fifteen years of age and had hung around haunting his old house ever since. He was stuck between this world and the next because something was left undone or someone couldn't let go.

I laughed and cried throughout the entire movie. It stirred many emotions in me. It reminded me of my brother, John. I wondered how different my life would have been if he had not died. I grieved for all that he had missed here on earth and how much I missed him. As the movie depicted the burdens and difficulties that face parents who end up burying their own children, I wondered why God had let me "find" that movie. After the kids were in bed, I cried in Todd's arms fearful for the future. He heard my concerns and then reminded me of God's constant companionship. This was only a movie and I was reading way too much into it.

As I lay in bed that night, I thought about John and Dad. I wondered why my family was called to so much suffering. After wrestling with that for a while without resolution, I began to reminisce about the good times we had as a family: horseback riding on fall Sunday afternoons; swimming with my entire family at grandpa's dock on hot August weekends and big family volleyball picnics on holidays.

As I relived all these memories I realized that these were parts of my life that I had never shared with Todd or the kids. I decided that the next day, Sunday, would be dedicated to John and my dad. I would get out all my pictures and spend the day telling my family about these two people that were so much of me, yet they had never met.

After breakfast the next morning, I got out all of my old photo albums that had pictures of John and my dad. I showed them pictures of my dad riding his horse, Laddy, in the Octoberfest parade as a Posse member and of John and I as we grew up together. I told them stories about the early fun times and the harder times. We discussed how both of them had lost their battle to cancer but won the race of life.

I felt John beside me all that day. He was so close that I could almost feel his breath as I went for a run that evening. His spirit remained very real and present with me throughout the difficult weeks ahead.

Tucker's surgery was scheduled for October 20th, at Sparrow with Dr. Harmon. If, however his blood counts were not high enough, surgery would have to be delayed. Tucker's fourth birthday was October 19th. Although I hoped that somehow Tucker would not have to spend his birthday in the hospital, I had learned to trust God timing. We had gotten pretty good at rolling with just a tentative plan and staying in the day.

At the same time another event came up on the radar screen. Some members of the community approached us about putting on a benefit at the school for Tucker and our family. They set the date for October 17th. They asked us if we could be there. I had no idea. Tucker's counts might be too low; it might not be smart with his upcoming surgery. I made no commitments but thanked them for their efforts and said we would at least be there in spirit.

Each day as I drove to work I considered and prayed about all of this...the surgery, the benefit, and that crazy *Casper* movie. Slowly, the Spirit led my thoughts to God's will for that day. I was to plan to go to the benefit. Tucker's counts would be high enough and we would not yet be in Lansing. I was to share my brother John and Tucker's stories as they related to trusting God with every detail of life.

The connection between Tucker and John's story was very more than a coincidence. John had said to the newspaper reporter a week before he died, "If God is taking me so young, he must have something really important for me to do." These words might relate to the coincidence that Tucker, the only male grandchild in my family, was "due" on John's birthday but born five days later; and that John died of cancer while Tucker was born with it. I wondered, Could John's spirit be working through Tucker? At times I thought possibly I was losing sight of reality as I pondered such things and I would try to dismiss it, but the Spirit kept pulling me back.

One night after the kids were in bed, I shared with Todd all these thoughts that were running through my head. I told him how clear it was to me that the Spirit wanted to work through this benefit and that it was an opportunity for us to share God's power and mercy with our family and friends and glorify Him through it.

Todd listened very intently then we prayed together about this opportunity. The next morning, he called many members of his family and invited them to the benefit. He told them that he had a feeling this would be a day that they would not want to miss. Todd's dad, brother and grandparents accepted the invitation and joined us for the weekend.

On October 14th, John's birthday, as I drove to work I prayed for direction in sharing this story. I just didn't know how I should go about it.

After I finished praying, I put in one of my favorite audiotapes. Immediately Kim Hill's voice filled my car as she sang:

*I wish the same for you,*
*Something to hold onto*
*a chance for love.*
*You and I, we are not so different.*
*We have the same questions about eternity.*

*I finally found the safe and the sound.*

As I listened, I heard her sing what I wanted to share at the benefit. I wanted to tell how I had learned to survive the evils of this world and doubts about eternity. How I had learned to beat cancer and death by finding God and giving it all to Him.

For a moment I contemplated singing this song myself. As soon as I drifted back to reality, I dismissed that thought. I loved to sing but I had no talent. God definitely would NOT be glorified through me singing that song! I then considered playing the tape; but that didn't seem quite appropriate. By the time I got to work, I dismissed the entire song idea.

God had other plans. That afternoon He put a person in my life that could sing that song if I was bold enough to ask. Her name was Melanie. Melanie was new to the area and currently going through treatment for breast cancer. She came to see me because she had developed lymphedema. As I was examining her arm, I asked her questions about her exercise habits. She admitted that the only regular exercise she gets is when she sings! At first I laughed at her answer, but from her expression I could tell she was serious, so I pried a little deeper. She explained that she was a cantor for the Catholic Church (which is a soloist that leads the congregation in musical worship during the mass) and a voice coach. She went on to explain consistent stretching and vocal exercises are crucial to a pure voice. As Melanie talked, my thoughts went back to the song in my car but I pushed any thought of asking her to sing this song aside. I didn't even know this lady!

After I described lymphedema and the treatment I recommended, I began making measurements of her arms so I could determine the extent of her edema and eventually the effectiveness of the treatment. While I took these measurements, we talked about adjusting to life in the Upper Peninsula. She shared with me many details of her life that had made the last year particularly challenging.

She told me of an experience she had just before moving here that really helped to put life in perspective for her. She sang at the funeral of a boy who was supposed to graduate from high school with her daughter. She said the entire service was magical. She could feel the Spirit throughout the sanctuary. All the passages of scripture and song seemed as if they had been hand-picked by God Himself. The service was not about despair and grief. It was about hope and the promise of eternal life. For example, she said, When my daughter read, "...*and then John said 'Now I looked up and I saw a new heaven and a new earth, for the first heaven and the first earth had passed away...*"

I didn't even let her finish her thought. By that time my eyes were brimming with tears as I blurted out, "Oh, Melanie does the Bible really say "*and John said?*"

She replied, "Yes, that comes from the 21$^{st}$ chapter of Revelations. John wrote all of Revelations as an old man. But what is so significant about that?"

I couldn't hold back my story any longer. I told her about John and Tucker's struggle with cancer and that today would have been John's 31$^{st}$ birthday. I told her how much the funeral she described reminded me of my own brother's funeral. I even went out on a limb and asked her to sing "my song" at the benefit.

She listened with a peculiar smile on her face, and then she agreed to go to my car with me and listen to the song after we finished working with her arm.

We ran to my car through spitting rain and listened to Kim Hill sing those same words that had spoken to me earlier that day. Melanie liked the song, and felt she could do it acapella if she could borrow the tape.

I couldn't believe I asked her or that she agreed to do it!!! As we walked to her car she said, "Thank you for this day, I really needed a friend in Marquette." I replied, "Don't thank me, thank God; He is the one responsible for us meeting. I know that I will!"

Melanie did an amazing job singing at the benefit. Her voice and the song's lyrics reinforced all the words that I spoke. Even her presence as (she called it) "a cancer poster child", with her short, fine new-growth hair was a testimony of beating evil with good.

Melanie and I have remained good friends and after Tucker's bone marrow transplant I "seized the day" and began taking voice lessons from her so that I too could confidently sing God's praises!

♥

By Friday night when Todd's family arrived, we were ready for the benefit. Tucker's ANC that morning was 4700 which meant his risk for infection was quite low and hence he would be able to join us at the benefit. It also meant we could all attend church together on Sunday morning.

That Sunday morning service was an awesome start to the day. Leon Jarvis, a coworker of mine and Catholic Brother, filled in for our regular pastor that morning. Leon had no idea that we would be in church or that Tucker's surgery would be soon, yet his sermon was on HOPE! He challenged us to give ourselves to God and to be excited about our faith. He empowered us to move with the Spirit and share how God is working in our lives with the world. His words set my heart of fire and prepared for that afternoon at the benefit.

During the time of prayer, we shared with the congregation that Tucker's tumor was now operable and that his surgery would be sometime in the next two weeks. In response to our news, Leon led the congregation in a corporal blessing for Tucker. The entire congregation turned toward Tucker and put their arm on the shoulder of the person in front of them until we were all joined by human touch ending at Tucker. As Leon lifted up a blessing for health, peace and love for our family, I looked down the pews and all around me and felt the love, concern and the power of prayer. My soul was filled with indescribable peace.

Leon closed the service with one of my favorite songs: "Here I am Lord". My tears flowed freely as I sang from my soul:

*"Here I am, Lord*

*Is it I, Lord?*

*I have heard you calling in the night*

*I will go, Lord, if you lead me*

*I will hold your people in my heart."*

♥

The setting for the benefit was a place that I had recently grown to love. It was our local public school, Superior Central. This rural K-12 school had opened their arms and supported us as Lauren started kindergarten this fall. They allowed me to talk to Lauren's class about why she would be gone so much. They did not object when I asked the kids to pray for Tucker. The teacher laughed with me as Billy, a bright little blonde classmate of Lauren's volunteered, "I already have been praying for him!" I was also permitted to pass out bookmarks and ask for prayers when I met with the high school student council and thanked them for the money they sent to help our family.

As I walked into the school gymnasium the afternoon of the benefit, I saw some of the teachers and the principal already there helping set up. I was humbled seeing these people who barely knew us, taking their Sunday afternoon to be a part of this day. I was overjoyed that these were the same people who would be interacting with my children in school and teaching them about this world. Their love for children and their neighbors was so evident".

Over three hundred and fifty people joined us that afternoon for a feast, music and silent auction. About half of them were friends from our church in Marquette and from our places of employment. The other half was people from the local area who came to support their neighbor. I remember thinking, these are the kind of neighbors Jesus called us to be.

Tucker was in the mood to celebrate that day. He wore his new leather cowboy vest and chaps that his Great Grandma had given him early for his birthday, along with his big black cowboy hat. He and Lauren were given plastic pop rockets as soon as we arrived. They spent the afternoon with a group of ten other kids popping the rockets up into the rafters of the gym and trying to catch them. Tucker played just as hard as all the rest of the kids. His bald head was the only external reminder of the disease that loomed inside of him.

After we ate and sang Happy Birthday to Tucker, I went up to the microphone. I took only a few notes and the plaque I had of John's story that hangs in my living room. I knew that my words could not be planned; I was to speak for the heart.

I started with a word of prayer. I read the prayer of St. Francis, the prayer read at my father, Virgil Francis's funeral and inscribed on his tombstone:

### Instrument of His Peace

*Lord, make me an instrument of Your peace;*
*Where there is hatred, let me sow love;*
*Where there is injury, pardon;*
*Where there is doubt, faith;*
*Where there is despair, hope;*
*Where there is darkness, light;*
*Where there is sadness, joy.*
*O Divine Master*
*Grant that I may not so much seek*
*to be consoled, as to console;*
*To be understood, as to understand;*
*To be loved, as to love.*
*For it is in giving that we receive;*
*It is pardoning that we are pardoned;*
*It is in dying that we are born to eternal life.*

After I finished the prayer, I shared Tucker and John's story; elaborating on the similarities between the two. I described to them how Tucker is fighting this evil. He is not worrying about what the future might bring. Instead, he is enjoying every day and staying in it. He is relying on both his earthly and Heavenly Daddy to get him through. He is doing just what God instructs us all to do.

I concluded by telling them how much I have learned by watching Tucker. He is showing me how to beat this. I challenged them to look at the trials in their lives and how they are reacting to them. I asked them if they are worrying and dreading the next day or are they taking their burdens to God and looking for His direction and will in every detail of life.

I quit talking when Tucker came up and grabbed my leg and said: "Mommy, are you almost done!!! You are talking too long...We want to play!" I figured that was the God's "sign" that I was to be done!!

Moments later, Kris Tidd, a good friend and coworker of mine, came and grad my hand. Her face was streaked with tears as she pulled me out the door saying "I've got a surprise for you!" Right outside the door was a **rainbow** crossing the horizon over the school! As I looked out over the rainbow, I smiled through my tears. I knew this rainbow was God's way of saying, *"Well done my good and faithful servant."* Kris and I and a few others watched the rainbow until it faded away.

Ten thousand dollars was donated to our family that night! Neither Todd nor I could believe the amount of love, encouragement and money we received from our small community. Later, as I drove home from the school, I reflected on the day and prayed: "Thank you for choosing me, for deeming me worthy of doing Your will. Thank you for providing for our family. Please help me remember this day if I ever forget Your presence or doubt Your love for me. In Jesus precious name I pray, Amen."

The next morning we were to leave for Tucker's surgery. As routine, I read *God Calling* while I ate my breakfast. It said:

*"...Learn that every act of faithfulness is a comfort to my heart..."*

After breakfast, I talked with Leslie, and it was decided that Tucker's blood counts should be checked before we left for Lansing. We agreed to go into Marquette for a blood draw and then wait at home until Leslie called us with the results. As we drove into town, I pondered that sentence in *God Calling*; I had strange feeling about this day.

When we got home from the clinic, there was already a message from Leslie on the answering machine. She said that Tucker's counts were acceptable, so we should pack our bags and come on down.

An hour later, as I stood in our bedroom packing, I got a nudge to call the clinic here and check Tucker's counts for myself. Leslie's phone call was just too quick. There is no way that the lab here processed the sample, got the results and faxed them down to her in the time that it took us to drive home. Leslie must have been looking at Friday's lab values.

This time I listened to the nudge and made the phone call to the lab. The nudge was right! Tucker's ANC was only 680. I called Leslie back and gave her the results from the current lab draw. She told me to wait at home; she would discuss these counts with Dr. Harmon and call us back. Early afternoon Dr. Harmon's nurse called and told us not to come. Instead, Dr. Harmon wanted us to recheck Tucker's counts on Wednesday with possible surgery on Friday. That meant Tucker could celebrate his fourth birthday at home with our family instead of in the hospital preparing for surgery!! After sharing the good news with the rest of the family, I went into the bedroom and knelt at my bed and said a prayer of thanks: "Thanks for the insight of my devotional...for the nudge...for our past experience with low blood counts (had we not made the mistake in July I wouldn't have been so cautious today)...and for God's continual love and mercy."

♥

We spent Tucker's birthday at home doing the things that we love to do. In the morning, Todd and Tucker took a "guy's adventure" on the neighbor's four-wheeler. They cruised down bumpy, rutted logging trails back deep into the crimson and gold woods. Tucker wore his cowboy suit and pretended he was the sheriff shooting the "bad guys" hiding amongst the trees as they dodged bumps and puddles.

While the guys were out on their adventure, Lauren and I made Tucker's birthday cake. Lauren was a very willing recruit, she loved to bake. Tucker requested an eyeball cake, a scary one for Halloween. We made the ugliest cake I've ever seen. It was so ugly we didn't even want to eat it!

Todd's Mom arrived just in time for dinner. We had homemade pizza and eyeball cake surrounded by lots of ice cream. After cake we opened presents. Our big surprise for the kids was a computer, thanks to Todd's family. They had sent us the money for it a month before and it arrived earlier that day. The kids were very excited and we all set it up after dinner. Over the next several months, Tucker and Lauren enjoyed many quieter moments playing preschool computer games together.

Tucker's ANC still was not high enough on Wednesday. This meant that his surgery would have to be postponed for at least another week. This also meant that Dr. Harmon would be back at U. of M. in Ann Arbor and Dr. Greenfeld would be Tucker's surgeon. We didn't know Dr. Greenfeld, but trusted that God had reason for this change.

Tucker's surgery was on October 27th. That morning I woke with a light soul. I knew that on this day a huge chunk of the evil, which plagued my child, would be removed. Thoughts of a miracle kept going through my head. I imagined that the tumor would fall out as soon as they opened Tucker up. *God Calling* encouraged me even more. It said:

### Days of Conquest

*"I see the loving striving, not the defects. I see the conquest of your particular battle. I count it victory, a glad victory.*

*I do not compare it with the strenuous campaigns of My great Saints.*

*For you it is a victory, and the angels rejoice and your dear ones rejoice, as much as at any conquest noted and rejoiced over by Heaven.*

*My children, count the days of conquest as very blessed days."*

I shared these words with both Kelly and Nicki, the child-life specialists that we had grown so close to. They marveled at how *God Calling*, once again, spoke directly to our situation. They shared my excitement for the outcome of Tucker's surgery.

A few hours before Tucker's scheduled surgery time, I went for a run down by the river. I was so full of positive energy that I could hardly contain my feet as I bounded down the street. My soul was on fire, I was so sure of a victory.

At noon, the surgery team came and took us to the surgical holding area. Just before they arrived we joined hands and prayed for God's strength and mercy for all of us this afternoon. We had much peace as we all followed Tucker's gurney down the hall.

Both Dr. Greenfeld and the anesthesiologist came to the holding area to talk with us before surgery. Todd and I had met Dr. Greenfeld the day before in Tucker's room and felt very confident that he was the man God wanted to do Tucker's surgery. Dr. Greenfeld had said to us: "My mentor in Pediatric Surgery taught me to hate cancer and be very aggressive about removing every bit of it." Todd and I agreed with this philosophy and gave him the permission to remove the right kidney if he had any concerns that the cancer had invaded it. Dr. Greenfeld thought there was about a twenty-five percent chance of that happening.

In the holding area right before surgery, however, was the first time that I realized that Dr. Greenfeld's first name was "John". The anesthesiologist also came in and introduced himself as "John". Moments later, as I carried Tucker down the hall to the surgical suite, I was full of peace knowing that God had picked these two men who bore the name "John" to care for my son that afternoon. I knew my brother's spirit would also be in that room.

As I kissed Tucker goodbye and adjusted the cross medallion around his neck I was suddenly overcome by the feeling that we would be called to make a sacrifice that afternoon. As I walked to the waiting room to meet Todd and Lauren, I tried to put that thought out of my head. I knew that I was allowing Satan to sneak in and cause me to doubt. I knew that if I doubted that I would be tossed and blown by the wind like a wave in the sea.

The surgery was expected to take three to four hours, so once I reached the waiting room we all went to the cafeteria for a quick lunch. Twenty minutes after we returned we got a call from the operating room. I listened anxiously anticipating that the nurse would tell of the miracle that I had imagined. She did not say that, she said that Dr.Greenfeld had just gotten to the tumor but things were going well.

We did not hear from the operating room again for two more hours. I tried to keep busy reading, writing and helping Lauren with her schoolwork, but inside the anxiety was growing. I couldn't quiet that voice telling me that we were going to be called to make a sacrifice.

Around Five p.m., the operating room nurse called back to let us know that Dr. Greenfeld had just removed Tucker's right kidney and that Tucker had lost a lot of blood but was still very stable. The nurse did not make an estimate of how much longer Tucker would be in surgery.

As soon as I hung up the phone, I looked at Todd with a shattered look. He took my hand and led me into the hallway so that I could fill him in without Lauren overhearing. I could feel my heart breaking as I told him about the kidney and the blood loss. We cried together for our little boy.

After we regained our composure, we went back to the waiting room. By that time the crowd of other people's family members had thinned out. This allowed Lauren and me to burn off some energy playing hide and seek around the waiting room chairs. We then settled down together in a chair, and I read to her. I was so glad my little girl was with me to keep me distracted. She will never know how much her innocent free spirit and love for her Mommy helped me that afternoon.

After two more hours however, I couldn't take it anymore. I felt my anxiety growing and my faith teetering. I went for a walk. I barely made it out of the waiting room before my tears began to flow. I cried, "My God, My God, why have You forsaken me? You gave me a rainbow, where are You today?" I knew that I was questioning God instead of trusting Him. I then walked quietly hoping for a wave of peace to wash over me.

As I walked, a song I often listen to entered my mind. This song was about sacrificing all, giving up all your kingdoms for God. Immediately I was convicted. Had I really made God my number one priority...even above Tucker's health? Was God more important to me than my family? I sobbed as I faced these very tough questions. I surrendered and prayed, "Oh Father, what a challenge you put in front of me. See how I strive and be merciful to me!"

When I went back in, Todd was talking to the waiting room volunteer. I watched as my husband shared our story. As I listened, I was envious of his rock solid faith. He was trusting in the Lord; and instead of worrying, he was witnessing!

Half an hour later, the volunteer showed us how to lock up the waiting room and then left. There the three of us sat all alone in that big room waiting to hear something. At that point, even Todd became anxious. Finally the phone rang. I picked it up almost afraid of what I would hear. The news was good! They had finally finished and Tucker was stable. Dr. Greenfeld would meet us in the conference room next door to fill us in on the rest.

We reached the conference room first and waited for Dr. Greenfeld with much anticipation. When he arrived there was a tired smile on his face. He said that the tumor was stuck on the Ascending Inferior Vena Cava. He ended up dissecting the vessel three times as he tried to get out as much of the cancer as he could. He remarked that Tucker remained amazingly stable throughout all of that despite losing over three pints of blood. Because he was so stable Dr. Greenfeld was able to take his time and do a thorough job.

As I listened to Dr.Greenfeld, I was humbled. I knew that God had tried to prepare me for the sacrificing of the kidney, but I wouldn't listen. All I wanted to think about was this miracle for which I was hoping. I also knew the true miracle was that Tucker could withstand such a surgery. It was God's presence that had kept him so stable.

With my eyes brimming with tears, I thanked Dr. Greenfeld for all of his effort and I handed him a bookmark of Tucker. I shared a little of our story and our faith. He read the bookmark and then said, "I think this time it will be different."

After we left Dr. Greenfeld, we went up to our new room in the Pediatric Intensive Care Unit (PICU). It was a locked unit with no phone access in the rooms. As we walked through the double doors into Tucker's room, we were both struck by the presence of our little boy. He looked so small and sick lying in that big bed in that big room. He was so swollen that his eyes were like slits and his fingers like sausages. He had on a nasal cannula giving him oxygen and his heart rate, respiratory rate and oxygen saturation were flashing on a monitor above his bed.

We all peered at him in disbelief. He didn't even look like the little boy we had played blocks with that morning in the playroom. Todd and I took turns holding his hand and stroking his head all evening.

I spent the night with Tucker holding his hand and reviewing the day. It had started with so much hope and promise and ended so painfully difficult. Through it all however, Jesus had been right there and God had been faithful.

I thanked God for choosing John Greenfeld as Tucker's surgeon and guiding him through this surgery. I thanked Him for keeping Tucker's body stable so that Dr.Greenfeld could do his best work. Most importantly, I thanked Him for teaching me what sacrifice feels like. What a different passion I now had for what Jesus, my Savior, did for me on the cross. I thanked Him for putting up with my lack of faith and having mercy on me and my family regardless of my weakness.

♥

The next day brought its own set of challenges and call for faith. Tucker was almost motionless all day. He only occasionally woke up and winced. His oxygen saturation and blood pressure teetered on the edge of critical all day. He remained very edematous and pale.

Todd and I spent the day trading off between the playroom and the PICU as Lauren was technically not supposed to be in Tucker's room. There were many times that day I wished some member of our family could have been there to help us with Lauren. However, that was not God's plan. My mom and sister had taken time off work the week before, when Tucker was originally scheduled for the surgery. When the date changed, their schedules could not.

Whenever I was in Tucker's room, I was holding his hand and praying as I watched the monitor above his bed. I feared that he would end up on a ventilator because his lungs were filling with fluid. I had seen that scenario so many times at work as a physical therapist working in ICU. I tried to trust God and not worry, but in my humanness, I failed.

Throughout the day my mood deteriorated. I tried to remember how I felt the day of the benefit and not to question why my beautiful little boy had to go through this living hell, but again I failed. In the afternoon I took Lauren over to O'Berski's. As I talked to Susie and watched Lauren and Matt jump on the outdoor trampoline in the crisp fall air, tears streamed down my face. As always, Susie's words put my soul at peace, but only for a wavering moment.

On the way back to the hospital alone in the car I fell apart again. I sobbed as I pounded on the steering wheel and cried to my God: "WHY GOD WHY? WHY ME? WHY HIM? I DON'T WANT THIS JOB! I'M NOT THE RIGHT CHOICE! YOU DIDN'T KEEP YOUR DEAL WITH ME! HE WASN'T SUPPOSED TO SUFFER LIKE THIS!

I'm not sure what God thought about this outburst; but He promises that His love for us is steadfast and His mercy is new every morning. I apologized later and hung on the promise of His forgiveness. I knew He never promised that life on earth would be easy. Rather, He promised He would carry us through and bear our burdens for us if we give them to Him. On this day, I fell to Satan because I took the burden back and did not trust God even after all that I had seen.

As I walked back to Tucker's room, from the car I reflected on *God Calling* from October 26th:

### *Deserters*

*"You must believe utterly. My love can bear nothing less. I am so often wounded in the house of My friends. Do you think the spitting and scorn of My enemies, the mocking and reviling hurt me? NO! They all forsook Him and said, 'I know not the man'. These left their scars.*

*So now, it is not the unbelief of my enemies that hurts, but that My friends, who love and know me, cannot walk all the way with Me and doubt My power to do all that I have said."*

These words convicted me. I knew that God was testing me in the fire just as he had tested Peter on the day of Jesus's persecution. He wanted to see how pure and strong my faith was. I was humbled by my weakness. Despite all I had seen, I still was not trusting God unconditionally without formulating my own plan and expectations. I was a "deserter" of sorts.

Early the next morning, Dr. Greenfeld came in and said that Tucker was holding his own medically, but now it was time to start moving him.

Movement would help reverse the third spacing of the fluid. That was just what I was hoping he would say. Now we were in my realm. That's what I did best; motivate very sick people to move!

Tucker was not nearly as happy to hear Dr. Greenfeld's orders. He wailed as I got him up into a wagon and wheeled him around the unit and down to the playroom. He did not feel like playing. He complained the entire forty-five minutes he was up. I didn't mind his complaining. It was nice just to hear his voice and have him alert.

We repeated this process at least five times both Friday and Saturday and reaped the rewards. By Saturday afternoon, all of Tucker's vital signs returned to normal and he was off oxygen. We were able to catch our breath for a couple hours.

That evening, Tucker started to complained of belly pain. Both Todd and I looked at his belly. It was bloated to the point that the steristrips holding the incision closed were stretched taut. His belly was very firm and tender to the touch. We brought this to our nurse's attention. She agreed with us and called the surgeon. Half an hour later, the surgical resident came in and examined Tucker. He said that either Tucker had a lot of gas trapped in his bowel or he had an ileus. An ileus is a paralyzing of part of the bowel. Often it is associated with too much trauma or a decrease in blood flow to the tissue and can lead to death of the tissue. The resident ordered an x-ray to differentiate between these two and encouraged us to walk Tucker more. He also ordered some drops to help reduce the gas.

Tucker was anything but thrilled to get up and walk again. Todd and I each took a hand and walked him slowly down the PICU corridor. He cried all the way, pleading with us to stop. Ten minutes later as they took the x-ray, I sat in the hall praying, "Please, God, don't let Tucker have an ileus". God was gracious. The x-ray showed no ileus. Tucker's problem was all gas. Within hours of receiving the gas drops and walking, he stopped complaining and his belly softened.

Sunday was Halloween; thankfully it brought no new "tricks". We continued to pry Tucker out of bed several times and take him down to the playroom. We made the most of the day; I brought costumes for both kids. Lauren went as a skunk. She and I had made her costume out of a hooded black sweatshirt and black and white fun fur. She borrowed Susie's air freshener for her odor! Tucker's costume was a "Duploblock" made from a box and plastic cups. He wasn't up to wearing the entire costume but he did wear the hat and we put the rest behind him in the wagon.

Lauren went around the pediatric unit spraying the nurses with air freshener after she "trick or treated" them. We all enjoyed handing out miniature teddy bears (sent by Todd's sister) to all the kids on the floor. We called it reverse trick or treating. Tucker stayed up three hours for the afternoon festivities.

At dusk, I got out for a run on the dirt track behind the hospital. As I ran around the track, my mind wandered back to days on the track with my brother. Suddenly I got the urge to run a "track workout" so I ran eight, half-lap sprints. By number five I could tell my legs were not as young as they used to be, but I was determined to reach my goal. As I sprinted down the back straightaway I imagined that I was racing John. Later, as I cooled down I contemplated the real race that I now ran; the race against cancer. I felt John's presence as I ran my final two laps singing *"My God is an Awesome God."*

When I arrived back in Tucker's hospital room no one was there so I took the extra quiet time to stretch and read *God Calling*. It was a familiar piece of scripture but tonight it had new meaning:

### The Voice Again

*"Thy word is a lamp unto my feet, and a light unto my path"*

Psalm 119:105

*"Yes! My word, the scriptures. Read them, study them; store them in your hearts, use them as you use a lamp to guide your footsteps.*

*But remember, my children, My word is more even than that. It is the Voice that speaks to your hearts, that inner consciousness that tells of Me.*

*It is the Voice that speaks to you intimately, personally, in this sacred evening time. It is even more than that. It is I, your Lord and friend.*

*"And the word was made flesh and dwelt among us." Truly a lamp to your feet, and a light to your path."*

I finished stretching with a smile on my face reflecting on these words. He was not only God but He was my friend! He deemed me worthy of His friendship and He wanted to light my way down this path.

♥

Monday morning started with great news. Dr. Greenfeld came in early to check on Tucker. He was pleasantly surprised at his progress. He agreed to discharge Tucker from the hospital if we would stay in Lansing for twenty-four hours.

We spent the morning packing up our stuff, and right after lunch Tucker was discharged. As we walked out the double doors of the PICU for the last time, the entire staff stood and gave us a standing ovation. Their gesture brought tears to my eyes. I felt the same admiration and respect for them.

We stayed with the O'Berski's that night and had a Monday night football party. Todd and I made homemade pizza, and Susie made her special ice cream shakes. It was a night of delightful family fellowship.

It was a very unique evening of Monday Night football. Walter Payton had died that morning at the age of forty-five of cancer. The half-time show was a memorial to this great football player nicknamed "Sweetness". He was nicknamed that because he was so talented yet so humble. Mike Singletary, Walter's longtime friend and teammate was interviewed outside of the hospital in which Walter died. My soul was warmed to hear him say: "Walter was at peace. He knew Jesus Christ and went to meet Him today!" After the broadcast Todd and I sat up and talked with Susie and Mike about the example that someone like Walter Payton sets in this world. He was truly a light, not because of what he preached but who he was and how he used his talents.

♥

Once home, Tucker slowly regained his energy and strength. The first few days, however were really rough. One night he just cried on the couch until he fell asleep. He looked pale, listless and gaunt (just like my brother John did before he died) as I carried him from the couch to his own bed. That night Todd and I held each other and cried as we mourned the suffering our child must endure. We so much wanted to take it away but we couldn't. The verse John 8:28 *"In all things, God works for the good of those who love him, who are called to His purpose."* kept going through my mind. I knew I just had to endure and trust, but it was hard!

One night as I folded clothes, I listened to a tape series called *Triumph over Trials by Joyce Myers*. These tapes empowered me to think of this trial as a training school for what God would eventually be calling me to do. I held on and continued to pray for strength, guidance and patience.

By the time we had to leave for the next round of chemotherapy (two weeks after surgery) Tucker was feeling pretty good physically; however, mentally he was still very fragile. We decided not to tell him it was time for chemotherapy until we had to. The day we left the weather was amazing; sixty degrees and sunny. Tucker spent the morning playing soccer, hiking through our woods and chopping wood with his daddy. We had a cookout for lunch and then Tucker was ready for a nap. While he was sleeping, we packed the car, slipped him into his car seat and headed for Lansing. When Tucker woke up two hours later he asked where we were going. Todd very gently told him that we had to go back to Sparrow for chemotherapy. He wasn't happy but he accepted it...for the moment.

We stopped in Mackinac City at the Mackinaw Trading Post, our favorite break place. This store is filled with the most unusual items for people of the north. That night the kids tried on raccoon and skunk hats and gloves. They looked so cute that the lady behind the desk came out with a digital camera and took their picture and gave it to us. The kids also found ceramic turtles that they could afford to buy. I was skeptical about these purchases especially after Tucker dropped his turtle right after purchasing it and broke its head off. He burst into tears. The clerk felt so bad that she gave him a new one. That, however, set the mood for the entire week.

The next morning as we were trying to leave McDonald's, Lauren dropped her turtle in the bathroom and its head broke off! Tucker was already crying when Lauren came walking out of the bathroom stall with a brave but crushed look on her face. She handed me her turtle and its head. I could see that her little heart was breaking. I turned my attention away from Tucker for a moment and comforted my little girl as she mourned her turtle. Just like with Tucker, I longed to take away her pain but I could not. I felt like crying too!

Things didn't get any better once at we checked into the hospital, Tucker just lay in bed watching an occasional video and sleeping. All he would say is "I just want to see "Copain"! (our dog) and a few times he volunteered: "Mom, I don't know if I can handle this." Once when Tucker was complaining, I asked him if he wanted to quit and go home. He replied, "No, I want to get better, but I just don't know if I can handle it!" I sympathized with him; there were moments I didn't know if I could handle this either.

Lauren was a godsend during that difficult week. She was an incredibly patient five-year old. She and I played countless games of dice, dominoes and Jinga. She never complained or acted out. She gave Todd and me something to do, and she was the only one who could make Tucker smile. God definitely knew what He was doing when He blessed us with Lauren as a daughter.

♥

We spent much of that week talking to Tucker about God's strength and Jesus's love. We tried to help him understand that Jesus was right there walking this difficult journey with him. Our words were only mildly helpful. He mostly just shut us out and laid there whimpering. I told Susie O'Berski of Tucker's struggle one morning. She had just the thing to encourage him: It was an audiotape story entitled: "The Great Bike Ride".

It was about a group of kids riding in a bike race to raise money for a children's hospital and to win new bikes. The kids were all put on teams. The team featured on the tape was named the "Hide and Seek Kids" because they were Christians who strive to hide God's Word in their heart and seek Him in all that they did. The "Hide and Seek Kids" had two special friends, GT and Guardian. They were guardian angels who helped them see God's lesson in all things.

The story began when the "Hide and Seek Kids" find out from the bully, Big Billy Baxter that the weak, sick kid of the school, Warren, is on their team. They are all very disappointed because they know that they all must cross the finish line together to win; and, they assume that Warren will be their weak link. What they don't know initially, but learn throughout the two-day, fifty-mile bike race is that Warren was weak physically but very strong spiritually and mentally because he was in the hospital a lot as a kid. He had to learn perseverance just to get better and be able to attend school with his classmates. Warren used his perseverance to encourage the "Hide and Seek Kids" during the race when they faced obstacles, and helped them overcome much adversity. In the end the "Hide and Seek Kids" won the race.

I listened to the tape with Tucker that afternoon. Tucker and I cried together as we talked about being tough and asking God for help. After we finished listening to it, he sat up in bed and started building Lego planes (something hadn't done all week). Warren's example spoke to him in a way none of my words could.

Tucker asked to listen to that tape several times the next day. He was still homesick, but his mood was brighter especially because he knew it was his last day of chemotherapy. When Dr. Scott came in, Tucker sat up in bed and asked him boldly, "May I go home tonight?" Dr. Scott, who hadn't heard a word from Tucker all week, laughed his big, hearty laugh and said, "Yes, as soon as that IV runs dry!!!"

That evening Dr. Scott also talked to us about making a change in Tucker's treatment regimen. In the original regimen, Tucker would receive five rounds of chemotherapy followed by some sort of radiation and stem cell transplant. Dr. Scott proposed that we do one more round of chemotherapy just prior to Christmas and then repeat all of Tucker's scans early in January to see if he was ready for the radiation and transplant.

Todd and I both immediately liked this idea. We knew that to beat this cancer we had to attack it with every weapon available the first time. One more round of chemotherapy meant more artillery going after the enemy. It also meant we wouldn't be in the hospital and starting the transplant over Christmas. We made the decision that very evening that we would follow Dr. Scott's recommendation.

With that good news, we headed home in a joyous mood. Our car was full of conversation about Thanksgiving, getting a Christmas tree and the first snow. These annual events which we had taken for granted other years were anticipated with a different joy this year. All that we had endured over the past five months had given us a new appreciation for the blessing of health and family.

♥

As Thanksgiving approached, I really felt the need to thank the people who were praying and helping us through this "storm". I kept my eyes open for the right opportunity to do that. The Thursday before Thanksgiving, my boss, Cathy, and I were discussing how the kids at St. Michael's Catholic School had adopted Tucker as their prayer project. I mentioned to her that I would like to thank those kids and let them know how effective their prayers had been. Two hours later Cathy called to tell me that she had gotten permission for me to speak at the all-school mass.

St. Michael's Church and school are right next to the hospital so just before noon the next day, I ran across the rainy parking lot and darted into the sanctuary. All the kids were already sitting and the altar boys were just lighting the candles as they sang "Lord of the Dance". I joined them singing this, one of my favorite songs, and then I sat and watched these young Christians lead the service.

At the very end of the mass, the priest called me up to the front. I walked up the long aisle to the front in my squeaky wet tennis shoes and with tears in my eyes told the kids how much their prayer and notes had meant to my family. I emphasized how God calls us to lift up our brothers in prayer and to believe with all our heart that our prayers will be answered. I thanked them for being obedient to God's command and consistently lifting up our family in prayer. I updated them on the treatments Tucker had left to undergo and asked them to continue to pray for us. Those kids heard my words that day. Many continued to e-mail Tucker and update their class on Tucker's progress for the rest of that school year.

♥

We has very few plans for Thanksgiving itself as Tucker had only finished his chemotherapy a week for the holiday and we knew there was a pretty good change that he would be neutropenic so getting together with friends was not a good idea. We hoped to have a quiet day at home just the four of us. Home was not a place we now took for granted and we were looking forward to time. The day before however Tucker's counts once again suggested that he needed to get a blood transfusion because a dangerously low hemo-globin. We knew the routine after last month so we made arrangements for the transfusion do be done that evening with the expectation of a morning discharge so we could still be home for our turkey dinner.

We had a different nurse than last time and she would not pre-medicate Tucker with Tylenol like the other nurse did even after I told her what the other nurse had said and pleaded with her to look into it. Because she did not, Tucker spiked a fever in the middle of the night. The next morning as I was packing up our stuff to be discharged, the oncologist on call came in and told me that Tucker would have to stay for the weekend to get IV antibiotics because of the fever. I was caught completely off guard by his words. I told him all about what had happened. He sympathized with me, but in the end said "Kim you are probably right that is why Tucker had a fever but if you are wrong he will be dead in 5 hours. We cannot take that chance!"

I was mad and frustrated. "Don't they understand how much time this kid has been in the hospital this year? How frail he is right now. This was not fair. He shouldn't have to pay for her incompetence!" I left the room and went to the nurse's station looking for that nurse. I made a scene that I am not proud of. Everyone knew how mad I was. Later, once Todd and Lauren had arrived and I filled them in on the situation, the oncologist came back in and offered a solution that we all could live with. He would give us an eight hour pass to leave the hospital, go home and have our turkey dinner, but we had to be back for pumpkin pie and the next round of IV antibiotics.

We agreed to the compromise and made the best out a bad situation. Our turkey was perfect as were the simple things that we made to go along with it. But mostly we enjoyed each other and this place we called home. We knew that this might be Tucker's last Thanksgiving and we cherished each moment of it.

Tucker was able to leave the hospital by Saturday afternoon and Sunday we got our first big snowfall of the winter. We were all so excited; we piped Christmas music outside and sledded all morning. The kids had a blast running up the hill with their sleds on their heads and racing each other down to the stream at the bottom of the hill. They were dressed in matching blue and red snowsuits. As I watched them I could hardly tell them apart. Tucker's color was so good and with his head covered there was no outward sign of cancer or the treatment side effects. I almost forget about our reality for a while. Later that day, I took my two dogs, Tugger and Jake, out skijouring. The snow was fast and the dogs were elated to be out. I marveled as I skied, at the simple pleasure of being close with nature and alone with God especially after the last few days we had spent at the hospital. Was this what it was like to ride God's Rainbow?

♥

Christmas is a time for giving gifts. It is the celebration of God giving us His only Son so that we may have the undeserved gift of eternal life. The Wiseman followed God's example and gave gifts of frankincense, gold and myrrh to worship and show their love for the Christ child. The reasons we give gifts remains the same: to show love and concern, to spread joy and hope to the world around us. Throughout Tucker's illness we experienced over and over the desire people had to show their love and concern; to spread joy and happiness to our family. But at Christmas we experienced this to a whole new level. It was humbling.

The first to express their love and concern was a group of girl scouts from Marquette. They conducted a can drive throughout the Marquette community and raised eleven hundred dollars. That meant that these girls collected eleven thousand cans! Each scout was responsible for giving out grocery bags with Tucker's bookmark taped on the outside to local businesses and schools. Two weeks later they went back and collected the bag full of cans.

I found out about the fundraiser when I walked into my hairdresser's and saw the bag in the corner almost full. Carol filled me in as she cut my hair. She told me that these bags were even sitting outside every classroom at a local elementary school! I was completely overwhelmed by this project! These girls didn't even know my family and yet they were putting all of this effort into a project to raise money for us. In addition this meant that the message of the bookmark was now that much more visible in our community. WOW!

By December 8th, the girl scouts were ready to share the fruits of their labor with us. We met in the lobby of the medical center after school. Tucker was very shy as he sat on Todd's lap and listened to the kids sing him *"We Wish You a Merry Christmas"*. He was also very quiet as one by one the girls came up and handed him envelopes filled with twenty-dollar bills.

Conversely, the girl scouts were not shy at all. You could tell by looking into their faces that this was their project, not their mom's. They felt joy because of what they were giving, not because of what they were receiving back from this quiet, little, bald boy.

All the adults who witnessed that afternoon commented afterward as we chatted around the Christmas tree what a great project this was for their kids. They were experiencing how good it feels to help and make a difference. As I listened, I marveled at how once again God was using for good what Satan intended for evil. He was showing these girls the spirit that lives within their souls and wants so desperately to guide their lives. I quietly thanked God for giving us this opportunity to help further His kingdom. I also thanked Him for each one of those scouts and their love for my family.

A newspaper reporter and photographer were present that afternoon. They interviewed the scout troop leader, some of the parents and kids, as well as Todd and me. The next day a 5x7 colored picture of the scouts handing Tucker the envelopes and an article appeared on the front page of the newspaper. The article spoke of hope and living for the day... of caring for your neighbor...of teaching our children values. It truly glorified God.

♥

After that article was in the paper, we received gifts in the mail almost every day. Many were from people we had never met. They were touched by our story and wanted to ease our burden somehow. There were others who knew us only slightly and wanted us to know they cared. One of those groups completely caught me off guard because of who they represent. Their action toward us went against the stereotype that today's society labels them with.

I received their gift at work on December 10th, my last day before we left for Tucker's sixth round of chemotherapy. My work schedule was very busy that day and I was very focused because I had many loose ends that I wanted to tie up before I left. As usual I checked my schedule at the front desk as soon as I arrived in the morning. I noticed that I was double booked at 1 p.m. When I questioned Peggy, one of our secretaries, she just smiled and said that the patient had requested me and that she was a friend of mine. I did not recognize the name and I didn't stop one minute to consider the God factor, but instead I started complaining to Peggy. I argued that there was no way I could fit in a new evaluation at that time and that I wouldn't even be here the next week to follow-up with her. Finally Peggy stopped me and said with a little grin said: "Just see her!" Peggy is a loving, beautiful Christian, and when I stopped long enough to see the twinkle in her eye, I saw the God factor and knew instantly that this had nothing to do with physical therapy. A little embarrassed about my behavior, I then said, "OK" and walked away with my tail between my legs.

After lunch, I went to the lobby to get this mystery patient, LeeAnn. She was sitting in the lobby with another woman. As soon as I saw LeeAnn, ours eyes connected, and we both smiled. LeeAnn and I knew each other because our kids were went to the same daycare. LeeAnn worked for Blue Cross Blue Shield of Michigan (BCBS). Recently we had gotten more closely acquainted as she helped me with my many health insurance questions. I knew her by face, voice and first name but not by last name. That is why I didn't recognize her on my schedule.

As I walked up to greet LeeAnn and the lady with her, I couldn't imagine what this was all about. LeeAnn immediately introduced the other women as

Rose and said that they had come to see me on behalf of the local BCBS office. She said that the entire office knew about Tucker's illness and were praying for us. They wanted to do something special for us this Christmas. With that they handed me a basket filled with cookies, candies and stuffed animals for the kids. They also handed me an envelope. In the envelope was a home-made card with a digital picture of the entire staff of that office pasted to the outside and all of their signatures on the inside. Also enclosed was a check for seven hundred dollars!

I was overwhelmed beyond words. All I could think of as tears welled in my eyes was that this was my insurance company. As a health care provider, all I had ever heard was what cold, hardened, greedy people insurance companies were. They didn't care about the patient, only making money. I never really believed that and now I had a very personal example to refute such judgment. I could only respond with tears and hugs and words of thanks.

❤

We were very grateful for all this out pouring of love on our family. However, we knew that we were not the only family who had a trial this Christmas. We had a desire to share our gifts with other needy families in our community whose story wasn't as public. One afternoon God gave me the opportunity to do just that.

I went to see Arlene, a patient with lymphedema whom I knew from previous admissions. After getting reacquainted, I examined her arm and then began giving her a lymphatic draining massage. As I worked on her arm we talked about our families and our faith. I told her about Tucker's cancer and how it had changed all my priorities and strengthened my faith. She shared the trial that her family was currently going through and then added that she couldn't imagine facing a trial such as ours with a child. In response, I gave her a bookmark and asked her to pray for Tucker.

The next day when I saw Arlene she said that Tucker's picture had demanded her attention all night. Whenever she looked up from the TV or from reading, she would see those beautiful blue eyes peering at her. Each time she looked into them, she said a prayer for him. Her words warmed my heart as I began working on her arm.

During this massage, I educated her how she should restrict some activities with that arm. She agreed, and said she was going to hire her granddaughter, Lisa, to help her with all of her Christmas cleaning. She went on to tell me all about Lisa and how proud she was of her for facing her problems and acting responsibly. She concluded by saying that she knew that Lisa could use the money from cleaning to buy her son some Christmas gifts.

Arlene's words stayed with me all afternoon. I thought about what it would be like to be a single mom and to spend every dime each month trying to make ends meet. I thought about how much money our family had recently been given and yet how this money could not buy the one thing we desired, a healthy child. As I drove home past Arlene's house, the verse jumped into my head: "Trust in the Lord and do good!" I knew instantly that I was to give Lisa and Michael some of the money we had received in order to brighten their Christmas. That evening my soul was dancing as I prepared a note that would accompany the money. I was delighting in the Lord and the task He had given me. It felt so good to be the giver for once and not the receiver. The next day before I left Arlene's room I slipped her an envelope and asked her to deliver it to Lisa.

Weeks after Christmas, we received a letter from Kristina Sharp and MFC First National Bank. Kristina was Lisa's mom. She relayed how our gesture toward her daughter had changed their entire family that Christmas. The focus of Christmas returned to love and kindness toward others because of what God did for humanity through His Son. She went on to write that she had shared our story with her coworkers at the bank and they felt compelled to take up a collection for us. Enclosed with the letter was four times the money that we had given to Lisa and Michael.

This story with Arlene's family does not end here. Weeks later I went into the bank and met Kristina. We immediately became "kindred spirits' and over the next several months became good friends. I would occasionally stop on my way home and update her on Tucker's progress.

Six months after Tucker finished treatment, I saw Kristina on the skywalk at our hospital. After we embraced and made small talk for a moment, she told me that her husband, Rodney, was having surgery to remove a brain tumor. I listened on in disbelief. Her story brought back so many memories. When we parted I promised her that I would pray for them and help in any way that I could.

The next day we received a request for a physical therapy evaluation of Rodney. I picked up the order and scheduled him for an afternoon visit. However, by the time I arrived at the ICU to see him, he had already been transferred to a less critical unit on the 8th floor. That meant he was doing well, but probably wouldn't be ready to get up and start moving until the next day. I decided to move on to the rest of my patients and wait until the next day to see Rodney.

I went back up to the eighth floor to see my orthopedic patients. When I went into room 816 to see the patient in the window bed with the broken hip, I noticed the gentleman in the door bed (behind the pulled curtain) had a bandage turban around his head. I had never met Rodney, and Kristina was not there, hence, I could not confirm that it was him, but the thought did cross my mind. That thought was confirmed minutes later when the doctor came in with the family and started talking about prognosis. I was trapped on the other side of the curtain, and did not want to hear this incredibly personal information, yet I knew that it was God's will for me to be there. The doctor told them that Rodney's tumor was incurable and that he had one to two years to live. I could hardly believe his words, I felt like I was reliving our nightmare. My heart poured out to my friend.

After the doctor left, I prayed for guidance and strength and then I opened the curtain. Kristina looked at me with surprise and disbelief; she couldn't believe I was there. She hesitated for a moment and then introduced me to her entire family (including Lisa) as Tucker's mom. She then looked at me with anguish in her face and said, "You heard! What are we going to do?" I hugged her and reminded all of them of our story and of God's power. I encouraged them not to let anyone steal away their hope.

The next day I came to work armed with the books and verses that had encouraged and empowered me when we first started down this road. I sat down with Rodney and Kristina and talked about how you beat cancer. Since then both Kristina and Rodney's faith has grown by leaps and bounds. Rodney's attitude is awesome and twenty years later, he is still beating cancer!

♥

On Sunday, December 13th we left for Tucker's last round of chemotherapy. Tucker's ANC on Friday had been way over 1000 for the third consecutive time in a week. Therefore, we confidently anticipated an uneventful week and timely return home for Christmas.

We arrived at Sparrow and "moved in" without incident. As always, we unpacked our stuff and headed directly to the playroom. Dr. Gehra and a medical student from the U.P. caught up with us there a few hours later. As Dr.Gehra examined Tucker, the medical student casually pointed out that Tucker's white blood cell count was only 1.2. She said his ANC was not available yet.

I was stunned. I couldn't believe that his blood count could be too low to start again! I had felt no nudge... I had followed protocol. Tucker's ANC on Friday was 2300 and seemed to be climbing. My immediate shock at this news quickly turned into curiosity. I wondered what God's plan was for this week. Half an hour later Tucker's ANC level was reported to be 702. As per protocol, it needed to be at least 1000 to start the chemotherapy. Dr.Gehra decided to give him a unit of red blood to see if that would help. His ANC would then be rechecked in the morning.

I stayed with Tucker that night. As I lay in bed with him I read my journal from August when this had happened to us the first time. His ANC was 700 when we arrived, and it took five days for it to rise over 1000. With that information, I shut my book and prayed to God for guidance. I knew that God had brought us down here for a reason. I just had to listen close enough to hear His plan. Later I read *God Calling*, and it too reassured me that God had a plan. The words from Jeremiah 29:11 comforted my heart as I listened for God's still soft voice:

> *"For I know the plans I have for you declares the Lord, plans to prosper you and not to harm you, plans to give you hope and a future."*

The next morning I awoke with an interesting thought: "If Tucker's ANC is still too low to start chemotherapy today, maybe we should go visit family instead of going home. We could then come back to do chemotherapy at the end of the week when his counts improved." As I considered this idea, Conda, our nurse came in and let me know that Tucker's ANC was only 675 this morning. Her news did not make me teary or disappointed; I was fully expecting this result.

Five minutes later while Conda and I were still discussing our options, Todd and Lauren walked in. I presented Todd with the idea of going to visit family. His first response was very tentative and cautious. He was afraid that the risk of exposing Tucker to possible infection sources was too great, especially with his compromised blood counts. After considering it for a while, he did agree to at least ask Dr.Gehra about this option.

Over the next hour, we got many little nudges about what God had planned for us that week. First I called my sister, Patti, to tell her to cancel her and mom's flight to Lansing this week to see us. She was very comforting and reassured me that no matter where we were she would find a way to get there and spend some time with me. Moments after I finished my conversation with Patti, Todd's mom called and said that Grandma Waage was doing very poorly and was considering quitting dialysis. We all knew that if she did, she would die in a matter of weeks.

I could see the sadness in Todd's eyes as he talked with his mom, and I knew how much he wanted to see his grandmother at least one more time. I silently started to pray and ask God if He was providing a way for Todd to see his grandmother.

Dr.Gehra came in mid-morning while I was showering. Todd discussed with her the idea of us going to Iowa instead of home until Tucker's counts recovered. Dr.Gehra thought it was a great idea! She reassured Todd that it was doubtful that Tucker's ANC would drop below 500 (which is the critical count for being prone to infection) and also volunteered that it should only take a few days to bring it back over 1000. She said that she would write us a prescription for a blood draw so we could check Tucker's counts while in Iowa.

When I returned from the shower, Todd was all smiles as he stood there packing Tucker's clothes into the suitcase. He told me what Dr.Gehra had said and then added, "I have been praying that God would provide me with a way to see Grandma at least one more time with Tucker and Lauren by my side and today He said yes! I smiled as I thanked God for directing our path so clearly.

I called my mom to discuss the situation with her. She agreed that we should go to Iowa. She comforted me as my tears flowed and I shared with her how I missed her and had looked forward to spending this week with her even, if it was in the hospital. Minutes later, my sister Patti called and said she would come to Iowa. As always, my sister was finding ways to help me. Her effort gave me back my smile as we repacked our stuff and left for Iowa.

As we drove, we thought up a funny way to make our entrance at the homes of Todd's family. We made a quick stop at a Walmart and bought two huge shiny Christmas bows to put on the kids. When we arrived in Iowa, our first stop was at Todd's dads. The kids stood at the front door with their bows on and began singing "We Wish You a Merry Christmas" as we hid around the corner. When Ken opened the door, he nearly fell over in surprise. His look of amazement and pure joy said it all. He had never experienced serious illness with a child of his own and it had become apparent since the beginning how difficult this was for him. Seeing the kids was the greatest gift we could have given him that Christmas. As I watched him play with them all evening, I thanked God many times for allowing us to come. That night as I fell asleep in Todd's arms all seemed right in the world. I had peace. Once again I pondered if this is what it meant to ride God's rainbow.

We repeated the Christmas bow entrance the next morning with Todd's mom and grandma. They both knew we were in town, but the missing element of surprise did not decrease their excitement of seeing the kids whatsoever. Unlike Todd's dad who cried tears of joy at their sight, grandma's smile grew bigger and bigger as the kids came into her makeshift bedroom off of the living room and greeted her at her bedside. That smile remained all morning as the kids shared all their news with her and played at her bedside.

That day was Todd's 37th birthday, and we spent most of it at his Mom's house, just as he had hoped. The kids enjoyed reading books and playing with their new Christmas gifts with Grandma Margie all morning. Then right after lunch, they helped make a birthday cake for their Daddy.

Todd's brother, Mark, arrived in the afternoon with his kids, Grant and Sydney. Grant and Tucker are the same age; and he, Tucker and Lauren have always been great playmates. Two minutes after Grant walked through the door, the three of them had already created an adventure with Tucker's new dinosaurs. Grandma sat in her recliner and watched their imaginary world develop. You could just tell how their youthful spirits fed her soul.

Grandma had told Todd when we first arrived that she wasn't sure that she could go to dialysis anymore. We certainly understood and let her know we all would support whatever decision she made. The next morning however, after having a day with several of her great grandchildren, it was obvious that she wasn't ready to quit. She didn't want to talk; she wanted her stockings and her breakfast! She wanted to be ready when it was time to go to dialysis.

After Grandma left for dialysis, we all went to "Pocketchange Amusement Park" in the mall. We went to the Carousel first. As I listened to the Christmas music and watched our kids' wave to me and laugh with their daddy and grandma, I once again had an overwhelming feeling of peace and contentment. Every inch of me was smiling!

The kids ran directly from the Carousel to the bumper cars. Lauren and I took on Todd and Tucker in a bumping match. The kids controlled the steering wheels and we controlled the foot pedals. As we crashed and bumped the side rails and each other, my sister Patti arrived. We all waved and shouted hello and then continued with our ride. I noticed as I climbed out of my bumper car minutes later that Patti's eyes were full of tears. After we greeted one another with a big hug she commented on how great it was to hear the excitement in Tucker's laughter and the twinkle in his eye. She felt our joy and was overwhelmed.

We split up for the afternoon. Todd, Marge and the kids went to do some Christmas shopping and Patti and I went our own way for an afternoon of shopping. Usually I hate to shop, but that afternoon I thoroughly enjoyed it. We were so happy to be together that our love shined for all to see. Many store clerks commented that we were the happiest two people they had waited on all holiday season! That night Patti and I stayed up until 2 a.m.

wrapping packages, laughing and sitting in the sauna. Just being with my sister, sharing stories about our kids and our faith, was magical.

I gained such an appreciation for my sister over those twenty-four hours. She and I had always been close. This was due to Patti's incredibly laid-back, loving personality. She has always loved me for just who I was, and was there for me when I needed her. During that short visit, however, we became even closer. She renewed my energy. Her silly stories made me laugh like I hadn't in months. Her loving ways toward others, like the people of war-torn Kosovo, whom she sent twenty percent of her Christmas money to, reminded me of the good in this world. When she left the next morning it was my eyes that were brimming with tears. I so love her!

♥

After we said good bye to Patti, we went to the local hospital for a blood draw and then returned to Marge's to wait for the results. As we waited, I thought of all the possible scenarios that could take place over the next week. If Tucker's ANC wasn't high enough today, we might be in the hospital over Christmas finishing up chemotherapy, or we might still be in Iowa waiting for his ANC to be high enough to start. I really wanted to be at our own house, especially this Christmas, but I told God that I would submit to Him and whatever His will was for us. Then I picked up the phone and called to get the results. I waited anxiously as the lab secretary looked up the results on the computer. When she got back on the phone, she said his ANC was 950, she hesitated and then corrected herself and said "wait, with the banded neutrophils it would be 1003!" I laughed with relief and shared with her the critical difference between those two results; under 1000 no chemotherapy... over 1000 and we could start today.

I shared the results with Todd and the kids and then called Leslie at Sparrow to tell her our good news. She happily got things set up for us to start chemotherapy the following morning. Once off the phone, I thanked

God for His mercy and direction. I knew this week was a gift from Him and these results today were a confirmation that we had followed His plan. Now it was time to head back to Lansing and hopefully be home for Christmas.

♥

Our week at Sparrow was actually enjoyable. We spent it celebrating Christmas with all the new friends we had made over the last six months. Tucker even felt like celebrating. He tolerated each chemotherapy drug so well that we asked half seriously if they were sure that they weren't just infusing water!

Each morning that week, Tucker liked to have breakfast watching *"The Grinch Who Stole Christmas."* Then we would head to the playroom for games and crafts. Kelly, Sheila and Nikki, always had something for the Sprangers to do. One day we emptied out their junk drawer and created musical instruments for the "Whoo" children. We laughed together for hours as our imaginations went crazy making "megawhotrumpets" and "bangawangbarmofters".

We did not know it at the time, but that was our last inpatient admission to Sparrow Hospital. On our last day, two coincidences occurred that made me both reflect and ponder the perfectness of God's timing.

The first coincidence occurred when we were in the playroom building a fort with the blocks. I kept hearing a "beep... beep" outside the windows. Finally, my curiosity won me over, and I went to see what was going on. My heart ached as what my eyes and ears were sensing registered in my mind. The noise was the backing up of heavy equipment. There were several of them directly below us, and they were destroying my running track. When Nikki came in a few minutes, later she noticed me watching them with tears in my eyes. She explained that the hospital had bought that property from the school district and had been planning this for a long time so all employees could park on-campus. After she left, I continued to watch them for a while as

I reflected on all times that this two-lane dirt track had been by sanctuary. I thanked God for allowing it to remain there over these last six months.

The other coincidence happened after Todd and Lauren left for the O'Berski's. Our night nurse came in to do her initial assessment. We were in the same room we had been in our first night there back in June, and this was also the same nurse. She and I talked for a long time just as we did the first night. The first time, however, she did most of the talking, and the conversation was mostly about medicine. This time I did most of talking, and the conversation was mostly about God and His love and power.

After she left, I laid awake for hours just like on our first night. This time I was not anxious or scared; the imprisoning walls of fear I had lived within ever since John died were coming down. Instead, I felt a peace that I had never felt before.... I WAS RIDING GOD'S RAINBOW! I prayed as I fell asleep that this feeling would never leave me.

The next day, December 23rd, we were discharged from the hospital. With our car packed to the brim with presents from Todd's family and the numerous generous people who give to the children's hospital around Christmas, we headed to the O'Berskis'. We had a beautiful evening with them celebrating the love we have for our children, one another and our Savior Jesus Christ. Todd and I agreed as we laid bed that night that it does our souls good to spend time with the O'Berskis. They give us hope and support all that is good within us.

The next morning we got up early and left for home. As our little blue Subaru carried us up I-75 North to the Mackinaw Bridge, we all were giddy with the thought of being home for Christmas. Never mind the lack of time to prepare; we knew that God would provide and that we would be at home together. As we drove through Munising (about 40 minutes from our house) we experienced an extraordinary winter sunset. The sun went under the horizon just as we drove down the hill toward Lake Superior. The pink of the sky illuminated the white snow and the dark green forest. The contrast was breathtaking. It reminded us all of why we loved this place we call home so much. We all quietly took in this beauty as we finished the drive.

We arrived at home just before dinner. Todd went into the house while I waited in the car with the kids. We had ordered some gifts that should have arrived while we were gone. Todd wanted to hide them before the kids came in. Twenty minutes later he still hadn't returned and we all had to go the bathroom! We got out of the car and raced toward the front door. Todd met us on the deck shaking his head. At first I thought he was shaking his head that we couldn't come in. As the kids raced passed him, he explained to me that he was shaking his head in disbelief at all that was in our house.

The refrigerator was stuffed full with Christmas dinner including a turkey. The counter had four or five different kinds of cookies for our eating pleasure. In the living room, Todd said the gifts were packed up so high he could hardly see the tree. Todd had spent that twenty minutes hiding them in our bathroom so the kids would be surprised the next morning. The generosity of our neighbors did not end there. An hour after we walked in, a neighbor came over with salads and pie for Christmas dinner. She was soon followed by another neighbor carrying a two-foot tall gingerbread house that she had spent the day making!

We had just enough time after visiting with our neighbors to eat dinner and then head off to the Christmas Eve church service. We sat in the balcony so that Tucker would avoid the crowd. The bell choir sat right behind us and rang cheer into the night air. The perspective from the balcony during the candlelight portion of the service was overwhelming. God's Spirit emanated as I looked down on all the individual flames burning. Each flame represented a different spirit, burning with the love of both the Father and Son! I thought about my flame and how much brighter it had grown this year.

When we arrived at home after the service, the kids were both sleeping. We tucked them in and then became Santa's elves. For the next three hours, we pulled out box after box that had been left at our house and put them under the tree. Many of the boxes didn't even have names telling us from whom they came. We wrote "From Santa" on all of them as we talked about how much this trial had taught us regarding love and generosity. When we finished, the entire living room sparkled with bows, tinsel, gifts and goodies. We spent the wee hours of the night enjoying a glass of wine next to the fire. It was the loveliest Christmas Eve I can ever remember.

Christmas morning came very early. In fact this was the first Christmas morning that the kids actually had to wake us. We cuddled up on the couch and watched the kids open gifts. We were just as surprised with what was in the packages as they were! The kids did not rush through the unwrapping. They took their time and played with each gift as they opened it. Once however, Tucker opened the battery-rechargeable four-wheeler, he had no interest in any other gift. He put it together with his daddy and then spent the rest of the morning riding it back and forth fifteen feet in our living room.

We spent the afternoon enjoying just being home: our dogs, the meal from our neighbors, sledding and a hot sauna before bed. Throughout the day I kept pondering how much different I felt this Christmas. Our Savior's birth and promise of eternal life had new meaning. I was not stressed by the usual Christmas stuff, but instead truly savoring every moment of the day.

♥

That Christmas, I also received a very special gift. It was confirmation that I had really heard God during that first run; that this trial was really about showing me and other's the power of faith. It was an email from Nicki, one of the child life specialists at Sparrow. It said:

*It is Christmas Eve night. I turned on my computer to check my email and then I started to look up some things on the internet. Even though I hadn't planned to, I keyed in Tucker's wed page address and read every last word. I've been waiting to tell you what impact your family has had on me, and after reading Tucker's website, I know that the time is now.*

*I grew up with very little religious background. My family didn't go
to church regularly. After my dad had a heart attack, and a near death
experience, he became a Catholic and joined the Catholic Church. My mom
then became a Catholic after my dad's second heart attack. I was a teenager by this time and resented any push toward religion of any kind. My
younger sister became a Catholic, and my older sister became a Catholic
before marrying a Catholic man.*

*All through college, I rejected organized religion for reasons that I felt
were sound. I guess, I can say now, that I have always felt a bit lost. There
has always been too much anger and negativity in my life.*

*Then out of the blue, I met your family. From the moment I met all of
you, I knew that there was something so special about you. And there definitely is. I know you have heard this kind of thing before, but maybe even
more so now. Being around your family, hearing your stories, and feeling
your faith in God has made me want to change my life. For the first time
in my life, I am believing in God. I am searching for a church that is right
for my family and I am changing my life for the better in so many ways. It
all seems to have come easy. It is amazing.....*

*I want to thank you for letting me know you and for introducing me
to God and the wonderful ways He shows His love. I am learning to pray,
and I am praying for Tucker and family. Thank you and I hope you have a
wonderful Christmas!*

*Love Nikki*

I had loved Nikki since I first met her. We had great conversations almost
every time we were in the playroom together. I never asked about her faith
and I wasn't trying to witness to her. I was trying to cope and she was always
a willing, available ear. As I read her email that day, I was humbled at how
God had used our trial to help Nikki receive grace. I was overjoyed at the
changes happening within her. What she did not know was what a gift her

email was to me. It gave purpose to all this suffering. With her words in my heart I enjoyed the rest of Christmas and prepared for the new year.

# Chapter 5:

# ...And the Earth Was Dry

*And it came to pass in the six hundred and first year, in the first month, the first day of the month that the waters were dried up from the earth.*

*Genesis 8:13*

The year 2000 was the beginning of a much-anticipated new century. I remember when I was in high school, and we would talk about the upcoming new century. I remember thinking how far away that was; I would be the ancient age of thirty-four when that new century rolled around. I wondered how I would celebrate such a notable New Year's Eve. I never imagined that I would spend the last hours of the old century finishing a blood transfusion at the hospital with my four year-old son so I could ring in the new century quietly at home with my family.

As Todd and I sat by the fire that evening we talked about how much richer life seemed now; that we really noticed the little things like a child's laughter, a beautiful snowy morning, and the warmth of spouse's touch. Our happiness was not dictated by our circumstance, it was coming from within to color every moment and make it joyful.

We also talked about what the new year would bring. We both certainly knew that our storm was not yet over, but rather the most difficult and risky aspects were quickly approaching. We felt a little like Noah trying to figure out how much longer we would be drifting and what God's will was for us. We both were very sure of God's presence. We were not afraid but more curiously optimistic and interested in what God had planned for us.

❤

It didn't take long for God to start revealing His plan. On January 2nd, I received a phone call from a slightly familiar voice. The lady on the other end introduced herself as Valerie Holoway. She said she had read the article in the paper about Tucker and the scout troops and had felt a soft spot in her heart for our situation. She explained that she practiced homeopathy and nutritional counseling in Marquette. As I listened to her, I kept thinking that her voice sounded familiar. Then it occurred to me that she was the lady I had overheard in the organic food co-op a few weeks before. She was talking with another patron and I could tell she was very knowledgeable about nutrition and healing. I felt nudged to go talk to her; tell her our story and get some advice.... But I didn't.

Thankfully Valerie did not disregard God's nudge to call me. She got my phone number from my neighbor and boldly reached out to me. Her phone call was a godsend. We talked for an hour that morning. The following day Tucker and I met with her. She did some testing on him to determine how his body was handling the chemotherapy. Her tests showed that his kidneys and liver were stressed and his lymph system was sluggish. Valerie recommended a few supplements and some major changes to our diet. The information and recommendations she made complimented the traditional medicine track we were on. We now knew the impact of certain life choices on his body and what foods would help his immune system and which ones wouldn't.

Tucker and I went right from Valerie's office to the organic food store. Our grocery list had things on it like "Ezekiel Bread", Stevia sweetener, soymilk, unsweetened plain yogurt, Tofu and fresh spinach.

My meeting Valerie probably did as much for me as it did for Tucker. Her ideas made sense to me and empowered me to think that I could be part of the cure planned by God. I took her recommendations seriously and did everything I could to incorporate them into our lifestyle.

♥

On January 9th, we returned downstate to have all of Tucker's tests repeated. These tests would tell if he was ready for the radiation and the transplant. I was still praying for the miracle of completely clean scans before the transplant. As we prepared to leave our home, I was a little anxious as I considered what an important week away from home this would be. We would either come home very hopeful and ready for the next hurdle, or discouraged and searching for hope. God set my perspective where it needed to be that morning through *God Calling*. It said:

*Be calm, no matter what may befall you. Rest in Me. Be patient and let patience have her perfect work. Never think things overwhelming. How can you be overwhelmed when I am with you?*

*Do not feel the strain of life. There is no strain for My children. Do you not see I am a Master Instrument-maker. Have I not fashioned each part? Do I not know just what it can bear without a strain? Would I, the maker of so delicate an instrument, ask of it anything that could destroy or strain?*

*No! The strain is only when you are serving another master...or carrying two days burden on the one day.*

*Remember that it must not be.*

We all stayed with the O'Berski's that week as Tucker did not have to be an inpatient. During dinner our first night, Mike and Susie told us about a family in the Lansing area whose three year old son had just been diagnosed with neuroblastoma. His name was Charles DeGroot. As Susie told us about Charles and his family, I was amazed with all the similarities there was between our cases.

The next morning we saw Dr. Kulkarni and got our tests and appointment schedule. She was delighted to see Tucker looking so well. She also told us about Charles and asked if we would go up to the pediatric unit and introduce ourselves. She thought it would be very helpful for his parents to see Tucker six months into treatment. We assured her that we would stop by that afternoon between tests.

Tucker was so brave during all of his scans. He marched into the appointments with his cowboy hat and boots on, and didn't even squirm as they injected the dyes and markers through his central line. He lay completely still for up to an hour as they scanned his body. He told them he didn't need anesthesia to lay still and he was right!

As we waited for the renal flow scan injection, I noticed another little boy and his mom waiting. His mom looked so wiped out. I wondered if that was the DeGroots. As I watched them and offered a smile, I felt so much empathy for her. The memories of those horrifying initial days were so vivid. I wanted to run over and hug her, but resisted the urge. It just did not seem like the right time.

I went up to Charles room late in the afternoon. Mark, Charles 'dad, was with him. Mark and I chatted briefly. I was amazed at how positive and accepting Mark seemed to be of the entire situation. He said, "There are people all over the world praying for this little guy!" and "I have seen so many good things coming out of this already, that I know it is God's will!" I wondered if he was sincere in his words or if he was masking the pain to cope. Whichever, that was between him and God. I just tried to love him and encourage him. Before parting, Mark and I agreed that it would be great to get our families together in the playroom some night. Mark volunteered that he owned two pizza stores in town and that he would bring the pizza! We made a date for later that week.

The next three days we spent in Ann Arbor repeating the MIBG scans. As we were getting ready to leave the hospital after the first day's scan, we saw Dr.Yanik in the hallway. He asked us if we wanted to come and look at the results with him. I wasn't sure if I wanted to or not, but Todd readily said "Yes!" As we all followed Dr.Yanik to the viewing area, my heart pounded. I prayed for peace and for Jesus to hold my hand as we looked at the results.

Dr.Yanik stopped at the door and asked us to wait outside the room for a moment. That gave us a chance to have a group prayer before we went in. Holding hands, we thanked God for this day and asked Him for His mercy. Moments later, Dr. Yanik opened the door and let us in. He had a big smile on his face as he said he didn't want to sound too hopeful, but this first day scan showed no signs of neuroblastoma! He showed us Tucker's initial scan and compared it to the current scan. All the areas of initial uptake that were very darkly shaded were now clear. It was the miracle that I had been praying for. I knew it was very dangerous to jump to conclusions, but I couldn't help it. I began to praise God (before the second day's scan) for this miracle!

The next morning Tucker insisted that I come in for the scan instead of Todd. I tried not to look at the screen, but Lahti inadvertently put the monitor right in front of me. I sang and read to Tucker throughout the entire test. Only two times did I look up and then out of the corner of my eye I saw the dots signifying increased uptake of the MIBG at the right tibia and on the left pelvis. My heart sank as I realized that my miracle had not come true-Tucker's scans were not clear.

I didn't tell Todd what I had seen on the monitor. I decided that both of us didn't need to be crushed until we knew for sure. We didn't see Dr.Yanik that day so we would have to wait until we saw Dr. Kulkarni on Monday to confirm what I saw. That afternoon, as we drove back toward Lansing to have dinner with the DeGroots, I remembered the words from God Calling that morning:

*Never despair, never despond. Be just a channel of helpfulness for others. Have more sympathy. Feel more tenderness towards others.*

I needed to embrace those words. I needed to stop fretting about what I thought I saw on Tucker's MIBG scan and instead be God's instrument for this other family who has just started this battle. I recalled the hope that our meeting with Karsha's family had given us during our first hospitalization, and I prayed that we would be that same kind of blessing to the DeGroots.

♥

We had a great evening with the Charles' family. Mark and Sue were about our age and we had much in common to chat about. Their daughter, Audrey, was Lauren's age and looked surprisingly like her. Tucker, Lauren and Audrey quickly overcame their leeriness of one another and built a block fort in the corner of the playroom. Charles was in no mood to play with them. He had received chemotherapy that afternoon, so he was very content sleeping or watching other kids from the wagon. The DeGroots also had a two –year old son, Jonathon (nicknamed the "Viking") who was there. After twenty minutes with him, we knew why he was called the "Viking". His entire face lit up and his eyes twinkled as he destroyed the kid's fort and pillaged the rest of the playroom. Mark and Sue did their best to contain him, and we all enjoyed his energy and zest for life!

Between caring for our children and helping them get acquainted, we found time to get acquainted ourselves. I was amazed as Sue shared her story how much we had in common. Her Mom had died of cancer when she was young, and she had always feared cancer coming back to haunt her. We had both grown up in the same religious denomination that neither of us now practiced. We talked at length about God and faith. As I shared with her, I chose my words very carefully. I wanted to point her toward Christ but not sound too preachy. I encouraged Sue to be open to Jesus and rely on Him to carry her through this storm.

That night was the beginning of a great friendship with this family. We have provided and supported one another as no else could. We have grown in our faith together and shared in all aspects of our lives. Sue and I talk often about Heaven and how we look forward to eternity together in a place where there is no pain or suffering.

♥

That weekend we had no plans and no obligations. Tucker was done with all of the testing, but the meeting with Dr. Kulkarni was not until Monday. We took advantage of that time spending it the O'Berski's. We were resigned not to waste it worrying about test results we could not change. Friday morning we all lay in bed tickling toes and playing guessing games until the smell of pancakes drove us out of bed. Upstairs, Mike treated us to his specialty: blueberry and chocolate chip pancakes!

After breakfast, I went for a walk with Susie around their subdivision. As we walked, we discussed how God was working in different aspects of our lives. Later, I read *God Calling* and marveled at how its words exactly reflected my morning discussion with Susie. It said:

*Glad indeed are the souls with whom I walk. Walking with Me is security. The coming of My Spirit into a life, and Its working are imperceptible, but the result is mighty...As you go on obeying Me and walking with Me and listening to Me, you will see how glorious, how marvelous My revelations are, and My teachings.*

♥

Monday came quickly and we returned to Sparrow for Tucker's bone marrow biopsy and the meeting with Dr. Kulkarni. The biopsy started as routine with me looking on and praying from the foot of Tucker's bed. As Dr. Kulkarni took the marrow sample, Dr. Guertin began to whistle "Amazing Grace". His song reminded me of how good God is. As I listened, I closed my eyes and felt a wave of peace wash over me. It made me smile.

After the procedure, Dr. Kulkarni came into the recovery room to discuss the test results from the last week. I tried to keep my peace as I anticipated her words, but I knew how much rode on these results. If Tucker's scans weren't clean or showed new tumor growth, the chance of the transplant curing him would be minuet.

God had mercy on us. Each test result showed His protection and His healing hand. Tucker's hearing, renal flow scan and echocardiogram showed no sign of damage to Tucker's other systems from the chemotherapy. The bone scan and abdominal CT showed no signs of tumor, and most impor-tantly, Tucker's MIBG scan showed uptake only in the growth plates and that was completely normal!!"

I could hardly believe my ears as Dr. Kulkarni shared these results with us! I had obviously misinterpreted the second day MIBG scans. The miracle that I had been praying for since August had come to pass; our mourning had turned to dancing and our sackcloth had been removed. In the deepest way, I wanted to shout God's praises from the mountaintops.

Later, as I reflected on the verses from Genesis that God had revealed to me regarding our trial, I marveled at the parallels in time. Like Noah, we were called to go through a mighty storm and then spent many months drifting at sea surviving only on faith and hope. Now we, like Noah, were in a situation where it appeared that storm was over, that the earth was dry!

As much as I wanted to celebrate this victory, I had to remember that this storm was not over and God in His wisdom was not allowing us to get out of the boat yet. I knew that we needed to keep trusting God and following Noah's example of patience and obedience as we experienced the unfolding of His will. For us that meant enduring MIBG radiation and a stem cell transplant.

♥

# Chapter 6:

# *The Fulfilling of God's Promise*

*And in the second month, on the twenty-seventh day of the month, the earth was dried... Then God spoke to Noah, saying, "Go out of the ark, you and your wife, and your sons and your son's wives with you. Bring out with you every living thing of all flesh that is with you...*

*Then Noah built an altar to the Lord, and took of every clean animal and of every clean bird and offered burnt offerings on the altar. And the Lord smelled a soothing aroma. Then the Lord said in His heart, "I will never again curse the ground for man's sake."*

*Genesis 8:14-18, 20*

On January 24th we began our journey through the uncharted water of MIBG radiation therapy at U of M Hospital. This was not only uncharted water for us; it was new for U of M as well. Although they had been using MIBG radiation for twenty years to scan for neuroblastoma, they were combining it for the first time with a stem cell rescue in the hopes of having better long-term outcomes. Tucker was only the fourth child to be enrolled in this experimental study. Karsha was the second.

Dr. Yanik was the principle investigator of the MIBG study. Prior to the start of the infusion, he met with us in the oncology playroom and went through the research protocol and consent form. Tucker and Lauren played in the dress-up closet while we talked with Dr. Yanik. I knew from being a member on our local Institutional Review Board that the consent form had to include all the possible risks of this treatment but even so, this was overwhelming. It felt surreal to agree to this potentially fatal treatment for our child as we watched him play so happily.

As I listened to Dr. Yanik, I kept my peace reflecting back on the scripture and the *God Calling* reading for that day:

*I am your guide. Do not want to see the road ahead. Go just one step at a time. I rarely grant the long vista to my disciples, especially in personal affairs, for one step at a time is the best way to cultivate faith.*

*You are in uncharted waters. But the Lord of all Seas is with you, the Controller of all Storms is with you. Sing with joy. You follow the Lord of Limitations, as well as the God in whose service is perfect freedom.*

After we signed the consent form and were going over final plans for the next day, Tucker let us know that he too was ready for this next battle. He burst out of the dress-up closet in full knight armor and exclaimed "Let's do this!"

♥

The following morning MIBG radiation was injected into Tucker through his central line and he was put in an isolation room behind lead shields. The entire room, including the bed, was wrapped in plastic and even the nurses were monitored for their amount of radiation exposure. Todd, Lauren and I watched the entire process from the doorway, as we were not allowed to go in the room until Tucker's REM count was under 3.0.

*God Calling* that morning gave us much reassurance for the day. It said:

*I am with you both. Go forward unafraid. Health and strength, peace and happiness and joy-they are all My gifts. Yours for the asking...*

*Be not afraid. Fear not. It is to the drowning man the Rescuer comes. To the brave swimmer who can fare well alone. He comes not. And no rush of Joy can be like that of a man towards his Rescuer.*

*It is a part of My method to wait till the storm is at its full violence.*
*So did I with My disciples on the Lake. I could have stilled, but what*
*a lesson unlearned? What a sense of tender nearness of refuge and*
*safety would have been lost.*
*Remember this- My disciples though that in sleep I had forgotten*
*them. Remember how mistaken they were. Gain strength and confi-*
*dence and joyful dependence and anticipation from that.*
*Never fear. Joy is yours and the radiant joy of the rescued shall be*
*yours.*

As I read this, I reflected on its relevance. Back in July, when we first learned about MIBG radiation therapy, I knew this day would come. Yet I had often prayed that God would remove this burden from us; that He would create a way for Tucker to be healed that would not include this technique of radiation infusion and isolation. God was answering my prayers in this reading. His answer was: *"No, you must go through this storm so you can grow closer to Me, the Rescuer."* I smiled as I realized His answer and promised that I would strive to rely on Him no matter how big the waves got.

Despite my promise, I struggled that evening as I camped with Lauren and Todd in the hallway outside of Tucker's door. I wanted to go hold my son's hand and help him deal with all the obstacles of this day, but all I could do was to stand at the door and change the videotape in the portable television.

That night after Todd and Lauren went to our room; I picked up my pencil and let my heart grieve:

### ISOLATION
*They infused Radiation*
*Then put my son in isolation.*
*They marked a line that I must not cross,*
*For 48 hours I am at a loss-*
*Not to see his smile...*
*Touch his hand...*

*Wipe his tear.*
*He knows that his mommy is near,*
*And that is enough for him...*
*But not for me.*

Tucker remained in isolation through the entire next day. In the morning, he was content watching television and playing with his trucks. However by afternoon he was frustrated and fragile. At one point he was crying because he had to go the bathroom and he could not get there because of all the Ivs and catheters. We rang for the nurses but they did not come. Finally, Todd and I went into the room to help him. That was against all rules and we got in a heap of trouble when the nurses finally did arrive. The risk manager for the hospital system came to investigate and scan us with a Geiger counter to see if we were emitting radiation.

The manager was a very tall, thin middle age man. As he questioned us he was a bit rude and arrogant. He looked at me and said: 'Why were you just sitting here in the hallway anyway?" I looked him right in the eye and said: "Where would you be in your four year old had cancer and had to be in isolation for two days as part of treatment!" He said nothing else and walked away. After that, the nurses responded much quicker and the rest of the day past without further incident although Tucker was ready to be done with this. I was thankful when he fell asleep early for the night.

After Tucker was asleep, Todd, Lauren and I made the best of the evening and our hallway hideaway. First we created Valentine puppets, then we painted our faces with our new face markers, and we ended the evening watching *"Mouse trap"*, a slap stick comedy. I can't imagine what the hospital personnel thought seeing the three of us curled up together on two recliners at the end of the hall laughing hysterically at the portable television that we turned from Tucker's view to ours. The laughter felt good!

Mid-morning the next day we heard Sue, the MIBG radiation technologist, come walking down the hall. Sue was a 4'10"ball of fire who was the workhorse of this clinical trial. She had taken excellent care of us all week and we were very thankful to hear her coming to rescue us that morning. She took Tucker out of the room and down to the Nuclear Medicine Department so she could measure how much radiation he was now emitting and complete some additional scans. It felt so good to be able to hold Tucker's hand as we accompanied him to Nuclear Medicine.

First Sue measured Tucker's radiation emission. We were all holding our breath and praying for a number lower than 3.0 REMs so Tucker could be released from isolation. As I held his hand and waited for Sue to tell us the number, I kept repeating the words: "ALL is WELL". Sue interrupted my words to declare that Tucker's radiation emission level was at 2.9REMs! We celebrated this victory with hugs all around! Sue completed a few more scans, and by early afternoon Tucker was discharged from the hospital. As we drove away, we thanked God for helping us through these difficult days and for growing our patience, trust, and focus.

We arrived home and quickly fell back into the routine of school and work for Lauren and me during the day, and evenings enjoying time as a family. We knew that we would have just ten days at home before Tucker started the stem cell rescue. We also knew that when we left for this next and hopefully last phase of treatment it could be several months before we would return home, and we may return without Tucker. The realization of these facts made each moment at home precious.

My morning time of reflection and prayer had become a sanctuary for me; a block of time and space completely dedicated to my spiritual health and relationship with the Trinity. I am no theologian but I could actually tell some mornings it was more like hearing from God, an authority figure directing my path, and other mornings it felt more like Jesus, an intimate friend and brother holding my hand. Day by day I became more spiritually ready for what was coming next.

I worked until the day before we left Ann Arbor. As I said goodbye to my coworkers and patients, I was humbled and awed by the care and love I felt from this community. I knew that God was answering all their prayers for my family because my peace was overwhelming. The final message of encouragement I receive before I left work was written on my daily flip calendar that sits on my desk. I read it right before I walked out the door. It said:

*You shall never regret not taking one more test,*
*or not working late one more night.*
*You will regret times not spent with a child or a spouse.*

I smiled as I walked out the door. I knew that I would return a different person but that I would never regret the next few months.

♥

We left for Ann Arbor on February 8th after Todd and I each had a chance to go on a final skijour. Skijouring is a crazy fun Nordic sport where you cross country ski with a dog pulling you. It is my favorite way to ski. You feel one with nature and you can cover a lot of ground FAST! As I skied over the same trail where I had first heard God's voice last summer, I reflected on our journey thus far. I felt confident that I had heard God's voice and I was learning the power of faith. I also knew that the stem cell rescue would be harder and longer than the radiation. It would test our endurance and stamina like nothing yet had. I contemplated the challenge of God's Calling from that morning:

*I am your Lord, your Supply. You must rely on Me. Trust to the last*
*uttermost limit. Trust and be not afraid. You must depend on Divine*
*Power only. I have not forgotten you. Your help is coming. You shall*
*know and realize My Power.*

*Endurance is faith tried almost to breaking point. You must wait, and trust and hope and joy in Me. You must not depend on man but on Me, on Me, your Strength, your Help, your Supply.*

*This is the great test. Am I your Supply or not? Every great work for Me has had to have this great test-time.*

*Possess your souls in patience and rejoice. You must wait until I show the way. Heaven itself cannot contain more joy than that soul knows, when after the waiting-test, I crown it victor, but no disciple of Mine can be victor, who does not wait until I give the order to start. You cannot be anxious if you know that I am your Supply.*

This reading foretold of the difficult days I knew would come. It urged me to turn only to God for my reassurance, my strength and my supply in those difficult days.

As I skied the last quarter-mile up our forest-lined road, I felt focused and ready. Later, as we drove away from our home waving goodbye, I remained focused. I knew I would miss my home, but the biggest asset I had, the love of my Father and my family, was traveling with me.

The next morning the rescue process began with the surgical insertion of a second central line. We were all in good spirits when we arrived at the surgical waiting room. We didn't mind starting our day in this place we were now so comfortable (with both Lahti and Betsy).

After surgery, Tucker was admitted to 714, a room we would call home for the next month. Lauren was thrilled because it was right across the hall from the "park". The "park" was an open playroom for all kids. It had a jukebox, a fort and a life-size rocking horse.

Tucker recovered from the anesthetic and surgery so quickly that he joined Lauren in the "park" by midafternoon and they allowed him to leave the hospital that evening for an early Valentine's dinner. We chose a cozy

Italian restaurant just a few blocks from the hospital. As we toasted one and
another with our water goblets, we thanked God for the love He had for our
family and the love we shared. We knew that this would be our last outing
together for a long time, and we enjoyed every moment of it including a big
piece of chocolate mousse cake for dessert!

That night I talked with Sue DeGroot on the phone. She thanked me for
the copy of *God Calling* I had sent her and share with me how it had spoken
to her today. Last night she had asked God to give her some sign that Charles
would be okay. This morning she woke up with much peace in her heart and
the darkness that had loomed since his diagnosis was gone. Later she read in
*God Calling*:

> "The Divine Voice is not always expressed in words. It is made known
> as a heart-consciousness"

Sue knew that the peace in her heart was from God and she thought it was
a sign that Charles would be okay. I smiled as I listened to her describe her
peace. I also knew that this peace was from God, and I prayed that she was
interpreting this "sign" correctly. Only time would tell.

During that phone call, Sue offered us a wonderful living option for the
month after Tucker finished the stem cell rescue that we would have to stay
within an hour's drive of the hospital. (Currently we had no plan for that
month. We figured we would cross that bridge when we got to it.) Sue's aunt
had recently bought a house across the street from Sue and Mark and it was
exactly one hour from Ann Arbor. She wasn't planning to move in until the
end of March. Sue said she would talk with her aunt to see if we could stay
there if we were interested. I thanked her for thinking about us and told
her that I would discuss it with Todd. I quickly added that I couldn't think of
one reason why we wouldn't take them up on this option. It would be a huge
answer to prayer.

I went to bed that night feeling God's arms around me. I wasn't afraid of
the chemotherapy that would be starting tomorrow. I welcomed it for I knew

that it was the beginning of the end. I could see God's handiwork in providing this home for us after discharge. I felt very secure and cared for.

♥

The next four days were full of meeting the people who would become our family for the next month: Adrienne and Theresa from the child life department, Viita, our primary nurse, and the families of Jacob and Elmira.

Adrienne was a professional artist who had decided a few years prior to volunteer her services to Mott's Children Hospital on a regular basis. Eventually they hired her because she added such a unique dimension to what they could offer these sick kids. Adrienne spent most of her time with the kids who were hospitalized a long time. She would make a huge poster with their name and favorite things as a door sign for each room. This poster was then laminated and hung over the window of each room,

Adrienne came to see Tucker early the second morning. She was tall, slender, older woman who just looked like an artist. Her clothes, her makeup and even her hair style, all reflected a flair for color and design. She took a picture I had of Tucker on a four-wheeler and painted a life size picture of it to hang over his bed. She also made him a huge wall graph to record his daily blood counts as well as daily "chores" that we would mark with a sticker when they were completed. Adrienne's work really impressed our kids and brightened up our room. Almost instantly Adrienne and I had a fondness and appreciation for one another's gifts.

Theresa was the Child-life Specialist. She was a smiley, giggly twenty five-year old Yooper want-to-be. I enjoyed her youthful lifestyle. It reminded me of a different time in my life. Theresa would close down the playroom to other kids for an hour and a half a day so that Tucker (who was neutropenic) and our family could have some playroom time. She had lots of cool projects like "Shrinky Dinks", dress up closet, K-nex and spin painting. We would sit and do the projects with the kids and tell her about life up north. Tucker really looked forward to going down to the playroom during that first week. It made each day pass quickly and kept all of our spirits up.

Viita was our primary nurse, which meant whenever she was working she was assigned to us. She was a feisty Italian gal with two little boys of her own. She and I spent much time discussing balancing our careers with our family responsibilities. We also talked at length about faith and trials.

Jacob was a cute eighteen month old who had just been diagnosis with neuroblastoma. Todd was asked by a staff member to stop in and talk with his parents as Jacob's case was quite advanced and they needed some hope. His parents, Theresa and Craig, told Todd their nightmare story of delayed diagnosing because of insurance protocols and reimbursements. They were bitter and angry. As Todd relayed their story to me, my heart poured out to them, yet I knew God's timing was perfect and that He could still do anything.

Late one night, I stopped by Jacob's room and introduced myself to Theresa. I tried to be God's tool and encourage her as the Schrem's had encouraged us. After that, Theresa and I became late night chat partners in either the laundry room or Jacob's room. I almost felt like I was back in college living in the dorms. Except, instead of going to class each morning, we were going off to battle... battle against cancer!

Jacob was admitted at least three times over the month that we were hospitalized for Tucker's stem cell rescue. Jacob couldn't eat anything and he kept throwing up blood. As I watch his struggles, I became so aware how "easy" we cruised through all the initial chemotherapy. I thank God for past protection He had given us that I wasn't even aware of at the time.

Elmira was a fifteen year-old from Romania who had CML (the most serious type of childhood leukemia). In Romania she had no hope for a cure because of the lack of advanced health care. Her aunt, however, lived in Grand Rapids, and she took it upon herself to get Elmira here and to get her treatment. Elmira also did not have any health insurance, but this did not stop her aunt. She solicited funds from all around the country to help offset the cost of Elmira's treatment. When we met this family, her aunt had raised 75,000 dollars! We talked much with her in the kitchen and the "park "over that month. Their story made me very grateful for health insurance and for the health care system we have in this country. My heart went out to Elmira's mother, as she did not know a word of English. I thought how scary it would be to come to a country without your spouse, without speaking the language, to go through all of this with your fifteen year-old daughter.

We shared a private kitchen with Elmira's family and at least once daily I ran into Elmira's mom there. We would try to communicate. After a while she started to offer me Romanian food and drink. At first I hesitated but eventually I tried some. It was …interesting!!

I only met Elmira once. On the day that she actually received her donor stem cells I stuck my head in the door and congratulated her on her new birthday. She was grinning from ear to ear sitting up in bed eating a piece of watermelon.

Unfortunately, things didn't stay that good for Elmira. During our third week in the hospital, her kidneys shut down and she was transferred to ICU. Just before we were discharged, she was moved back to our floor and we were hopeful that she was over the worst of it. In April, once we returned home, we received a letter from Elmira's aunt. Elmira had passed into Heaven.

As I read her aunt's letter, I couldn't help wondering what God's plan was in all of that. Why had he called this aunt away from her family and into this huge project... why had he cared for Elmira through all preliminary treatment...why had He tested this Romanian Mom so...for this to be the intended end? The answers to these questions eluded me. I echoed the words of a of a Steven Curtis-Chapman song as I entertained these questions:

*"God is God and I am not,*
*I can only see a part of the picture He is painting. God is God and I*
*am man so I will never understand it all,*
*for only God is God."*

♥

During the first four days after the central line was put in, chemotherapy was infused continually into Tucker. I could see as each day progressed, the toll that these medications (which are actually toxins) were taking on his body. Although his blood counts were staying in an acceptable range, he was turning paler and weaker. As I watched him deteriorate, I found comfort in God's Word (John 15: 1-17) and in a *God Calling* entry from that week:

> *Think of My trees stripped of their beauty, pruned, cut, disfigured, bare, but through the dark seemingly dead branches flows silently, secretly, the spirit-life sap, till lo! With the sun of spring comes new life, leaves, bud, blossom, fruit but oh! Fruit a thousand times better for the pruning.*
>
> *Remember that you are in the hands of a Master-Gardner. He makes no mistakes about His pruning. Rejoice. Joy so the Spirit's reaching out to say its thanks to Me. It is the new life-sap of the tree, reaching out to Me to find such beautiful expression later. So never cease to joy. Rejoice!*

I later realized that these words regarding pruning and improving the fruit were not just about what was happening to Tucker, but to all of us. The fruit referred to is the fruit of the spirit described in Galatians 5 22-23:

> *But the fruit of the Spirit is love, joy, peace, long-suffering, kindness, goodness, faithfulness, gentleness, and self-control.*

Each day trying to survive in this difficult environment with all its uncertainty pruned our branches. Our peace, joy and love radiated from the Spirit living within us, not from our daily circumstance. Our gentleness, kindness, and goodness became purer and more genuine as we cared for our children and got to know the families around us. Our self-control, faithfulness and long-suffering grew as we witnessed God's purpose in all circumstances and the reward of complete faithfulness.

♥

My mom flew into Lansing on February 12th to spend a week with us. Lauren and I made a road trip to Lansing to pick her up and to do a little cooking at the DeGroot's home for our next week's meals.

This was our first time out of the hospital in a while. It felt so refreshing to be away from the city and driving through the rolling hills, past red barns and farm fields. As soon as we pulled into "Home Again Farm" (the name stenciled over the barn door) I knew that we would love living here while Tucker was recovering. There was a warmness and joy that radiated from that farm that I immediately sensed.

Sue and I cooked for an hour while Lauren played with Audrey and Charles. As we cooked, Sue shared with me that this day was the anniversary of her mom's death. She told me how drawn she felt to my mom since she learned that they both had the first name "Phyllis". I invited Sue to come to the airport so she could meet my mom. She gladly accepted the offer. We decided to make it a real party and bring Lauren and Audrey along with us.

My mom's plane was late so Sue and I sat and chatted as the girls ran around the airport. We enjoyed watching their budding friendship and we thanked God for giving them soul mates with which to go through this cancer experience. Both Sue and I agreed that it surely would have been nice to have a peer who understood when we, as children, went through this illness with our parents.

When my mom's plane arrived we gave her a hero's welcome. She was very surprised by the additions to the welcoming party, but very happy to meet Sue and Audrey. Later Sue told me that it did her soul good to meet my mom; to see a woman who had survived the loss of a spouse and a son to cancer. Watching my mom interact with Lauren and experience joy reinforced within Sue that no matter what the future held for her family, she could still thrive. I now know that what Sue saw in my mom was hope. Hope for a better tomorrow...hope in God's grace...and hope in eternal life.

Our week with my mom was nicer than I had even hoped. Before she arrived, I was quite uneasy about how she would do in this environment. I didn't know if she could handle seeing all of these sick kids. I was afraid that it would bring back too many agonizing memories. I didn't know if she could handle seeing Tucker at his physical worst. I didn't know if she could just be supportive of Todd and my decisions on how to care for our family in this setting and not give unsolicited advice.

I under-estimated my mom; she handled the environment beautifully. She did a great job finding her way around that big hospital and being Lauren's buddy and kindergarten teacher. She handled seeing Tucker during his difficult days and she really lifted his spirits. She held her tongue. She took on the role of supporter and encourager. She told me that I had the patience of a saint and that she had never seen a husband and wife team like Todd and me. Coming from her, those words meant so much.

That week together changed our relationship. I realized what a strong, loving mom she was and what grace she had exemplified as she held her family together during times of trial. I really appreciated her strengths and loved her for who she was. Similarly, she realized the gifts and calling that God has blessed me with and she treated me like a grown woman. She loved me for who I had become, not for what she hoped I would be.

My mom's visit included the climactic event of our entire hospitalization, the actual stem cell transplant. It was no coincidence that my mom was there to witness that event. This disease had been "her cross" to bear throughout her life just as it has been mine. She knew that a transplant could beat this evil, but she had never experienced it. Twenty-five years ago, my dad's doctor offered him one of the first bone marrow transplants. He turned them down because it was too experimental and he was too weak by that time. The doctor had also mentioned a transplant as a possible cure for my brother's cancer. It however, progressed so fast that it never became a reality. My mom wanted to see this miracle event that had been only an unreachable possibility for her love ones in the past.

The actual transplant was so anticlimactic that to some it may have been a letdown. I, however, was not letdown at all. I felt God's hand on the entire event. The morning started with some unexpected visitors. We were all in the room just waiting for the stem cells and the physician, when a faint knock came at the door. Todd went to door. I could see from where I laid in the bed with Tucker, that he was very surprised by who was at the door. Moments later, our minister from Marquette, Larry Jones, peaked his head in. I was just as thrilled and surprised to see him as Todd. Larry wasn't allowed in Tucker's room because of Tucker's low blood counts. Hence, Todd and I joined him outside the room for a time of prayer just before the transplant began. Larry prayed for healing for Tucker, peace for Todd and me, wisdom for the physicians, and through all of these things, glory to our Lord who makes all things possible.

After we finished praying, Todd asked Larry how he knew that Tucker's transplant was this day. Larry replied, "I didn't! This is God's timing. I just happened to be here today because our daughter has an appointment with a neurologist in an hour, and we were in the area!" We all laughed in amazement at God's incredible timing. Then we said our good-byes and quickly returned to the room, as the transplant was ready to start.

The transplant took only about thirty minutes. It was as simple as thawing the stem cells that were collected last fall and putting them into Tucker's central line through a syringe as Tucker lay sleeping in his bed snuggled between Todd and me. Lauren and my Mom watched at the doorway.

The cells were a beautiful cherry red and radiated life. As I watched the fluid disappear from the syringe into Tucker's body, I felt a surge of life within my soul. Finally something other than a toxin was going into Tucker. Winter was nearly over and spring was coming! This fluid represented new life, like fresh sap running through his veins.

Later I was inspired to write this poem about the event:

### The Seeds of Life

*Licorice red, Flowing Seeds.*
*Being sowed into his marrow to*
*satisfy its need.*
*Divinely they move through the bloodstream*
*Finding where to:*
*Rest...Grow...Thrive...Give life!*
*These seeds are not so different from*
*the ones we plant each day.*
*Seeds of faith, hope, peace and joy.*
*We plant in the hearts, souls*
*and minds of others.*
*In the hope that they too will:*
*Rest...Grow...Thrive...Give life!*

That truly is what happens during a stem cell transplant. The chemotherapy (given before the transplant) kills any remaining cancer cells that may exist within the body. It also, however, destroys all of the remaining bone marrow and stem cells that live in the marrow. Stem cells are like seeds; they are the mother cell to all the blood cell types (red blood cells, white blood cells and platelets). Without them/ a body cannot live. When the stem cells are infused into the body, they bring it back from the brink of death (with no ability to make blood cells or platelets) and restore life. How that happens is the true miracle. The stem cells have an affinity for the bone marrow; which means that when once infused, they travel through the bloodstream until they reach the destined bone marrow and there they plant themselves. The marrow is fertile soil in which they can grow and begin producing blood cells again. That entire process speaks to the divine wisdom behind life. Life is no accident. Cells knowing where fertile soil is, where they can grow is no coincidence. Every time that I think about these "seeds of life" finding their destined home, it reinforces my belief in a higher being (God) and His infinite wisdom.

♥

After the infusion of the stem cells was completed, Tucker slept for three hours. Lauren, Mom and I went to the gift shop and bought Tucker some presents to celebrate this new "birth" day. I got him a three-foot tall column light that was filled with water and plastic fish. When turned on, the water aerated through the column and made the fish dance. The light beamed through the water alternating from pink to blue to yellow. The base of the light was what really caught my eye. It was a ceramic scene of a beautiful little blonde-haired boy swimming with the whales and dolphins through the ocean.

Tucker had always loved whales and dolphins and had even decided to ask the "Make a Wish" Foundation for a trip to see the whales. I knew that he would love the lamp and that it would help him dream of better days.

Lauren bought Tucker a little rubber whale key chain whose eyes popped out whenever his belly was squeezed. My mom bought him a big Happy Birthday balloon.

When Tucker woke up, he was very surprised and elated with the gifts. We set the lamp up on the nightstand next to his bed and used it as a night-light. Its warm tones transformed the room from a sterile hospital room to a friendly underwater hideaway. Tucker spent hours watching the fish dance in the column and Todd played the mandolin by its light late into the night.

That evening as we quietly celebrated our victory, my mom commented that she thought that Tucker was probably over the worst of it and she was awed by how well he was doing. I agreed with her that he was tolerating it all extremely well, but deep in my heart I knew that we had not come to the worst of this trial.

My intuition was right. The next ten days were extremely difficult. Each day Tucker's blood count posted on his wall graph dropped lower and lower until his white count reached zero and stayed there for many days. His platelet and hemoglobin levels were kept above critical levels by intermittent transfusions. Once his counts bottomed out, we knew that his risk for infection and bleeding were much greater. It became a waiting game to see if the stem cells would grow and begin making new cells before an infection or system failure would take his life.

♥

All of us had our own challenge during the next week. Tucker's challenge was to endure all of the physical pain associated with a stem cell transplant. This included very high temperatures, diarrhea, vomiting, and mouth sores so bad that he couldn't even open his mouth. Tucker rose to the challenge. He complained and cried only when we dragged him out of bed for a shower. Mostly he lay in bed and either listened to his GT Tape about the bike ride or watched a *"Superman"* movie. I was encouraged by his choice of music and movies. They told of perseverance and the good guy winning at the end. Tucker somehow knew at age of four that he needed to surround himself with that kind of hopefulness. He was not giving up the fight.

Lauren's challenge was to be incredibly patient and resist the temptation to become jealous of all the attention Tucker was receiving. She did her very best and even overcame her shyness around strangers. She especially came out of her shell with family who stayed with us over that time.

Todd's and my challenge was to withstand the evils of worry and fear, and not allow them to steal away each day's joy. The only way to do that was to surrender all to God. We became keenly aware that every detail of our lives was in His hands. We grew very close to Him because we spent all our time just hanging with Him and or caring for our family. We didn't make any decisions until after praying about them. We had no other priorities. Our walk with Him and following His will for this family became our only goal.

God used nature to encourage us during that time. It was only mid-February, yet signs of spring and new life became more prevalent every day. My soul was rejuvenated during my daily run into the arboretum just outside of the hospital. As I heard the sound of gurgling water in the river where the ice had been, and saw the tulips rising from the ground, I could sense God saying, *"Don't worry, the seeds are growing!"*

One day while I was running up a hill in the arboretum, I closed my eyes and imagined that this hill was our trial. I ran as far up the hill as I thought we were through this trial. The hill was so steep and winding that I couldn't see the top from the bottom nor from where I turned around that day. As I ran back down, I reflected on how similar this hill really was to our trial: we had no idea where the top was or what was around the next corner. We had to run with faith and perseverance, believing that the top was within our grasp and that we could handle, with God's help, whatever was around the next corner.

Every day I returned to the hill and ran it again; each day I went higher and higher. With every bend I rounded, God spoke to me about endurance and running the race set before me. He became my greatest coach and cheerleader! On Saturday, the 26th of February, I had the opportunity to take Todd running up "my hill". When we were almost to the highest point I had been, Todd sprinted out in front of me and by the time I caught him he had completed the ascent! He laughed as I told him that meant that our trial would soon be over. He replied, "If that is all that it took, I wish you would have run all the way to the top sooner!"

♥

God also provided us with a much-needed diversion over that week. It came in the form of a project. Adrienne, the artist, asked our family if we would make a poster board display for "Children and Health Care Week". She gave us a three-foot poster tri-fold and encouraged us to use all of our artistic ability to make a board that tells our story.

We all got involved in this project. We decided to tell our story as it related to the story of Noah. Todd painted with watercolor the pertinent scenes from Noah's trial. Lauren drew our apple tree and cut out strips of colored construction paper for the rainbow. Tucker and I picked out pictures and poems that told our story. Tucker even climbed out of bed and sat up and used my little paper cutter to crop pictures! Creating this board was very therapeutic. It was a "trust in the Lord and do good" thing, a ministry project. It gave purpose to my days and made craft time with Lauren even more fun. Most importantly, it reminded me of how faithful God was and how far we had already come.

I still have that board. It sits behind my dresser in the bedroom. The pictures are now faded and glue has gotten crusty. It has no material value. I have pulled it out now and then over the years when I need a reminder of God's grace and mercy. My response to it is always the same: a smile, a tear and an over whelming gratefulness for God's faithfulness.

♥

When we started this trial, I had no idea when or how it would end. The Spirit had told me as I read about Noah to remember the dates: the first day of the tenth month, the first days of the first month and finally the twenty-seventh day of the second month. I had peace and confidence that, like Noah, our trial would end with joy and a sign of God's love, however I had no expectation of how that sign would come. Sometime around Feb 20th, "day five" post stem cell infusion, as I was filling in Tucker's daily wall graph, I was inspired with what this sign would look like. Tucker's day of engraftment would be on twenty-seventh day of the second month. Engraftment, marked by the rise in the white blood cell count, signifies the beginning of new cell growth within the bone marrow. I grabbed a pen and wrote "2/27" on the appropriate square of the wall graph and circled it. Then I picked up my bible and read that part of the scripture in Genesis again. As I read and meditated on the words, I received more insight about the significance of this date of engraftment. Tucker's engraftment on the 27th day of the second month would be confirmation that our storm was over, just as it was for Noah.

All week after I circled that date on the graph, health care professionals who came in our room would ask why that date was circled. I would boldly tell the story and the significance of the date. This sparked many interesting conversations and varied replies. Most admired my faith but were skeptical about this Divine insight. They didn't believe that God reveals Himself in this way in our times; those encounters only happen in biblical times. I disagreed. God wants to give all Divine insight, most people, however, are too busy, distracted or loud to hear His still quiet voice.

♥

On Friday February 25th, Todd's Mom, Marge, and my sister, Patti, arrived. The timing of their visits was excellent because we all needed some rejuvenating. Tucker had an especially difficult morning before they arrived. He was tired of feeling sick and emotionally he was very fragile. We listened to the GT tape as we did his morning care and then we attempted to play Legos. Tucker tried to play but he had very little energy and his mouth hurt so much he couldn't even muster a smile. As I interacted with him, my heart felt so heavy. I missed my happy, easy-going little boy. It seemed like an eternity since I had seen his true spirit. The pruning and the winter were getting very long for all of us.

At noon I left and headed to Detroit to pick up Patti from the airport. I was actually happy to go. I needed a break from the hospital and the incredible stress of the situation. As I drove I quietly confessed to God my fears and asked Him to calm this storm and give me peace.

Patti's flight arrived without incident and as she walked through the arrival gate, joy welled within me. I love her silly light-hearted way! I knew she would have me laughing a gut-wrenching laugh within an hour. It didn't even take that long. On the drive back to the hospital, Patti told me of her flying adventure. She got fogged out in LaCrosse the night before and her luggage went to Minneapolis and Detroit without her. The comical part was that she had put deer sausage and a knife in her suitcase as a treat for us. She then made up a hilarious story about her suitcase getting ripped to shreds as it went through security with drug sniffing dogs. I laughed so hard I nearly cried. It felt so good!

Patti had the same effect on Tucker. On Saturday morning she and I were playing with "Play Do" on his bed hoping to engage him in some activity. Patti started making the characters from the "Mr. Bill Show". I followed her lead and soon we had all the main characters. Then she began catapulting Mister Bill off a teeter-totter. This caught Tucker's eye and a few minutes later he was giggling, as Mister Bill laid crumpled into pieces at the base of the teeter-totter. After Mister Bill ran into a Lego wall and his legs broke off, Tucker picked up some "Play Do" and began playing with us. This was the first glimpse of my Tucker I had seen in days. It brought tears of joy to my eyes. By the end of that day, Tucker's fever broke, his mouth was feeling a bit better and his urine output was up. All of these positive changes encouraged me that the day of engraftment would indeed be the next day, the 27th of February.

Todd and I were both able to stay with Tucker that night as Marge and Patti stayed with Lauren. We told our nurse to wake us when Tucker's morning blood counts were back from the lab. Tucker slept well, and hence so did we. Around six a.m., Heidi gently touched me on the shoulder and said: "Tucker's counts are up!"

I sat up smiling and rubbed my sleepy eyes as the reality of her words set in. Tucker's WBC count was at 600. God's revelation to me had come to pass! He had pointed me to Noah's storm at the very beginning of this trial for instruction and encouragement. The words became our reality:

- The duration of the initial 40 days of thunder, lightning and rain that comes with a cancer diagnosis.
- The 151 days of waiting and floating at sea through six rounds of chemotherapy.
- The water (tumor) shrinking enough that by the first day of the tenth month removal of the tumor was possible.
- All the scans and testing being negative/ Tuckers body free of cancer at the beginning of the year.
- And today, the 27th day of the 2nd month... the day that Noah was told that his trial was over and a new covenant was established between God, Noah and every living thing. God promised that He would never flood the earth again .....**Tucker engrafted !**

As Todd and I stood at the window watching the sunrise, tears rolled down our cheeks. We were awed and humbled how the creator of the universe cared enough about us to answer our prayers in such a perfect way. We were watching our personal prophesy being fulfilled. We knew at that moment that our storm was over. That we had stepped onto God's rainbow and were riding it. We bowed our heads in reverence and thanked God for choosing us worthy of such a gift.

# Chapter 7:

# *A New Life*

*As for you, be fruitful and increase in number,*
*multiply on the earth and increase upon it.*

*Genesis 9:7*

The next week was a spiritual "top of the mountain" week. I felt so close to my Maker. My desire to know Him more intimately was overwhelming. *God Calling* spoke of Christ's desire for love and companionship. It said:

> *"I came to draw men unto me and sweet it is to feel hearts drawing near in Love, not for help, as much as for tender comradeship. Many know the need of man; few know the need of Christ."*

These words struck a note with me. Jesus had walked with us through one of worst nightmares that any parent could imagine. He encouraged, provided, and loved us. His presence was strong yet gentle. Now I had a deep desire to meet His need for deep comradeship. Each morning I would ponder what that meant and how it would look in my daily walk going forward.

By the middle of the week, Tucker's doctors began to talk about discharging him from the hospital, Tucker's counts continued to rise every day, and his fevers and mouth sores became less of a concern. The only remaining obstacle was regulating his TPN, a nutritional supplement infused right into the bloodstream.

They allowed us to take Tucker out of his room for the first time in three weeks. We put him in a wheelchair and took a tour of the floor (this seemed like a grand milestone). As we wheeled him down the long hall, we could hear an approaching helicopter. We followed the noise down to the launch pad on the top of a slightly shorter building. Fascinated by the noise and the size of the copter, Tucker intently watched it land. For the next ten minutes we all watched as the crew worked around the idling copter. Then without even loading or unloading a patient, it took off again. It was as if the helicopter had landed and sat there just for Tucker that afternoon. It was a great little blessing for my sweet boy.

The next day brought a blessing for me. My sister, DeeAnn, and her husband, Ron flew in from California to spend a week with us. DeeAnn had been so instrumental in my faith journey over the years; constantly putting a book in my hand or a song in my heart. She had challenged me to make my faith a priority. I had not seen her since Tucker was diagnosed and I was really looking forward to sharing with her all the ways that God was working.

Lauren and I picked up Ron and DeeAnn from the airport. It was an abnormally nice spring day, and both Lauren and I enjoyed soaking in the sun and warmth as we waited for Ron and DeeAnn's plane to arrive. I marveled at the difference in the weather in just one week. The week before when I picked up Patti, it was a cold and blustery winter day, much like our situation at the hospital. Now a week later, spring had come to us at the hospital and to the world all around us.

♥

On March 6th, Dr. Levine came in early and examined Tucker. After checking all his labs and giving him a good once-over, he told us we could start packing... Tucker was being discharged. When Tucker heard this news, a smile broke out across his entire face. He was more than ready! We spent the entire morning packing up the room that we had called home for the last month. We packed the thousand paper cranes that the Girl Scouts in Marquette had made for Tucker, the Valentine silhouettes of the kids that hung on the bathroom door and the fish lamp that had transformed this room into an underwater aquarium. We filled box after box with Legos, plastic dinosaurs, stuffed animals, and videos. When we finished, the room looked so bare and sterile that I kind of felt sorry for it. It was now just a hospital room again.

Before we left, our nurse, Viita went through all of the discharge instructions. She stressed the importance of watching for fevers and the importance of coming to the clinic if his temperature was over 100 degrees. She told us not to be surprised if Tucker needed frequent blood and platelet transfusions. In fact, she confessed, "Most kids end up being readmitted to the hospital at least for a couple days sometime in their recovery". I was so tired of the hospital, I couldn't even imagine having to be readmitted, but I knew better than to worry or be preoccupied by this possibility. That bridge would be crossed if and when we ever came to it. For now, I was just thankful for this day and the chance to leave the hospital at least for a while.

♥

We arrived at our new home across the road from the DeGroots late in the afternoon. This space that God had provided for us was perfect. It was in the country with fresh air and wide open fields exactly sixty miles from Ann Arbor (the maximum allowable distance). It was an empty, new home, which meant that there were no plants (with associated molds and mildews), or other kids' germs to which to expose Tucker.

Sue had found all the essential furnishing we needed to be comfortable. In fact, the only room in the house that was completely free of furniture was the living room. We took advantage of that space and built our finest and most permanent HotWheels track complete with jumps, loops and a Lego city around it.

Our first full day at the house was a true gift from God. As I read *God Calling* that morning, a warm feeling overtook me as if my Savior was giving me a hug. The reading said:

### *"Surprises"*

*Many there are who think that I test and train and bend to My Will.*

*I, who bade the disciples take up the cross, I loved to prepare a feast for them by the lakeside- a little glad surprise, not a necessity, as the feeding of the multitude may have seemed. I loved to give the wine-gift at the marriage feast.*

*As you love to plan surprises for those who understand, and joy in them, so with Me. I love to plan them for those who see My Love and tender joy in them.*

*Dear to the heart of My Father are those who see not only My tears, the tears of a Savior, but the smile, the joy- smile of a friend.*

The day that followed was like a feast by the lakeside. It was eighty three degrees (the normal high for March 7th was 39 degrees and the previous year it had been −13 degrees!). Tucker's morning doctor appointment was flawless; he needed no transfusions and had no fever so we made it back to the farm just after noon.

We all spent the rest of the day outside soaking up the sun and letting it rejuvenate our spirits. Lauren and I took the DeGroot's horse, Star, for a ride through the open fields surrounding their house. The sun, light breeze, and smell of spring felt almost too good to be true after living in a hospital for a month. We sang and laughed together as Star trotted along.

Tucker didn't have enough energy to run or play. At first he hobbled around like a ninety year-old man, wanting us to carry him everywhere. He did however have enough energy to ride in the DeGroot's golf cart. Todd took him, Charles and Jonathon for a ride around the horse pasture and down by the pond and fire pit while Lauren and Audrey ran out front with the dogs. They all laughed as they cruised over bumps and made quick turns. When

Tucker got off the cart an hour later, his twinkle and enthusiasm for life emerged for an instant as he told the story of their adventure.

That night for dinner Sue grilled chicken while Todd and Mark got out their guitar and mandolin and had a little jam session.

As I witnessed this all, my senses were almost overwhelmed by the goodness of life: The smell of grilled chicken...The laughter of children at play...The sun warming my back...A yard full of toys... and a nice glass of wine!

This "perfect day", this surprise from God, set the stage for the next three weeks on North Diamond Road. The "golf cart ride" became the "golf cart chase". The "Jam sessions" became a part of the routine for Todd and Mark as they worked together in Mark workshop building two wood kayaks.

Each morning when Todd went to "work" in the workshop, I took on the role as a stay-at-home mom. This was a role I had never had the chance to play before as I had always worked full time. The mornings that we didn't go to the clinic, we had school time. We started each day with the calendar and checking out the weather. We made a weather spinner like I had seen in Lauren's classroom and we would look out the window each day and decide whether it was sunny, cloudy, rainy or snowy. After we lost Tucker's attention, Lauren and I would work on her "red" word flash cards and reading her first sentences. For recess we would join Tucker in the living room building with Legos or playing HotWheels. As Tucker started to feel better and have more energy, our recesses became more active. One day we made up our own "Superman" game. I was "Luthor", Lauren was "Lauren Lane" and of course Tucker was Superman (complete with the shirt that he had painted in the hospital!). As I ran around the house jumping over Lego cities trying to capture Lauren Lane, Superman would chase me and peg me with his secret weapon, superballs!

Our afternoons involved playing outdoors with the DeGroots. We would all meet on the paved circle of Mark and Sue's driveway. Mark always had some surprise toy for the kids. One day he shot off his model rocket and we all chased it with the golf cart. Another day we all chased his remote control racecar around the drive. Every day the kids spent hours driving the battery powered jeeps, scooters and bikes around and around the private little circle. I delighted in this play as much as all the kids did. As a physical therapist, I saw the incredible value in play and how it was restoring my son.

At each of his clinic follow-up visits in Ann Arbor, the physicians were amazed. Tucker had not needed even one blood transfusion since his discharge from the hospital. His blood counts climbed higher with each appointment, as did his emotional and physical wellness. When one nurse asked me what our secret was, I smiled and told her how God had provided the therapy. It consisted of sun, Legos, laughter, other little boys, fresh air, and LOVE!

Eating was Tucker's only lingering problem. Addressing Tucker's lack of any appetite or desire to eat was a lesson in pure patience. He had mucositis which is an inflammation and degradation of the inside lining of the gut. It was a side effect of one of the chemotherapy drugs that he had received before his transplant. The doctors told us that mucositis can take months to heal.

Even the smell of food would make Tucker nauseated so he would hide in his bedroom when I was cooking. Each evening at dinner, we would ask Tucker to try sitting at the table with us. He tried but usually he didn't last long. After five minutes, he would need to go back into the bedroom.

One afternoon Tucker announced that he was going to eat dinner with us that evening. Prior to the transplant one of his favorite foods was spaghetti, and this day he told me if I made spaghetti he would "snarf" it all down in one bite! I was a little skeptical about that but I was more than happy to fix spaghetti and give it a try. In actuality, he only ate three bites of spaghetti and two bites of applesauce. Just the same, we all celebrated Tucker's victory.

♥

The next day was also a day of celebration. It was Lauren's sixth birthday! Dr. Levine saw Tucker in clinic that morning and was very impressed. He said that Tucker now only needed to be seen weekly and that could be done at Sparrow Hospital back in Lansing. Tucker and I were ecstatic as we left the clinic. No more drives to Ann Arbor three days a week!

Before we rushed home to share this great news, we had a little errand to take care of at the hospital gift shop. Tucker had picked out a very special hobbyhorse (that neighed), which he wanted to get Lauren for her birthday. I told him if he walked all the way to the gift shop from the clinic that I would buy it so he could give it to her. He struggled down the last long corridor; but he made it and with pride bought that horse for his sister. As I cheered Tucker down the hall, I recalled my years of running track and of all the finish lines I had crossed. I was very impressed that Tucker would do this not for his own gain but so that he could get a gift for his sister. Again, my little boy was teaching much about love and perseverance. He too had learned what it meant to ride God's rainbow.

Lauren's birthday party that evening with the DeGroots was a celebration of simple blessings: Milestones like losing your first tooth on your birthday... Good friends and good food around a table and the simple, humble courageous spirits of children.  We had the party at "our house" complete with a rainbow-colored butterfly cake, a piñata and of course HotWheels and Legos. Lauren loved her hobbyhorse and all her new Ferbie friends.

♥

The next ten days were golden days at "Home Again Farm" which neither of our families will ever forget. Tucker was eating better each day and Dr. Gehra cut his TPN way back so that he only had to wear the food pack at night. This, along with Tucker's improved energy, allowed him to run and play with the other kids. Both Tucker and Charles were required to wear masks when they were out in public but at home they did not have to and they could just be kids. Charles was no longer neutropenic, so he did not have to be isolated from the rest of the kids. With our boys in less critical situations, Sue, Mark, Todd and I were free to just enjoy our days and deepen our friendship.

One day, the "girls" all went into Mason for a girl's day out! We all got haircuts at "Jon's Place". Afterward, we went to the candy/toy store and then out for lunch. It was a chilly spring day, but just being able to spend some quality time with our daughters warmed our souls. We giggled as they picked out new haircuts from the books in the waiting room and then sat very timidly in Jon's chair while he cut their hair. We admired the almost-real looking baby dolls in the toy store and enjoyed Sue's favorite "Jelly Beans" from the candy store. At lunch we discussed six year-old stuff like tooth fairies and how Ferbies communicate with one another.

The next morning the "girls" went on another adventure, this time to a neighborhood church. The speaker, Doug Routledge, was the guest pastor that morning. His full time ministry was with a youth program at a farm a few hours away. He had a word that day from God for both Sue and me.

He started talking about Super Heroes. First, he described all of his personal favorites, and then he told us who he felt was the greatest of all Super Heroes. It was Superman! He went on to describe all of the attributes of Superman. I sat there grinning as I had thought much about Superman over the past month. I had watched all of the movies during Tucker's transplant and now played it with the kids daily in our living room.

After Doug described Superman's attributes, he asked if anyone knew Superman's weakness. Many in the church volunteered that Superman's weakness was "Kryptonite". Doug then came to his first point. All Super Heroes (even Superman) have weaknesses... All except one... Jesus Christ is the only Super Hero without a weakness. Jesus Christ is God in human form, and He is without sin or weakness. Jesus Christ, the greatest of all Super Heroes, still lives today and desires to have a personal relationship with each one of us.

Doug then made his second point. Because Jesus Christ is so human He can relate to us wherever we are. To illustrate this point, Doug asked those who are cancer survivors to raise their hand. Sue and I both raised our hands. (Although neither of us had ever had cancer personally, we felt as if we were survivors.) Doug then described chemotherapy and radiation and told how only other cancer survivors could understand what that was like, and how that experience changes a life. Sue and I looked at one another and smiled, as we knew all too well the truth of his words. Doug went on to say that even more than a fellow cancer survivor understands, Jesus understands. He knows our soul and our every thought. He has beaten the most difficult foe, our adversary, and yet His might has not made Him estranged or deaf to the sufferings and plight of His children.

In conclusion, Doug challenged us to examine our personal relationship with Jesus Christ. Were we reaping all the blessings of a close relationship with Him? Had we asked Him into our hearts? Were we spending time with Him on a daily basis? Were we giving Him our burdens or trying to rely on own strength?

I pondered Doug's words all that afternoon. I came to the conclusion that in order to *ride God's rainbow* one must develop an intimate relationship with Jesus. He is the light of the world just as the rainbow is. When He shines in a storm something beautiful happens; what was intended to destroy and cause fear and destruction is replaced by a breathtaking phenomenon of light. The storms in life: sickness, death, divorce, financial struggles can bring fear and destruction but if we turn to Jesus, let him carry us through and take our burdens for us, then those storms lose their power.

Sue was encouraged by Doug's words to bring her fears and concerns to Jesus. Throughout this trial with Charles, she has been more apt to find a human ear to bend with her concerns and fears than her Savior's. Only recently had she accepted Jesus as her Savior and admitted she was powerless. Now she needed to continue on this path and truly develop a friendship with her Savior.

After the service, we went up and met Doug and shared just a little of how his sermon had spoken to us. He thanked us and encouraged us to return the next week when he would present "The rest of the story"! We assured him that we would be back.

♥

That evening the DeGroots invited the Shrems (Karsha's family) and us over for dinner. All afternoon I anticipated what that evening would be like. Our families were now all in such different situations. Karsha had come out of remission and was at the end of treatment options without any real medical hope of recovery. In Doug's words, "They are trying to keep the cancer controlled long enough for some miracle drug to be discovered to cure her." Charles was just ready to start his third round of chemotherapy. He and his family had many difficult challenges yet to face. Sue was already dreading the transplant, which was slated for late summer. Tucker was all done with treatment and still very fragile. We were now focusing on what we could do to build up his system and keep the cancer from returning.

Despite the differences in our children's current medical statuses, the evening was lovely. We loved and supported one another as we talked briefly about our situations and how they were impacting our families. Before dinner, Sue said a prayer. As I listened to Sue, my soul smiled. She had come so far in her faith during these few short months that I had known her. Her prayers were no longer laundry lists of concerns but moreover a humble thank you and a request for blessing. After Sue finished we all very spontaneously lifted up prayers for each other's family. It was truly beautiful.

During dinner we went on to other subjects and enjoyed the evening and our children. As I played Barbies with the girls, I reflected on the current mood in this home. It was obvious to me that Jesus lived in all our hearts and we were all confident that God's plan ultimately was good. It was with this reassurance that we were all living for the day and making the most of it.

♥

On Monday, we had a doctor's appointment at Sparrow. Dr. Kulkarni was very pleased with all of Tucker's blood counts. She hinted that our return to the U.P. was not far off! During the upcoming week, Tucker would have one of his central lines removed and we would finish weaning his TPN. If all of this happened without incident and his counts kept climbing we would be allowed to go home after next week's appointment.

Three days later, Tucker had surgery to remove the central line. That morning had striking parallel's to the morning of his first surgery to biopsy the tumor. It was the same surgeon and the same surgical suite. Once again I was there alone with Tucker. My only companions being my Bible and the book *God's Story*. As I carried Tucker down the long hallway to surgery and gave him a kiss goodbye, I felt like time had stood still and I was repeating the same experience all over. I assured myself as I left and walked back to the waiting room that this nightmare was nearly over, not beginning. As I waited, I reread chapter eight in *God's Story*: "He Calms Your Fearfulness". As I read, I shook my head in dismay at how the words on these pages had become so real in my life. I was awed by the way Jesus had comforted me and given me peace during the roughest days of my life. Like Noah, we had made it through the storm and were now witnessing the rainbow. Tears filled my eyes with tremendous gratitude.

♥

God commands us over and over again in Scripture to bring to Him all the little details of our lives and rely on Him to provide. Believers are good at doing that when God is the only option however, God doesn't want to be the last option; He wants to be the first option!! We were learning that part of *riding God's Rainbow* was simply bringing our needs to Him and then watching how He delights in answering our prayers. God took the opportunity during our last week in Lansing to drive that command and promise home to us.

After Tucker's Monday appointment, Todd and I began discussing how we were going to get all our stuff back to Marquette. All we had was our little Subaru hatchback which was totally unable to fit even half of the stuff we had accumulated over the past six weeks. We threw out a couple of options and then the Spirit nudged me to pray for a solution instead of trying to create one. I suggested this to Todd and he was receptive, so that evening and the next morning we prayed together for God to provide a way for us to get all our stuff home.

Tuesday afternoon God answered this prayer s only He could do. We took all the kids to Potter's Park that afternoon as a special treat. The entire afternoon was a joy. It was warm enough that we could get rid of our jackets and run in the sunshine. The animals were also frisky and happy to feel the sun. Many of them, including the peacocks, put on a little show for us as we walked past their cages. The park was abnormally busy for midweek because many of the Lansing schools were on spring break. Even the concession stands were open. Of course we had to take advantage of that and so outside of the lion's cage we stopped for ice cream.

As we all sat there in the sunshine licking our cones, a lady walked past and smiled at me. She looked vaguely familiar, but I couldn't place her. My soul took notice but my brain did not! Moments later she was having a conversation with Lauren like she knew her. I took another look at this woman..... It was Heidi Paquette, Lauren kindergarten teacher from back home! Lauren was too shy to talk with her, but I wasn't! It was so good to see a face from the U.P. We stood there and chatted while we enjoyed our cones.

Heidi shared that her entire family was down here for Spring break. Her husband came down early in the week for meetings while she and the kids had just arrived. Heidi also volunteered that she had intended to contact us while they were down here but figured that we were in Ann Arbor, not Lansing. I updated her on our situation and why we were now in Lansing. Shaking her head in disbelief she said, "I can't believe we met here, I just happened to be going by this park and something told me to drive in."

As we parted she said as an afterthought, "Is there anything we can do to help you out?" Jokingly, I replied, "Not unless you have an empty van!" She stopped in her tracks and said, "We do! My husband drove the van down, and it is completely empty." Todd and I looked at each other and laughed. This certainly was not an option we had considered for getting our stuff home. We had trusted God to provide and He did!

♥

Sue and I made attending the little church and hearing the second part of Doug's sermon a priority the next weekend. We arrived early to get a good seat (right up front!) and waited with anticipation for what God for us that day. We were not disappointed.

Doug spoke on the Great Commission and its pertinence for us today. He started his sermon by looking out into the congregation (but it seemed like he looked right at us) and said, "There is no such thing as a coincidence. And it definitely is not a coincidence that you are sitting in this church today. God has something He wants you to hear, so listen closely: God's plan for salvation includes His Son and YOU!"

He went on to tell a very funny story of how he imagined the great commission got dreamed up by Jesus in Heaven and how the angels reacted to Jesus' crazy plan: "How could one man and twelve disciples spread the good news of salvation across the world?" He went on to explain that the only way that all souls across this world could be saved was if believers stepped out boldly and shared the good news in their words, actions and deeds.

He challenged us to let the Holy Spirit, our advocate sent by Jesus, to work through us and be the disciple that God wants us to be.

Doug's words immediately reaffirmed for me that this trial had not been a coincidence; that God was using it to bring us and others closer to Christ, and that He wasn't done! He could continue to use our witness to bring others to Him as long as we were willing to share our story. Certainly, the temptation as we headed home was to try to move on with life and put this entire experience behind us. However, I knew this was not God's desire. He wanted to use the wisdom and faith we had gained for His glory! He would give us opportunities to share...to make a difference for others going through a trial...to offer hope and shed His light. We just needed to be empty vessels waiting to be filled.

I pondered these things the next day as I went for my morning run. I read *God Calling* before I left the house. Very appropriately, the reading was titled Go Forward! And the scripture verse quoted that day was Philippians 4:13:

*"I can do all things through Christ that strengthens me!"*

With enthusiasm, I underlined that scripture. This trial was nearly over and we had overcome all adversity with Christ's strength. More than that we had found God's rainbow and we had learned what it meant to ride it.

I also underlined the last words of that day's reading: *You are only beginning a new life together. Joy, joy and joy.* As I went out the door for my run, I had so much joy that my feet barely touched the ground. Once I finally settled into a pace, I thought about what this new life would be....what had I learned about riding God's rainbow. I identified four things that would be essential if I was going to stay on this rainbow:

1. Daily fellowship with Jesus. Don't drift away and get caught up in a life of busyness. Make daily prayer and reading of God's word a priority.

2. Live for the day and seize it! Don't take on two days' burdens. Cast all fear and anxiety to my Savior and trust how he is caring for me.

3. Leave the planning to God. His plan is always better than mine. Lift up my concerns and desires to Him and then enjoy the blessing He bestows upon me.

4. Be God's vessel. Never miss an opportunity that God provides to do His work. Only in this way will my life be truly complete!

♥

Tucker's Monday morning appointment was flawless. He had completely weaned off of all TPN during the last week and his weight was climbing. He recovered well from the central line removal surgery last week and his blood counts were great today. Dr. Scott marveled at how good Tucker looked and joyfully released us back to the care of Dr. Chen in Marquette.

That afternoon was bittersweet. I was excited about returning to our world, but I knew that I would never again have a season like the one that had just transpired. It was a season of resting and growing in faith, sharing Christ and bearing other's burdens. It was an opportunity to be a stay-at-home mom, a teacher, a nurse, a minister and a good friend in a whole different world than I was accustomed. In many ways, I would miss this world.

The next morning we went forward. The date was March 28, just one day before Sue's aunt would be moving into this house. It was cold and drizzly as we loaded the Subaru to capacity. Mid-morning all the DeGroots came over and we said our final good-byes and with tears in our eyes, headed north.

# Chapter 8:

# *Home*

*Whoever dwells in the home of the Most High will rest in the shadow of the Almighty. I will say of the Lord, "He is my refuge and my fortress, my God in whom I trust."*                    *Psalm 91: 1-2*

It felt amazing to be back in our little home in the woods. Our ten sled dogs were so happy to see us. They had been well cared for by our neighbor but they were happy to have their people back. Our house dog, Copain, was especially happy to come back to his house with his people. We all had a big slumber party with Copain in the living room our first night home.

Here in the woods we didn't have to worry about isolation, quarantines or neutropenic precautions. We could just keep Tucker at home and allow the beauty of this place to heal Tucker's body and keep him safe. We did just that for the next two months.

God immediately put in front of us an opportunity to be fruitful and share our story, Just two days after we got home, I got the oddest phone call. At first I thought that it was a phone solicitor and I almost hung up. But I was nudged not to; so instead I patiently listened to her "sales pitch". She was a representative from St.Judes' Children's Hospital and she was calling to ask me if I would consider organizing a bike-a-thon fundraiser for St.Judes.

As I listened to her I could hardly believe my ears. I had just spent two months listening over and over to Tucker's GT Tape about a bike-a-thon fundraiser for a children's hospital and now she was asking me to do the exact same thing!

After she finished giving her pitch, I stopped her and asked a few questions: "How did you get my name? What did she know about our family?" I needed to know up front if this was man's doing or God's. All she knew was that ten months ago my name had been given to them by my secretary and that she had tried several times in the past but I was very difficult to reach. She knew nothing of Tucker's illness or of the incredible timing of this call. After I told her briefly about our last year and of our return only yesterday, she apologized for calling. I reassured her that there is no such thing as a coincidence; she had called on this date for a reason. I told her that I would pray and discuss this opportunity with my family and then get back to her.

The next day I went back to work. My colleagues warmly welcomed me back. They had heard of God's faithfulness so many times from me over the previous nine months and now they were curious of how His hand had moved during the transplant. I was more than happy to glorify God in the details of the last two months!

Sharon, a social worker who had followed our whole journey very closely, stopped me in the stairwell and inquired about Tucker. After I filled her in, she shared with me how her children had vigilantly prayed for Tucker daily and how she was really hoping that they could meet him sometime. As she talked, the Holy Spirit nudged me regarding the "bike ride" opportunity. A bike ride would be the perfect setting for all the kids who prayed for Tucker to meet him and witness the effectiveness of their prayers. Psalm 37, the verse that I had memorized that was on a wall hanging in Susie O'Berski's kitchen, came into my mind:

Commit your way to the Lord; trust in Him and He will do this: He will make your righteousness shine like the dawn and the justice of your cause like the noonday sun.

I thanked Sharon for her family's prayers and as we parted I promised her that I would look for an opportunity to get our kids together.

That evening after dinner, we all talked about this bike ride possibility. Both of the kids were very excited and wanted to begin practicing their pedaling immediately! Todd and I decided that this was definitely a "God Thing" and that we needed to pursue it. Later when I was snuggling Lauren in her bed, it popped into my head when we should have this ride. June 11, the one year anniversary of Tucker's diagnosis and after his quarantine was over. I quietly slid out of bed and went into the kitchen and looked at a calendar. As I flipped to June an uncontainable smile came over me as I discovered that June 11th this year was on a Sunday. How perfect to have this celebration of God's love and faithfulness on God's day.

The next day, I called St.Judes and committed to putting on a ride. Over the next two months our family worked on all the logistics of the event. We recruited the help of our church youth group and many of our work colleagues. We solicited donations from local businesses including a bike painted like a brown and white Jersey cow that said "Got Milk" from the local dairy. Usually, I detest soliciting, but this time I didn't mind it because it was also a chance for me to testify of God's love and mercy.

My most interesting soliciting experience was with the producer of the GT Tapes. I hunted down King Communication's phone number through a Christian bookstore. When I called the number, a child answered the phone. Reluctantly, I explained who I was and that I was trying to find the creator of the GT Tape series for which I was looking. After I finished, the little boy said, "I'll go get my mom". While I waited for her, Satan kept tempting me to hang up. "Don't make a fool of yourself to an adult you don't even know. She probably has never even heard of GT and the Halo Express". I resisted this urging and waited patiently remembering that those who persevere always prosper.

When the boy's mom answered, I first asked if she was associated with Kings Communication. She responded yes and then introduced herself as Debbie Kingsriter. Kings Communication was the company that she and her husband had started when they were living in Minneapolis and he was playing professional football for the Minnesota Vikings. They wrote and produced these tapes using kids from the local area as the characters including both of their own kids.

I then introduced myself and told her how we came upon these tapes. I thanked her for putting so much effort into them and let her know how all of them, but especially the *"Great Ride of Faith"* tape, had ministered to our family during Tucker's illness and treatment. Then I told her about this bike ride opportunity and how it had come about and finally I asked if there was any way I could get more of the those tapes.

When I finished talking, there was no reply. For a moment, I thought we had been disconnected. She finally replied, "Isn't our God awesome! How He uses each of us to help bear the burdens of others!" She then told me that not only was her daughter's name Lauren but that the *"Great Ride of Faith"* tape was inspired by her son. He was born with a heart condition and spent much of his childhood in the hospital including several heart surgeries. Like Tucker, her son's survival was iffy. They had to rely on God's strength and mercy to carry their family through. God answered their prayers and her son survived his heart condition and now is an avid athlete with incredible perseverance and wisdom.

We talked for the next thirty minutes about our families, trials and how these experiences have changed our journey. I found this woman very inspiring. She had used the talents, gifts and trials in life to witness in a powerful way. She donated thirty copies of the "Great Ride of Faith" tape to our bike-a-thon.

♥

The week before the bike-a-thon we went back down state for Tucker's three month post-transplant checkup. We stayed with the DeGroot's again but this time we camped in their backyard. Each morning Todd, Tucker and I would be on our way to Ann Arbor by sunrise for Tucker's scans and biopsies. Lauren stayed with Sue and Audrey. In afternoon we would arrive back in time for the kids to drive jeeps around the farm; swim in the pool, and have team squirt gun fights. The kids love being together and just picked up where they left off in March.

The stressful part of the week, of course, was finding out the results of Tucker's tests. Todd and I both knew that the medical world had offered us all they had to cure Tucker's cancer. If these tests showed any sign of reoccurrence that would be a strong sign that it was not God's will for Tucker to survive this disease. I had contemplated and prayed much about these test results. The more I prayed the more insight and peace I gained. I knew in my heart that this storm was over and that Tucker was cancer free. I did not need the reassurance of modern health care tests. Todd and I agreed that repeating these tests was important not for us personally but to further medical knowledge.

The other important part of this week was that if all was well Tucker could stop wearing his mask out in public and he would be allowed to go places like parks and church again. Isolation and wearing a mask is very hard for a four year old to understand especially when no one else has to wear one. We told him it would keep him safe...From what? From dangers he could not see. He trusted us but was very tired of wearing a mask whenever he left the house.

We had our appointment with Dr.Yanik at the end of the week to discuss the test results. He said that Tuckers' blood counts looked good so he could stop wearing the mask and could resume normal four year old activities in the community. YAY!!!! Dr. Yanik, however could not tell the state of Tucker's cancer because many of the reports were not yet available. He was very apologetic. I assured him that we were completely fine without knowing the results. We were confident in God's love for us and were trying to stay in the day. Knowing the results would make living in the day much harder either way. If the results suggested that the cancer was back, it would be extremely difficult to not worry about the future. If the results were clear of cancer, it would be easy to begin to plan a summer full of activities and not live for each day and only that day.

Dr. Yanik seemed to understand what we were trying to say, but he didn't really buy it. He had to make sure that we KNEW the results. Later that same day he left a message on the DeGroot's answering machine that all of Tucker's tests were clear of any signs of cancer. We all celebrated this news but pledged to each other that we would continue living for the day..., making the most of each one just one at a time!

♥

The next several days called us to do exactly that: "live for the day". We had no control over what took place, we just had to trust God and go with the flow. We arrived home from down state just an hour before our families arrive from Iowa and Wisconsin for the bike-a-thon. The evening was chaotic but fun.

The next morning on a whim, we all went to an interdenominational faith walk in downtown Marquette (without any mask!). The walk went right down Main Street and finished in Lower Harbor Park, the same park the bike-a-thon would finish in the next afternoon. The weather that morning was beautiful. It was sunny and seventy degrees with a deep blue sky contrasting with a dark blue Lake Superior. As I enjoyed the walk, I envisioned this kind of weather the next day during "Tucker's Ride of Faith".

That "vision" was not to be. In fact an hour after we finished the "faith walk", the wind drastically changed and the clouds and cold fog rolled in. By that afternoon there were tornado warnings! The next morning we woke to forty degrees and drizzle. We didn't let the weather deter us. We packed the bikes into the car and headed to church. We were finally going to get to go to church as a family. During church I kept peeking out the window hoping for a change in the weather. It never came. By the time the bike-a-thon began at one o clock, it was even colder and windier. I wondered if I should even let the kids ride on such a blustery day. A friend came to our rescue and brought the kids some long underwear and gloves so they could at least try it. Both Tucker and Lauren bravely got on their bikes and pedaled straight into the wind determined to make it to the park.

We were not alone in this craziness. Everyone who had volunteered to help or had signed up to ride still showed up. The reception, complete with ice cream and pop was still held at the park afterward (although we all longed for hot chocolate instead of ice cream!). No one seemed upset about the weather except me. Although outwardly I wasn't showing it, inside I was completely confused and discouraged. I thought today was God's big day; the day that He had chosen for revival in our community. I envisioned the beaches and park packed with people, all curious about this event. I was ready to witness of God's great power and love and change hearts for Him.

But that wasn't God's plan. Not one person who didn't have to be, was out by the lake that day. I contemplated all of this as I rode the course. I was filled with a new insight: *"This weather is like your trial. It is a nasty storm. As you ride through a storm you learn about perseverance, and personal suffering. You also find out which of your acquaintances are hardy enough to ride with you. Look around, these people are the people I have chosen to help you and your family. Enjoy this victory with them."* As I rode into the reception and looked around I noticed that people present were almost all believers. I smiled and thanked God for this insight.

The reception was truly a celebration of our victory over this disease. The love and joy within that small pavilion warmed all of our hearts (and hands!) A friend told me the next day, "I kept looking for a rainbow, but then I realized it was formed by the love of the people there."

## Chapter 9:

# *Remember the Covenant*

*Whenever the rainbow appears in the clouds, I will see it and remember the everlasting covenant between God and all living creatures of every kind on the earth.*

*Genesis 9:16*

God blessed us with many rainbows over the year of Tucker's illness. These miracles of light were my constant reminder of God's love and His promise to me that I was always in His care and that He had ultimate control over all things. Over the next two years we would be called to remember the promise of the rainbow many times as we experienced suffering that we couldn't understand and tried to be obedient to God's leading. Each day we came to a greater appreciation for the fragility of life and God's sovereignty.

In July of 2000, just before we were to leave for family reunions in Wisconsin and Iowa, we found out that our dog Copain had cancer. He was thirteen and had been looking sick for the previous two months, so it was not completely unexpected. Nonetheless, it could have been anything but cancer and I could have handled it. But this news was devastating. Our vet told us at diagnosis that Copain's cancer was very advanced and he expected Copain to live less than two weeks.

After debating what we should do about our trip we decided to take Copain with us. He always loved trips. As soon as he saw us get the suitcases out he would run around the house in circles and try to escape to the car whenever the front door was opened. He had not gotten to travel with us much over the past year because we were always heading to some hospital. This time, however we did not disappoint him. Once the truck was packed,

Todd picked up Copain and put him on my lap. Cope was very weak, but he managed a feeble tail wag and then fell asleep. He laid on my lap the entire drive. As I stroked his pure white fur, I recalled what a true companion that dog had been. He was Todd's first pet; the dog Todd had always wanted but never gotten when he was a kid. He was our baby during our first four years of marriage. Once Lauren was born, he accepted the transition to "dog" with grace. His only need was Todd's love and attention. He would do almost anything for that including any kind of trick. His specialty was playing dead after being shot with a loaded finger!

I also reflected on how hard this past year had been on this true companion. He was well cared for by friends, but he missed Todd and his family. Every time we returned, he would run like crazy around the yard in pure joy. All he wanted was to be with us, yet it seemed he somehow understood and accepted the separation and his temporary homes.

Once we arrived at my mom's that evening, Copain began to fade fast. Todd and I slept out in the truck with him that night. He labored just trying to breathe. As Todd and I pet him, we talked about what this would be like if it was Tucker we were watching die instead of Copain. We considered the mercy that God was bestowing on us by taking our old dog instead of our child.

At dawn, Todd left with Copain and his guitar. He drove to the veterinarian and sat on the tailgate playing his guitar with Copain on his lap looking over a green valley and oak covered hills until the office opened. It was Todd's way of saying goodbye to this true companion. Copain died that morning.

We buried Copain in my mom's backyard, where we had buried many other family pets in my youth. My mom made him a little white cross and the kids decorated his grave with flowers. On that day the watch that Tucker had given me for my birthday stopped ticking. When I tried to get the battery replaced, the jewelry store clerk told me that the battery was not the problem. She asked if I would like a replacement watch at no cost. Without hesitation, I refused her offer. This watch had sentimental value far out weighing its market value. I put the watch back on my wrist and continued to wear it on a daily basis despite that it had no worldly function or value.

♥

I returned to work after that vacation to some very distressing news. During the week that I was gone, two of my coworkers had been diagnosed with cancer! Both were single women in the prime of life. One was an occupational therapist named Kim who worked on the rehab unit. Unknown to many of us, she had been diagnosed with optical myeloma when she was in college. Now, three years later, this cancer reared its ugly face again. The other was a physical therapist assistant named Hope. She appeared in excellent health; working full time, exercising with me at lunch in the gym and teaching dance classes at night. During the previous week, she had a seizure in her sleep and was brought to the hospital by ambulance. The next day a MRI revealed a brain tumor.

Neither of these two women was extremely close friends of mine. Hope and I had worked together for eight years but never really in the same department. Occasionally we would work a weekend together. Just before I left for vacation we had done just that. I remember our discussion at lunch was about Tucker and his illness. I also remember watching Hope work with a rehab patient in the afternoon and having a "feeling" that Hope would soon be in a storm. Without knowing why, I reacted to that "feeling" by praying for Hope's faith and strength.

Kim was new to our department, but from the first time I met her I knew there was something special about her. She had a zest for life, a presence which made me smile. Whenever we saw each other in the hall one of us would say "Hi Kim S" and the other would respond "Well good day Kim S". This greeting would bring a smile to both of our faces!

As soon as I found out about Kim and Hope's medical conditions, I began praying for each of these colleagues and asking God to show me how I could help them. I didn't want to pry into their personal business but rather be an encouraging voice and available shoulder. I bought them each a copy of *God Calling* and began leaving occasional encouraging notes on their desks. Kim and I began to chat frequently about beating this disease. She shared with me a book called *There is no Place like Hope* by Vickie Girard, three-time cancer survivor. It is a great little book about beating cancer in mind-size bites. It premises is that cancer is fought on three battlefields: the mind, heart and body. The mind and heart must beat cancer first if the body even has a chance. Kim got Hope and me both a copy of this book. Its perspectives opened up the door to many conversations about nutrition, treatment and faith between the three of us.

I was very transparent with both Kim and Hope about the "God Factor" in our fight against cancer. I shared insight I had gained about life and priorities during the year of Tucker's illness: Life is just a finite piece of time that is gone in a vapor. Without faith in Jesus Christ our Lord, there is no Divine help through storms in life and more importantly there is no hope for eternal life. Kim and Hope listened with interest but would rarely vocalize their beliefs and insights with me. One time Kim looked at me and said: "I wish I could be as sure of this faith stuff as you are! I just can't believe without proof." Her words saddened my heart. I could not open her eyes or her ears. Only God could do that. I began praying for her salvation in addition to her healing. I knew she would not be able to receive the blessings God had for her unless she gave up her doubt.

Kim's cancer never went into remission again. Despite Dr. Chen's best efforts, it quickly spread into other parts of her body. She fought with incredible grace for fifteen months. She captained our "Relay for Life" team the next summer despite being weakened by her disease. We walked hand in hand that night around the track with Todd, Tucker, Lauren, and Dr. Chen surrounding us. Neither of us really knowing what the future would hold just embracing the beautiful evening and the support of good friends.

Kim worked up to her last month of life. She gave all she had to help others! Whenever I saw her she would ask about Tucker and Charles. She never complained or let on how much she was struggling. Like my Savior, she suffered with grace. I pray that in the end she was rewarded. On November 13, 2001, Kim slipped away with her mom and dad by her side. She will always be a colleague whose smile and love for life will be imprinted on my heart.

♥

Hope's journey was very different than Kim's, but not less difficult. Her cancer responded to radiation but was not completely destroyed by it. After she received as much radiation as they could safely give her, there were still signs of active disease. The only option was surgery and that option was risky. Hope's tumor was not encapsulated but rather it fingered out into her brain. Hope decided to take her chances and go ahead with the surgery.

In June 2001, two years after Tucker's diagnosis, during the Relay for Life, Hope had that surgery at the Mayo Clinic. Often that night as I walked around the track I thought and prayed for this friend and colleague. I prayed for strength and perseverance for both her and her husband.

I had no idea that night how appropriate those prayers were. Hope's battle was just beginning. Her battle wouldn't be for life, but for function. The surgery was successful at defeating the cancer but at a great price...the loss of speech, and the use of her entire right side.

Hope returned to our hospital about a month later to be rehabilitated. Her hospital room was just two doors away from my office. Each day I would stop in and see her and either I would read "*God Calling*" to her or just hold her hand and tell her about all the stuff happening at the hospital and in Marquette. As I spent time in her room, I contemplated the mood within my workplace. Two years before my colleagues had watched my family's fight against cancer and witnessed God's compassion and mercy on us. A year later they began that same battle with Kim and Hope. Now, another year later, they were witnessing the devastating effects of cancer for both of them. I was sure many were questioning the fairness of these afflictions and how God worked.

I had no answers to these questions except that I indeed knew that life was not fair. But I also knew that God never said that it would be. He said that suffering should not surprise us because we live in a fallen world that includes all sorts of dark, difficult, ugly things. Believers are assured that God will walk through these things with them but not that He will take them away. God's hope is that we will eventually rejoice in our suffering as we will see them as the moments in life that we turned to Him for strength and wisdom; and we watch Him make good out of what Satan intended for evil.

Hope became an extraordinary example of this. Before her cancer, I found her to be a bit whiny and self-centered. After her cancer diagnosis I never saw that side of her again. She never really regained her ability to speak clearly but her she never stopped trying and she did so with such grace. Her boyfriend Andy really stepped up and stood by her. They were married and together they lived a much simpler life. This disease did not destroy their lives. Joy radiated through them as they lived one day at a time. Hope lived fifteen years like this before her cancer returned and took her life.

During treatment, the Schrems, DeGroots and Sprangers were the three amigos...a Divinely created support group for one another. I thought, although never vocalized, that God had a special job for each of our afflicted children and that each would miraculously beat their disease. Because of this sentiment and the incredible love we had for these families, the painful journeys that we joined them on over the next two years was the most difficult to understand and to have peace with.

Despite the cancer growing within Karsha, she continued to feel well through the summer of 2000. We got together for dinner or a picnic with the

DeGroots and Schrems whenever we were in town. Each time, Karsha looked thin, but happy and full of life. Doug and Romani would tell us of a new drug or treatment that they gave them hope. Our family continued to pray for Karsha and her family holding on to the hope that God still was going to miraculously move and heal her.

At nine a.m. on October 19th, 2000 Tucker's fifth birthday; Karsha slipped away to heaven. Sue DeGroot waited to call and tell me the news until after Tucker's birthday party was over. I knew that Karsha had gone into the hospital a week before because of pain but I had no ideas that she was this close to passing. Her physicians had hoped to get her pain under control so she could go home one last time. They had told Romani and Doug that she would probably live a month or so.

The night before Karsha died, she told her Mom not to worry...Jesus was there! Romani told me later that the peace and strength Karsha displayed could not be mistaken. Truly Jesus was right beside her.

Romani's words gave me some comfort but Karsha's passing negated so many false assumptions that I had made. Our children would not all survive their disease .... Would any of them? Were we all being called to become great witnesses for Him? The purpose in putting our families together now seemed unclear. I was very confused.

During the days following Karsha's death, as I struggled with the reality of it, I found my peace and instructions for going on from a verse in Proverbs:

> *Trust in the Lord with all your heart*
> *Lean not on your own understanding*
> *Acknowledge Him in all your ways*
> *And He shall direct your paths.*

As I sang these words, I was inspired with this thought: *"Don't try to figure this out. You can't, not with human perspective. You must trust that in all things I work for the good of those who love me. Your job, Kim, is to acknowledge Me in all your ways and allow Me to direct your path."*

The next day, as I went for my afternoon run I contemplated what I had heard the Spirit whisper the day before. I asked God to direct my path. Immediately I was impressed to look up the story of Jesus restoring life to a young girl in the New Testament. When I returned home from my run, I found the story in both Mark 5 and Luke 8. With great interest, I read how Jesus took the little girl's hand and told her to get up. Just before restoring her, He healed an old woman who had touched His cloak. His words to her were:

*Daughter, Your faith has healed you, go in peace.*

*Mark 5:34*

As I read these words, I felt the Spirit call me to try and restore Karsha, even at her funeral. I knew it was a ridiculous idea without God. But with Him, all things are possible. In the book of Acts, there are many examples of Jesus' disciples carrying out His work of healing and restoring. Our God remains the same, if He used His followers to heal and restore before, He can today as well.

I meditated on this throughout the next morning as Todd and I flew down to Lansing. Mark and Sue picked us up from the airport and we all went to the funeral together. Karsha's casket was still open when we arrived. Doug met us at the door of the church. His shattered look and mumbled words were heart breaking. Romani was near the casket talking with family and friends. As soon as she saw us, she came over, embraced us and began to weep.

Romani and Doug's pain was more than I could bear. As I tried to comfort Romani, memories of my brother's funeral and the incredible pain of goodbye flooded my soul. I so wished I could take this pain from my friends, but I knew that only Jesus could do that.

Before the service started, Sue and I went to Karsha's casket together. I had shared with Sue my revelation about restoring Karsha. She agreed that God could do it, but would He? Karsha looked like a petite china doll lying in that casket. I put my hand on hers. Her hand was so cold and stiff, the spirit so removed, that it startled me. As I rubbed her hand I remembered our park adventure with the "gang" only months before. Karsha pretended to swim across the field to our imaginary island. I recalled our "Barbie party" in the DeGroot's parlor with Lauren and Audrey. I thanked God for those cherished memories. I then squeezed Karsha's hand and said quietly, "If it is God's will, Karsha rise up from this casket." I waited a moment not knowing what more to do and somewhat afraid about what might happen....Karsha did not rise.

The funeral service began shortly after I let go of Karsha's hand. Susie O'Berski joined us for the service. Just seeing her made me feel better. The service began with the song "Lord of the Dance":

*I am the Lord of the Dance you see.*

*Dance, Dance wherever you may be,*

As they played this familiar melody, I closed my eyes and I could see Karsha dancing in the front of the church instead of lying in the casket.

Throughout the service, people of all ages kept coming forward and sharing how Karsha had changed their perspective on life. Her quiet intro-spective way was so refreshing in this loud, busy world. It was truly amazing to see the number of people this nine-year-old had impacted during her short life here on earth. Susie O'Berski sent me note days later, which gave me perspective and some thoughts to ponder. Her note said:

*...God never makes a mistake. Karsha was on this earth just as long as she was supposed to be. It appears from her funeral that she did more good in nine years than many people do in eighty. Remember Kim, it is not the quantity of life, but what you do with the days you are given...*

"*God Calling*" the morning of Karsha's funeral was equally insightful. It said:

### Hill of Sacrifice

*You must trust to the end. You must be ready to go on trusting to the last hour.*

*You must know even when you cannot see...You must be ready, like my servant Abraham, to climb the very Hill Sacrifice, to go to the very last moment, before you see My Deliverance.*

*This final test has to come to all who walk by Faith. You must rely on Me alone. Look to no other arms, look for no other help. Trust in the Spirit Forces of the unseen, not in those you see. Trust and fear not.*

As we stood at Karsha's burial site on the top of a hill, I recalled these words: *"You must trust to the end. You must go on trusting to the last hour. This final test has to come to all who walk by Faith... Trust and fear not!"*

With tears streaming down my face, I prayed for Romani and Doug: "Dear Father help our friends stay close to you and one another. Strengthen their faith; help them to keep trusting in You."

♥

Todd, Mark, Sue and I did not go to the luncheon after the funeral. We did not feel like being social or making small talk. We mourned the loss of Karsha and fought fear for our children's future. So instead of going to the reception we went to a Chinese restaurant for a quiet lunch.

We discussed the implications of Karsha's death. We all agreed that we never thought that Karsha would die of her disease. Karsha had paved the way for Tucker and Charles' treatment. She had been one of the first kids to try MIBG therapy in combination with a stem cell transplant. Her success with this protocol was why they would consider it for Tucker. Karsha always seemed to beat the odds and bounce back; we couldn't actually believe that her fight was now over.

As the four of us talked I could tell that Sue was really struggling with the "what ifs". I shared with her the message in *"God Calling"* that morning and encouraged her to continue to trust and fear not. I knew she agreed with me and was striving to do so, but I also knew that Sue was a worrier and that the following weeks would be very difficult.

Todd and I were scheduled to take the seven p.m. flight back to Marquette. The flight was delayed two hours and then once we were in flight we were rerouted to Milwaukee because of fog. We didn't have any luggage, (not even a toothbrush!) and we were stranded in Milwaukee. Fortunately, the airline put us up in a local hotel.

That night I cried myself to sleep in Todd's arms. The entire world seemed so dark. I missed our kids. I missed Karsha. My heart broke for Romani and Doug and I didn't think that I could handle much more. As I lay there in the darkness contemplating all of this, Jesus whispered: *"you who are heavy burdened give it to Me, I will gladly bear it for you."*

When we finally got home the next day around noon, the sky was brilliant blue, the sun bright and the air, brisk. As I got off the plane and breathed in this air I was encouraged with this thought*: "It is a new day, move into it. Trust and fear not."*

We picked up Tucker from the greenhouse where he had gone to work with our neighbor, Diana. Tucker jumped into my arms as soon as he saw us. Then he ran and got the Hyacinth bulb that he had planted for me. I almost cried as I watched him run and play. I love that boy with all my heart and I appreciated at a new depth the mercy God has had on our family.

♥

When Charles was first diagnosed, the proposed treatment plan was very similar to Tucker's. In fact, many times the physicians at Sparrow used Tucker as an example when telling the DeGroots what to expect in the future. As, however, Charles went through treatment two big differences occurred in their cases. First, Charles' tumor could not fully be removed and second Charles MIBG scans were negative other than the tumor itself. Because of these two differences, Charles physicians decided against MIBG radiation and instead external beam radiation followed by a stem cell rescue using a very different drug regimen than Tucker had.

Sue was thrilled when she learned that Charles would not have to undergo MIBG radiation. She had feared the three days of isolation ever since she heard about it. I was not thrilled, but rather had a pit in my stomach and definite anxiety about this change. Todd felt the same way. We both had been in the room when Doug Schrem had told us, "Don't fear MIBG, fear neuroblastoma! Kids are resilient, they can get through anything! But neuroblastoma is relentless. You have to give it every gun you have the first time!"

I didn't tell Sue of this apprehension; I didn't feel that it would help her at the present as the doctors decided on the protocol, not her. Instead I kept praying for wisdom and discernment for Dr.Yanik and the rest of the team at Sparrow and Ann Arbor.

Charles was scheduled to begin his stem cell rescue in early September 2000. Just prior to the transplant he had a routine bone marrow biopsy. This biopsy revealed two cancer cells in marrow that had been clean of cancer after the first round of chemotherapy. This result was incredibly concerning to Dr.Yanik. Sue couldn't understand his concern. She said, "Tucker had two suspicious cells after his transplant and no one was too excited about that. Charles has his entire stem cell rescue left. Surely that will destroy whatever residual tumor cells are in the marrow." I agreed with Sue because her rationale seemed logical, however, I knew that there was much I didn't understand about this business. I had much confidence in Dr.Yanik, so when he went on high alert so did I.

Charles cruised through his stem cell rescue. He engrafted on September 27th, 2000, nine days after receiving his stem cells. Five days later (on the first day he was allowed to leave his room) he celebrated by running down the hall with his Dad and playing with Theresa in the playroom! I could hardly believe Charles strength and resiliency. Tucker couldn't even walk by the time he was allowed out of his room. He only had enough energy to ride in a wheelchair down the hall and watch the helicopter.

Charles was released from the hospital in early October. He went home and never looked back. His counts improved with each doctor's appointment. The physicians and nurses at the clinic all raved about his progress. Dr.Yanik said at one appointment, "Charles has tolerated this treatment better than ninety-nine percent of all kids I've worked with, what a pleasure this kid is!"

After Charles fully recovered and was past his one hundred days of restrictions, the DeGroots seized the day and took a kid's dream vacation to Disney World (Compliments of the "Make a Wish" Foundation)! They spent five days enjoying the "Give the Kids the World" and Disney. Charles (the king of cotton candy), Audrey and Jonathon were treated like royalty. They were allowed to go to the front of every line at all of the attractions. They could eat whatever and whenever they wanted for free. At bedtime they were even tucked in and read a story by "Clayton Rabbit". Mark and Sue called and told us of their adventure when they returned home. Even their voices sounded rejuvenated. They desperately needed that week of fun.

Two weeks later the DeGroots were on the road again. This time their destination was the Upper Peninsula! It was their first visit to our home and the first visit our families would have that would not involve doctor's appointments, blood draws or central line flushing as an evening ritual. Instead we spent three days enjoying winter and each other U.P. style!! Mark tried skijoring and Todd and I took Sue dogsledding. Todd drove the team from the front sled and Sue and I shared the back sled. Sue was very leery when we started. She told us that she was very not athletic and that she would probably fall off. Once we got into the woods and I taught her how to take turns, push with one foot and steer the sled, she really started to get into it. It was a brisk, sunny winter day. As we slid through the pristine forest with hardly a sound, Sue commented: "I can see why you guys enjoy this...this is such a 'Todd thing' to do... he looks like 'Nanook of the North!'"

The entire weekend was carefree and fun. We went to the Valentine Tea at our church, Lauren's winter fun day at school and the start of the local dog sled race. We celebrated Audrey and Lauren's seventh birthdays and took a group sauna complete with a dip in the snow bank!

In between all these activities we took time to share with each other about our spiritual journeys and life after cancer. On Sunday night we had a great discussion about the purpose of the church and the reason to belong to one. Mark and Sue had gone to church with us that morning. It was a treat for the congregation to meet this family that they had heard so much about and had been praying for so long. Mark and Sue did not belong or regularly attend church back in Mason. Mark couldn't understand the purpose of the church. If someone has a personal relationship with Jesus, why would he need a church? We tried to explain how our church assists and guides our relationship with Jesus; how it provides accountability, mission and ministry for all members. It also is a source of incredible strength and support during times of trouble.

That conversation could not have come at better time. Mark and Sue revisited the subject the next day as they drove back to Mason. They decided to look for a church in their community. Within a month they had found a church that they were very excited about. It was a nondenominational Christian church that welcomed Sue and Mark with open arms. Over the next two months, Mark and Sue developed many new relationships with strong believers within their community. It was a delight to talk with Sue and hear about the church and her involvement in the women's group.

We went down to Lansing during Spring Break for Tucker's one-year follow-up tests. We stayed with the DeGroots and repeated the routine of leaving early in the morning for tests and getting back to the farm for afternoon fun. Tucker tolerated all the tests very well. Dr.Yanik saw Tucker at the end of the week. After examining him and looking at the test results he marveled at how well Tucker was doing.

We had a celebration dinner with the O'Berskis and DeGroots at the DeGroots farm that evening. It was such a blessing to share our victory with the two families that had been God's hands and feet the year before to help us through. Sunday before we headed back North, we joined the DeGroots at their church. Together, we praised God and thanked Him for His mercy.

When we left Mason that day, we knew that Charles six-month follow-up scans were scheduled for the end of April. I began to pray about those tests. I was a little concerned because Charles looked quite pale when we were there, however his energy was great. I knew that God's plan for Charles was good. My prayer was for continued strength and peace for Mark and Sue, and that Charles' sickness would not be unto death but for the glory of God.

♥

Two weeks later as we sat at the dinner table the phone rang. I answered the call and heard the words that I feared and was not prepared to hear. It was Sue. Dr. Kulkarni had called that afternoon and talked with Mark. Charles' MIBG scan revealed a new tumor. It was in the abdomen but not at the site of the original tumor. Dr. Kulkarni said that she did not yet know how they would treat this new disease, as Charles was so fresh from his transplant. She said she would discuss it with Dr.Yanik and get back with them regarding recommended treatment.

I couldn't utter a word in reply. There were no words that would express my sorrow and disbelief at that moment. Despite the loss of Karsha, I had remained confident that both Tucker and Charles would win this battle against cancer. This news was devastating, for we all knew that you have one chance to beat neuroblastoma and if it returns, it is with vengeance.

I listened as Sue cried and vented. I had no answers. I wanted to wrap my arms around her and take away her fear and sorrow, but like with Romani, I could not. I felt grossly inadequate at that moment, a humble human.

After I hung up the phone, I carefully shared the news with Todd and the kids. I wanted Tucker and Lauren to know so they could be praying appropriately for their buddies but I didn't want to fill them with fear regarding Charles or Tucker. Their response to the news was one of hope. They had a very trusting eternal perspective free of fear. Once again, I yearned for the faith of these children.

The next week was a nightmare, even from eight hours away. Mark and Sue met with Dr.Levine at U of M. He was very honest and recommended that they not treat the tumor. He said that a relapse this soon after a transplant was a very serious problem. He predicted that even with treatment, Charles had two to six months to live. This was more information than Sue was ready to handle. Dr. Levine's words penetrated her heart like a dagger. She left the clinic overwhelmed with grief and fear. Over the next several days, Sue tried to process this news and hold it together enough for her kids.

Mark and Sue did not share this news with Audrey or Charles at first. They wanted to wait until they were coping better and until they had met with Dr.Yanik and got his recommendations.

Sue was sure that Dr.Yanik would offer them more hope and at least some possible treatment options. He did exactly that. He didn't give them false hope but he offered a well thought-out treatment regimen of a new oral chemotherapy that had shown promise with other types of cancer followed by MIBG radiation through a study at Philadelphia Children's Hospital.

When Sue shared with us Dr.Yanik's recommendations, I had mixed emotions. I was glad that he had restored her hope; yet, I was saddened that he recommended MIBG radiation. I couldn't help wondering if Charles had gone through the same treatment regimen as Tucker the first time, if his disease would have stayed in remission. I knew these types of thoughts were futile. I could not change the past; instead I needed to focus on how I could help the current situation.

I had such empathy for my friend. She had seen so many difficulties in her young life: the divorce of her parents, her Father's suicide, her Mom's long battle with and eventual death from cancer and now this. I wanted to convince her of God's love for her and help her to rely on Him. I knew that only in Jesus would she find the peace and strength to get through these trying days. However, why would she believe this? Sue felt completely abandoned by God and questioned His love for her. She had grown so much in her faith and had followed Him as best she knew how. She thought she would be rewarded for her faithfulness with a healthy child I couldn't blame Sue for feeling that way, but I knew that was not God's heart. I believed that God, along with the rest of us, cried daily with Sue. I continued to pray that Sue would one day see it that way.

I wasn't the person that God would call to help Sue during this new battle. I lived eight hours away and my son was in remission. I could not help with her everyday needs and my words of encouragement were cheap. God, however, had other Christians in mind to help and support her. These were the people at Vantown Community Church; the very people that Mark and Sue had just joined in fellowship with a few months ago. These individuals acted as Christ commands all Christians to in the parable of the Good Samaritan. They gave sacrificially to help their neighbor. They helped care for Audrey and Jonathon, they brought joy and planted flowers at the DeGroot's home, they were a shoulder and an ear for the hardest days, and they generously sent money to help the DeGroots through this financial challenge.

As Sue and Mark shared with us all the support they were getting from their church, my spirit was filled with awe and joy. I marveled at God's timing with the conversation around our kitchen table in February. I thanked God for leading our conversation that night and leading the DeGroots to that church.

♥

In the middle of May, we went camping with the DeGroots in Petosky. Everything about the weekend was magical, as if it was created by God just for us. The location and weather were incredible. It was early in May yet it was eighty degrees each day. Because it was early in the camping season, the Lake Michigan beach and State Park were freckled with only a few other campers. We spent Saturday building sandcastles and combing the beach for Petosky stones and crayfish claws.

Saturday evening we enjoyed sitting around the campfire eating pudgie pies and listening to Todd and Mark play their guitars. After dinner Sue and I took the kids back to the beach for a sunset stroll. First we watched the kids roll down the sand dune to the beach. The girls climbed and rolled first and fastest. They giggled incessantly as they made their way toward the bottom. Tucker and Charles were two steps behind, striving to keep up and Jonathon struggled just behind them with determination. As I watched Charles, I could hardly believe that this deadly disease loomed within him. He had great energy and color. He ran and played all through the day and again this evening without missing a step.

Sue went ahead to the beach with the kids while I stayed back so I could videotape the moment. For a while I zoomed in on just Sue and Charles as they walked into the sunset. Charles' innocent voice could be heard in busy chatter as Sue looked on with hope and peace in her expression. As I filmed, I wondered what the future held for these two. I prayed for God's mercy and thanked Him for making me so painfully aware of all the blessings I have.

On Sunday before we parted, we all drove up to Harbor Springs for ice cream. We found a quaint little ice cream and chocolate shop just off the harbor. After we all had gotten our favorite dip, another patron took a group picture for us. It was the perfect picture of each of us showing our true colors. The kids "rainbow" and "blue moon" lips and faces complimented their pink noses and happy smiles. The adults looked a little rough without morning showers, but very content.

Sue sent us that picture in a frame which had engraved on it Jeremiah 29:11: *"For I know the plans I have for you,"* declares the Lord, *"plans to prosper you and not to harm you, plans to give you hope and a future."* Below this verse was the word *"JOURNEY".*

Every time I look at this picture with those words, it gives me perspective. We can never go back to that incredible day in May in 2001, no matter how much I would like. It was a day in each of our journeys. A day we were able to travel our roads together. But on the next day, we each would travel our own road. The only common thread that would guarantee that our roads would cross again is God. God promises that His plan is to prosper us, to give us a hope and a future. God cannot lie, He cannot break a promise. That would be a sin and it would separate Him from Himself! If we travel that road with Him at our side then, no matter what, we will have a hope and a future.

♥

Throughout that summer, Charles continued to try different oral chemotherapy drugs to stop the growth of this cancer. Unfortunately not any of them were effective long term. Charles' cancer kept growing albeit at a slower rate than expected. It was decided that MIBG therapy should be tried anyway. Dr.Yanik recommended the study open at Philadelphia Children's Hospital using MIBG in cases like Charles. Sue and Mark prayed about it and God answered yes by opening the door financially and logistically so they went ahead and scheduled it for mid-August, just after Charles' fifth birthday.

The DeGroots had a grand celebration for Charles' and Jonathon's birthdays. They had family and friends from all over the area to their home for a huge cookout and party. It was a true celebration of life that now seemed so precious.

A few days later the entire family plus Mark's fifteen-year-old niece, Krystal, got in the van to begin their Philadelphia adventure. They had done their research and decided to make this into a vacation as well as a hospital trip. Krystal was along to help with childcare and to see Philadelphia with the family. This trip was an adventure, and it started way before anyone had expected. Five hours into the trip, Charles started to complain of a stomachache. Mark and Sue didn't think too much of it and didn't really know what to do about it at this point, so they kept driving. After eight hours, Charles was screaming in excruciating pain. Mark found the nearest local hospital off the highway and went to the emergency room. Within hours, Sue and Charles were flown to Philadelphia via a helicopter. Mark and the rest of the family got back into the van and finished the drive. Charles was admitted to Philadelphia Children's Hospital through the emergency room and immediately the oncology team began to work with them.

They did a CT scan and found that the tumor in Charles' abdomen had grown so fast over the last two weeks that it was now pushing on other organs and vessels in the area causing this excruciating pain. The morphine helped but just took the edge off. Dr. Maris recommended that they continue with the planned MIBG therapy and see if that would slow the disease progression down.

The next day they started the MIBG therapy. In Philadelphia this procedure does not require strict isolation, instead, Charles needed to stay behind the lead shields but Mark or Sue could be in the room. Hence, one parent stayed with Charles and the other took the rest of the family to the Ronald McDonald House and then out to explore Philadelphia. On their second night at the Ronald McDonald House, Jonathon fell off of the bed he was jumping on and split his head open. Sue had just warned both he and Audrey of the danger of such an activity. When she picked up Jonathon to comfort him, she was overwhelmed by the amount of blood that was coming from the gash on his head. Her nerves were already fried from the events of the past few days. She could not believe that this was happening to her. She ran out in the hall looking for help and thankfully there was an employee just outside her door.

They helped her to the emergency room with Jonathon, while Krystal stayed with Audrey. The physicians in the emergency room looked at Sue funny like she looked a little familiar. Once they realized who she was and her "adventure" this week, they shook their heads in disbelief.

Sue called us from Philadelphia that night when she returned from the Emergency Room. As she told me about this adventure/nightmare, I was amazed at her calmness. I "heard" peace in her voice and her words. When she finished, I asked her about this peace that I sensed. She laughed and said, "I just lived through some of the worst days of my life and I have felt the hand of Jesus carrying me. I now know that I can get through anything!"

♥

The MIBG radiation therapy did shrink Charles' tumor substantially. In fact, Dr.Yanik and Dr.Merias were very optimistic about further MIBG treatments for Charles. The only limiting factor in regard to how many MIBG treatments he could have would be his blood counts. When his system required stem cells in order for his red and white blood cell numbers to rebound then it would not be safe to give him any more radiation.

Charles' health returned with the shrinking of the tumor. He no longer required morphine for pain control and he returned to the active carefree Charles that we all adored. For Halloween, Charles dressed in his pirate costume from Disney World and did what Charles does best; charm candy out of women!

Charles continued to do well through October and November. We went down in early December for Tucker's year and a half appointment and scans. Our week together was so much fun. A stranger in the house would never guess our situations. Sue volunteered that it was hard to see Tucker so healthy...it was so unfair. I agreed with her and I was thankful that the difference in our journeys was not destroying our friendship.

One night we all went to a local Christmas tree farm and picked out the DeGroot's tree. The kids were all bundled up in their hats, scarves and mittens. With his hat on, Charles looked just like the rest of the kids. He ran with glee between the rows of trees, giving his opinion on each and enjoying our game of tag. As I played with him and the rest of the kids, I marveled at how good kids are at living for the day and finding the fun in the moment. I believe that it is why I love being around kids and how they keep adults young. They don't worry about getting the perfect tree or what the neighbors think. Guilt, fear or bitterness does not imprison them. Before we left the tree farm, the owner gave each of the kids a small slice of tree trunk to use to make Christmas ornaments. The next day we all sat around the kitchen table painting our ornaments and discussing the Christmas story and miracle of Baby Jesus. When we returned home, I added these new ornaments to the boughs of our tree. As I placed them, I realized it was these kinds of memories that make life so sweet. I believe they will stay in my soul when it leaves this world. They will definitely resurface each year at our home as we pull out those ornaments and put them on our tree.

The day after we left for the home, Sue and Charles flew back to Philadelphia for another MIBG treatment. As they flew, Sue asked God for a sign that all was well. Moments later, Charles told her to look out the window. They were flying above the clouds and the sun cast a shadow of the plane on the clouds. Around the shadow was a rainbow. Later that night as Sue read Oswald Chamber's *Utmost for His Highest* daily devotional she could hardly believe the words. It was titled *"Rainbow in the Clouds"* and it began with the verse from Genesis 9:13: *I set my rainbow in the clouds, and it shall be a sign of the covenant between me and the earth.* Sue stored that "sign" in her heart.

This time the MIBG treatment was uneventful, Charles tumor was under control and he tolerated the treatment fine. Mark, Audrey and Jonathon did well at home thanks to Sue's incredible organization and their many friends.

Unfortunately, Charles did not recover from this bout of radiation like he had after the August treatment. His blood counts struggled to recover because his bone marrow was so beat up from two years of chemotherapy and radiation.

Sue and Charles began to "live" at the infusion center where he would receive blood and platelets almost every other day. Neither of them complained about this necessity. They were kindred spirits who loved spending time together. They spent hours playing checkers, reading, building with Legos and watching Charles' favorite "ScoobyDoo".

As this went on through January it became evident that Charles would not be going back to Philadelphia for more MIBG treatments. If God was going to cure Charles, it wasn't going to be with MIBG radiation. I kept praying for God's mercy and strength for the entire DeGroot family.

God answered my prayers. Charles held his own for the next month; and Sue and Mark showed a strength and peace that I would never have imagined two years before when we first met.

My conversations with Sue were no longer focused on the "the what-ifs" of the future, but rather on the present. I knew her heart was breaking with the realization that her precious Charles may be leaving her soon, but she refused to let the fear wreck the day she currently had.

During one of our late night phone conversations in mid-February, Sue told me about a "ladies night" that some of her friends had arranged for her. They had back stage passes and tickets for the Steven Curtis-Chapman concert in Ann Arbor on March 14th. I could hardly believe that Sue was going to meet Steven Curtis-Chapman!. I recalled how Steven's music had impacted her life and her walk during this trial. My sister DeeAnn introduced Sue to Stevens's music when she was visiting us during Tucker's stem cell transplant. Once

DeeAnn returned to California, she sent Sue the "Speechless" C.D. on a nudge from God. That nudge was right! Steven's music ministered to Sue like nothing else could. It made God's Word alive in her heart; it gave her hope, direction and encouragement. It was as if God spoke through the lyrics of each song.. After I hung up from that conversation, I couldn't get it off my mind. I had a "feeling" about that concert. Somehow I knew that God was going to use Steven to minister to Sue in a powerful way.

Charles was admitted to Sparrow hospital on March 6th at his request. His legs and head were aching so much that he asked to go to the "fun hospital". Mark and Sue took him without reservation. Sue called us from the hospital and told us the news. After a long silence she added, "Kim, I believe that it is the beginning of the end."

Two years before on that very day, we had moved into Sue's aunt's house on Diamond Road. It was the start of our month together. What a contrast of feelings I had this night two years later. I relived many of the moments we had together that month: golf cart chases around the field, rocket blasting, evening trips to the Dairy Hill for ice cream, kite flying behind the barn, our trip to Potter's Park.

DeGroots' situation now almost seemed surreal. I could not believe that this was truly God's plan; that both Charles and Karsha would die of their disease. I wondered if choices and decisions we make keep God's will from being realized or if God's will always prevails? I did not know the answer to this theological question and in some ways I didn't want to know. If it was truly God's will for Charles to die now, I questioned His mercy. If on the other hand, it was not His will and Charles died anyway, then I questioned His power.

I knew better than to let my mind ponder such thoughts. I knew that my earthly perspective was much different than God's. I was in no position to judge the fairness of God's will or question His power. Instead I needed to trust His heart and rely on Jesus to carry all of us through.

Sue's intuition about Charles' condition was right. Once admitted, he began to fade fast. The leg pain and headache they attempted to manage with narcotics and even then it was constant and severe. Despite the pain, Charles got up each day and went with Mark or Sue into the playroom and built with Legos. He was determined to build this one last Lego spaceship. He would sit with his hand on his head trying to control the pain as he searched for the piece he needed.

Mark called on Friday night and relayed this and other stories about Charles' courage and peace. He and Sue knew that the time was near, but they also could feel Jesus' strength upholding them. Todd was not home that night. After some hesitation, he decided to go to a Christian Men's retreat for the weekend. He knew that the only thing that could save Charles now was prayer and what better place to lift Charles and the DeGroots up but with a group of men committed to God's best.

I believe Todd's decision to attend the retreat was the right one. Todd used this situation to glorify God and to recruit others to pray for this family. The conversation surrounding the DeGroots was not only about the tragedy of the situation but more so about how God's strength has upheld them. The conversation challenged and encouraged other men to lead their family in faith and obedience and to trust God even at their darkest moment.

At home I too was focusing my time and attention on prayer for these friends, but in a unique way for me. I had been reading a book about fasting and really felt led to fast as I focused my prayer. I began my fast on Friday night after I had put the kids to bed. Throughout the day on Saturday, I stayed close to the phone and far from the refrigerator! I became acutely aware of how dependent my body was on food and how powerful the feeling of hunger is. I also gained insight into the degree of hunger for God's Word that is possible when the Spirit controls the flesh.

As I cooked lunch and supper for the kids, I was so tempted to just try a small sample of the meal. It was as if Satan was sitting on my shoulder tempting me with the aroma and sight of the food. I resisted his tempting and retreated to my bedroom to pray while dinner simmered. I prayed for God's will in Charles life; that Charles would not die because of a bad treatment decision or the lack of green vegetables in his diet, but rather because God was truly calling him home. I prayed that Charles' life, no matter what its length would glorify God. I knew that God loved Charles (who wouldn't love that kid!) and that Charles was His child, on lease to Mark and Sue. I prayed that God in all His wisdom would do what was the best for the DeGroot family and that they would rely on His strength.

Sunday morning I woke up early. We had all slept out by the fireplace in the living room so I had to crawl out of my sleeping bag without disturbing the kids. Once upright, I nearly passed out. I was nauseous and the room was spinning. I had to sit down on a kitchen stool and leaned over the counter to rest my head in my hands. As I sat there, I contemplated the intelligence of this fast. Was God hearing my prayers differently because I was fasting? Was my suffering having any impact on the DeGroot's situation or was this some dumb exercise in self-denial that was fruitless? I thought about breaking my fast, but the Spirit within me said *"not yet"*. So instead, I washed my face, pulled my self together and returned to the living floor to stretch and pray. At six thirty, I felt a change in my spirit; not miserable or mournful but instead an incredible peace. I knew immediately that Charles' battle was now over. I didn't call Sparrow for confirmation; I just bowed my head and thanked God for His mercy and His love.

When I got home from church, there was a phone message from Mark. Charles had died peacefully at six fifteen this morning with friends and family at his side.

I talked with Sue later that day. She was tearful, but not overcome with grief. She told me of Charles' last twenty-four hours: Charles woke up on

Saturday morning and asked Mark if he could put on one of his ScoobyDoo ties. After much debate over which tie to wear, Charles decided to wear both! He put them both on over his pajamas and then got back up on the bed and asked Mark to turn on his favorite ScoobyDoo cartoon. Charles began watching the show with much interest but soon fell back asleep. An hour later, Mark noticed that Charles' breathing had changed. The nurse came in and verified that indeed his breathing had changed. He was not sleeping; he had fallen into a coma. He remained in that peaceful state until the next morning when he took his last breath.

After I hung up the phone, I again sat at the kitchen counter with my head in my hands. It was over. Charles had really died just like Karsha. But the suffering too was finally over, and oh, how gentle God was with them all at the end. I could think of no better way for Charles to slip away than with his Scooby tie on and a vision of Scooby in his head.

♥

Our family left for Charles' funeral on Tuesday. I was very anxious about the trip. I didn't know how Sue and I would react to one another. My words could not take away her pain and my little boy was a constant reminder of the unfairness of this life. I asked God to give me the right words and keep Sue's heart open to us.

When we arrived at their farm only Sue and the kids were home. Mark was out working on funeral arrangements at the church. The living room was filled with pictures and crafts made by Charles that Sue and some of her friends had put together to display at the visitation and funeral. Sue was on the phone when we arrived, so the kids and I looked through the posters of pictures while we waited. When Sue got off the phone, we embraced. It was a long embrace full of meaning: I love you....I'm sorry...this hurts so much...Can we all go to Heaven now?

We then proceeded to look together through the posters that Sue and her friends had compiled as she told me how her week had gone. It was evident from her words and actions that she was still "numb". She was going through the motions, preparing for the funeral, etc. but inside her heart just couldn't believe that her precious Charles was now in Heaven and that they wouldn't see one another again until Sue joined him in eternity.

All four kids just seemed indifferent to the loss of Charles. Lauren and Audrey greeted one another with their typical smile and giggle and then began looking at pictures together without acknowledging at all what had happened. They did not appear to be grieving or have any emotion to the loss of Charles but rather a "matter of fact" attitude of his death. They enjoyed all the memories that the pictures brought back to life.

Tucker also showed no emotion, but very insightfully, took Jonathon under his wing like he was his new appointed big brother. They played together all afternoon with HotWheels and on the computer with such contentment. This was a huge change for the both of them. Usually Tucker was trying to keep up with the girls and Charles and Jonathon played independently.

All week, I expected some kind of expression from the kids of their loss. It never came. Retrospectively, I know that it was not that they didn't care about Charles, but rather that the finality of death is too abstract for them to understand so it doesn't sadden them like it does adults.

A great example of this came a week after the funeral. During Jonathon's snuggle time he asked Sue why they buried Charles body. Sue replied: "Because Charles is in Heaven so he does not need his body anymore." After a moment, Jonathon said, "Well, why don't we just put it in the basement so we can take it out and look at it once in a while!" Sue and I laughed about this comment, but it truly displays how Jonathon's little three-year-old mind conceptualizes death. Jonathon thinks of Charles as a body, not a spirit -like a toy that he can put on the shelf and take back out and play with at his convenience. The basement is the place where they keep stuff that they really don't need any more but might want someday. Charles' body now fits into that category for Jonathon. These two boys were not that close, nor did they play together much, but still Jonathon wants Charles around like he always was even if he is in a box in the basement.

♥

Mark returned home a few hours after we arrived with all the arrangements finalized. It appeared from his initial comments and expressions that he also was somewhat "numb" to the fact that his little boy had died. He, however, also possessed an unmistakable energy straight from God. As he told us about the details of his day he almost glowed. It was apparent that he was drawing strength and energy from the way that Charles' death was glorifying Christ and how their trial was impacting other's faith.

After Mark finished telling us about his day, he looked over at Todd and me and said, "Hey, have I got a great surprise for you two!" I couldn't imagine what good surprise Mark could possibly have for us and I waited almost in disbelief at his attitude and strength as he shared the plans for the next evening. The visitation was being held at their church in the late afternoon. Mark's surprise was that he had a ticket for me to join Sue and her friends at the Steven Curtis Chapman concert while he, Todd and the kids were at a bluegrass jam session at a family friend's house.

At first both Sue and I hesitated with Mark's plan. It didn't seem quite right to go to a concert the night of your son's visitation. That hardly seemed like mourning. However, as Mark pointed out, this is not just a concert. It was Steven Curtis Chapman's music that had opened Sue's spirit to God's love and mercy and challenged her to "take the dive" and surrender her life to Christ. She played his music whenever she drove; it encouraged her and gave her an eternal perspective. It was too much of a coincidence that this concert was the night before Charles' funeral. As Mark pointed out all of these things, I recalled silently my little "feeling" the night Sue first told me about the concert. I, too, thought it was more than a coincidence and wondered how God was planning to use Steven to minister to Sue. In the end Mark convinced us, and Sue went ahead and made the arrangements for the next evening.

♥

The visitation was held at Mark and Sue's church. As a non-believing friend told me later, "I couldn't understand it. I was expecting an incredibly sad and somber event. I know how devastated I would be if my five-year old had died. The environment that night was not like that at all. It was an atmosphere of hope and joy, not despair; a celebration of life, despite its shortness."

Mark and Sue were totally responsible for the tone that night. Mark was "God's soldier" and he was not going to allow Charles' death to be in vain. He was going to shout from the mountaintops how God had blessed him with this little boy and of the gift of eternal life that would reunite Mark and Charles someday. When the people from the funeral home put on some somber reflective "funeral" music, Sue went out to her car and gathered all her Steven Curtis Chapman CDs. She brought them to the funeral director and asked him to play this music instead. The music, the posters, the conversation and laughter all set the mood in that church. There was joy, and hope. It was a celebration of life and the innocence of childhood. I know that God smiled down on Sue and Mark as He whispered, *"Well done my good and faithful servants!"*

When the visitation was over, Sue and I along with her friends Pam and Marty changed our clothes and jumped in Pam's van to begin our road trip to Ann Arbor. I had met Pam and Marty several times in the past, but really didn't know them. As we drove, we all shared our testimonies of faith and some of the experiences that colored our lives.

We arrived at the Hill Auditorium in plenty of time to meet Steven Curtis Chapman before the concert. After a very cold wait on the front stairs of this old majestic building, the producer of the concert came out and escorted all that had back stage passes to a room behind the stage where we would meet Nicole Nordmann, (the opening act), and Steven.

When Steven and Nicole walked in with the show producer, they both began greeting and signing autographs at the other end of the line. Suddenly, Steven turned and decided to start at our end of the line instead. He walked right over to Sue and welcomed her to the concert. Sue immediately began to cry. Steven responded with such compassion as Pam filled him in on the story behind Sue's tears. Steven listened intently as he knelt at Sue's side. He seemed to forget that there was an entire line of people waiting to meet him, or that he had a concert beginning in twenty minutes. After Pam finished, Steven said: "Sue, I think that God has something for you in this service! This is a very special night. Things have come together for this show exclusively that I never dreamed would. Listen closely to the message for I think it will help make sense out of all of this and encourage you in your journey!"

Before Steven moved on, he signed a copy of the program for Charles' funeral service and he allowed us all to take a group picture with him.

The concert was all that he promised. Nicole Nordmann told the story of her good friends, a married couple who had the story book life, until he was diagnosed with and died from a brain tumor just two years after they were married. After the story, Nicole sang a song that she had written for these friends. It was about the seasons of life. The last season was spring, a time when new life rose from the dead of winter. In the lyrics she described how eternal life is always the final victory for all believers. As Sue listened she kept nodding, as she was reassured of His promises.

Steven's message was *"Live out Loud!"* He shared many stories of over-coming tragedy and living the life that God intends. The most amazing story was that of the Elliot Family. When Steve Elliot was five years old, his family along with four others left the states and traveled to Brazil in the hopes of bringing a savage tribe of Indians called the Melani to know Christ. After about a year of trying to communicate and befriend the Melani, tragedy struck. The savages murdered all the fathers, including James Elliot, Steve's Dad.

The women and children were tempted to give up the ministry and return back to the U.S., but they did not. As they were making the decision of how to proceed, two Melani women came out of the jungle and made peace. That was the beginning a beautiful relationship that brought many of these savages to accept Jesus as their Savior.

Steve Elliot grew up in the jungles of Brazil with the Melani. He had a passion for this ministry just like his dad. As an adult he tried life back in Florida, but found he always longed to go back to Brazil and finish the work that his dad and aunt started. Once he was married and had a family he did just that and another generation of Elliots grew up with the Malani people.

When his daughter was eighteen she left Brazil and went back to the U.S. to tour with a band for a year. Steve missed his daughter immensely and anticipated her return to Brazil. The night she returned was a true celebration with all her family and the Melani. It was also her last night on earth. She died of a brain aneurysm. Steve was devastated by the loss of his daughter. He couldn't understand God's heart in all of this. He had followed God's plan, yet he had to endure so much loss, that of a father and a daughter. As he was trying to work through all of this, he received a letter from Steven Curtis Chapman and some of his CD's. Steven had read the book The Gates of Splendor written by Elizabeth Elliot about their work with the Melani and he wanted to know more about the ministry. Steve Elliot listened to the music that Steven had sent and found the same encouragement and hope that Sue had found.

This story was not told on stage by Steven Curtis Chapman, but by Steve Elliot himself. After he told the first part of the story, the Melani savage who had murdered his Dad came out onto the stage and sang in Melani his version of the song *"I want to be a God Follower"*. As I listened I could see all the good that had come from the loss of Jim Elliot's earthly life, that truly God had a plan for good behind this evil.

After Steve Elliot told about his daughter, he looked out into the audience and said: "For that woman out there, who lost her five year old son to cancer this week, I encourage you to let God write your book and I promise you the last chapter will be awesome." At that Sue nodded and cried with understanding.

Steven Curtis Chapman ended the three-hour service with the song Step by Step. That is my favorite praise song, the one I love to sing in my car at the top of my lungs. My heart was on fire as I joined Steven and the rest of the audience in singing:

*Oh God you are my God and I will ever praise you.*
*I will seek you in the morning and learn*
*to walk in your ways.*
*Step by step you lead me and I will*
*follow you all of my days!*

After the concert was over, the four us walked back to the car bursting with hope and joy. Sue said, "Well I think we kicked Satan in the butt tonight!" She knew, as we all did, that this concert's timing was no coincidence. God did care for Sue and He used the willing hands and voice of Steven Curtis Chapman to encourage her and give her eternal perspective.

♥

The funeral service the next morning was different from the concert, but no less powerful. Mark and his Uncle Lester, a Baptist minister, led this service held in a Catholic Church. That church was chosen because it was the only one in Mason big enough to seat the anticipated numbers. In attendance were many doctors and nurses from Sparrow and the U of M Hospital. Their presence was very special to Sue. It confirmed to her that Charles wasn't just another patient and that her loss was shared by many.

Dr.Yanik sat right behind us and next to Doug and Romani Schrem, Karsha's parents. After the service he looked at both the Schrems and us and said "It has been an honor to sit by such fine people." I could only smile and choke back my tears. Oh how mutual the feeling was.

Mark started the service with his testimony of God's love and Divine plan for his family. This testimony in word and in action got everyone's attention. We each wondered if we would have the faith or strength to lead the funeral service for our child. Mark spoke directly about Divine strength and the goodness of God. He described the joy that he actually had in his heart despite his circumstances. He knew that this feeling was by God's Grace and that God's purpose in today was that others would ask for and receive this Divine Grace.

As Mark spoke, the mood in the church changed, just like at the visitation the night before. Suddenly people were not there to support the DeGroots but rather to find out about this Grace that was upholding the DeGroots at their darkest moment.

Uncle Lester provided that information in a dramatic way as he followed Mark with a powerful message on salvation and the consequences of not accepting Jesus Christ as your Savior. At the end of his message, he gave an invitation for all to accept Jesus into their hearts this minute and led a prayer of salvation.

Again, I could almost feel God applauding Mark and Sue's faithfulness from Heaven. They were kicking Satan around and making incredible good out of what he intended for evil.

♥

Charles was laid to rest in the Dansville cemetery. It began to rain just as we all got in our cars and began the processional to that spot. As I looked out the window, I wondered if the rain symbolized Jesus tears as he bore Sue and Mark's pain. This pain however turned to joy as a rainbow replaced the rain just as Sue and Mark's car drove into the cemetery. Later as I thought about the timing of that rainbow and recalled the verse from Genesis:

*Behold I set my rainbow in the clouds as a sign of My everlasting love*
*for you!*                                                                    Genesis 9:13

I marveled. God had made His presence so clear to our families. He had been at our side, growing us closer to Him, step by step. I closed my eyes and bowed my head in reverence and thanked God for being our true companion.

That evening after everything was over, we went back to the DeGroot's house to wind down and reflect on the day. While I was playing with Jonathon a small strange incident occurred that ended this chapter in life for me. Jonathon was hanging on my wrists and I was swinging him around when he grabbed my watch for leverage. The watch band broke and the entire watch fell on the floor and broke beyond repair. That watch... which Tucker gave me the day our cancer journey began three years ago... which seemed to have God's timing, now ceased to keep time forever. I picked up the pieces of time, just as I knew that Sue and Mark needed to do, and put them in place where I would never lose them, as I prepared myself for whatever tomorrow might bring.

# Chapter 10:

# *Only Believe*

*But when you ask, you must believe and not doubt, because the one who doubts is like a wave of the sea, blown and tossed by the wind.*

*James 1:6*

When I started this book I had no idea what roads we would yet travel or how this book would end. After Charles died, I thought that we had finished this chapter of our lives. God knew otherwise; He knew other fierce storms would come up. He knew that our faith, like a muscle, would become stronger as we endured darkness and relied on Him to pull us through. Just six weeks after we said goodbye to Charles, the first of these storms struck. It definitely was not anticipated... as it was not Tucker.

At that time, I had been writing almost every evening after the kids were in bed. Several times I had told Todd how therapeutic this writing was both as a tool for processing and expressing all that I had learned through our journey. On that particular night Todd had built a fire early and we all watched home movies. Later, after the kids were in bed, Todd and I returned to the floor near the fire. As we snuggled there, Todd asked me if I was going to write. I hesitated and procrastinated as I was tired and the fire felt so good.

We both remained quiet by the fire for a few minutes and then he said: "I am really glad that you are writing. I am curious, what have you learned?" I shared with him what I had recently been working on; the wisdom from *God Calling* that gave us perspective in the middle of the storm:

> **Suffering Redeems:** *All sacrifice and all suffering is redemptive, to teach the individual or to be used to raise and help others. Nothing is by chance. Divine Mind and its wonder working is beyond your finite mind to understand.*

*Another Start:...Why do you fret and worry so? I wait to give you all that is lovely, but your lives are soiled with worry and fret. You would crush My treasures. I can only bless glad, thankful hearts. You must be glad and joyful!*

*Practice Love:...No limit to My Power. Do all you can and leave to Me the rest. Peace will come and Trust. Fear not, I am your Advocate, your Mediator.*

*If Men Oppose: Only believe. The walls of Jericho fell down. Was it axes or human implements that brought them down? Rather the Songs of Praise of the people and My Thought carried out in action. All walls shall fall before you, too. There is no earth-power. It falls like a house of paper, at Miracle-working touch. Your faith and My power- the only two essentials. Nothing else is needed.*

As I shared these things to Todd, I expounded on how true each of these commands and reassurances had become for us. I noticed as I was talking that Todd was really concentrating on my every word and even his breathing was changing; like something was wrong.

When I finished he said in a very weak voice: "Don't ever forget these things Kimmy, don't ever forget!" I then knew for sure that something was wrong. I looked up from where I was snuggled in his arms and said: "Don't tell me!"...I needed not say anymore, I knew by the look in his face. Todd had CANCER!

I could see the tears in his eyes and my heart fell into my stomach. I could not fathom that God would allow another storm to envelop us so soon. I listened numbly for the next half-hour as Todd told me the details.

He had gone in for a regular physical a week ago because he was overdue for one and he had a toe nail that was infected again after it had been ripped off during a game of tag last summer.

During Todd's physical, Dr. VandEnde found a lump in his left testicle and he asked if anyone had ever noticed that before? Todd said that no one had ever said anything and they agreed that a baseline ultrasound should be done for future reference. Dr. VandEnde did not seem overly concerned with the lump so Todd did not schedule the ultrasound urgently but rather set it up at his convenience, which was in one week.

However, as Todd drove home that afternoon from his doctor's appointment, he started to reflect back on his last month. He had not really been feeling very good. Just like with Tucker, not acute or dramatic symptoms, but rather subtle symptoms of unexplainable weariness that he could not shake.

He had not taken the dogs out sledding for the last month despite perfect sledding conditions. He would look at those big strong dogs busting with energy late at night (the time that he usually would take them out) and opt against it. He was just too tired to hook them up.

He also did not have the energy to finish the home projects he had initiated. In the past, while I worked on the book in the evenings he would be out in the garage working on the kayak or finishing up the painting he started while the kids were in school, but now he was too tired. He knew that he should have been done with our home repairs a month ago. He was frustrated with himself because he just couldn't find the energy to get these things done.

After Todd realized this, he became more concerned about the lump and he wished that the ultrasound was sooner. Now he would have to wait an agonizing week to find out if there was really anything wrong or if he was just imagining the worse. He didn't share any of this with me because he couldn't bear to scare me before he knew more. He spent the long hours of that week praying, reading and preparing himself for whatever the next week would bring.

By the time he went for the ultrasound he not only knew that it would illuminate some sort of tumor but he also had a "feeling " on why God would allow this to happen to us again. In fact, he told me later, "I would have been very surprised if the ultrasound would have shown nothing."

After the ultrasound, the technician told Todd to expect a call from Dr.VandEnde by Friday or Monday regarding the results. That definitely was not the case. By four o'clock that afternoon a colleague of Dr. VandEnde's called with the test results. Todd was not surprised to hear the news, that his scan was positive for a testicular mass. She scheduled him to see an urologist the next day.

At that point in Todd's story I started to cry. I looked at Todd and said: "I don't know if I have the energy to go through this again!" I rolled over and sobbed. As I cried, God reminded how exactly right I was. He whispered: *"You don't have the energy, I do! You are powerless. Give me your burden...In your weakness you will find My strength.*

After a good cry, I laid in Todd's arms trying to focus on God's strength and all that I had learned about riding His rainbow. I knew I had to keep my mind from racing ahead to what might happen and seeing myself as a young widow just like my mom. I was scared. Todd having cancer was even a greater fear for me than one of my kids having cancer. At that moment, as if he had telepathy, Todd uttered these same thoughts. He said: "Kim, do you remember early in our marriage, before we even had kids that you told me your greatest fear would be if I would ever get cancer? Do you also remember that when Tucker was sick, you told me that this was tough but because we were a team that you could endure this? Again you were saying that your greatest fear would be if I had cancer. Because of all of this Kimmy, my greatest fear has been to ever have to tell you that I have cancer. Telling you this is the hardest thing I have ever had to do!"

Suddenly the tone of his voice changed as he started to reveal to me the insight that God had revealed to him over the last week that made sense out of all of this. He said: "Kim, this is spiritual warfare! Before Tucker got sick, I don't know if even believed in that term but now I know with all that I am that this is exactly that. Kim, think about how effective of a tool that you have become for God over the last two years. Satan knows that this is his best shot to turn you against God. He knows your greatest fear, he knows my greatest fear and he is going to put our faith to the ultimate test."

I did not sleep much that night. With the same pit in my stomach as I did when Tucker was diagnosed, I cuddled up to Todd and cherished just being able to be there with him. I reminisced about how he had rescued me from the darkness in my life after John died. He was my knight in shining armor. I tried to focus on God's love and His promises to me but I failed miserably. Satan had his way with me until the morning light. Finally at dawn I got up and showered, made my tea and went out into the living room to stretch. As I lay there on the floor I felt completely powerless and exhausted. Then one of my favorite songs popped into my head:

> *The steadfast love of the Lord never ceases. His mercy never comes to an end, it is new every morning. Great is His faithfulness.*

> *Lamatations:3 22-23*

The words "*faithfulness*" and "*new every morning*" gave me much comfort. I closed my eyes and asked God to carry me through this day.

I drove to work with Steven Curtis Chapman "Declaration" CD blaring words of encouragement into my soul. I sang until I actually started to feel empowered by the Spirit. I don't think that Satan could have possibly got into my head during that ride; the music was even too loud for him!

At work, I had a scheduled meeting with my staff first thing in the morning. I debated whether or not I should tell them this news. As I thought about it on the way to work, I was reminded of the verse that God gave in regard to Tuckers health:

> *This sickness is not on to death but for the glory of God, so that He may be glorified through it. John 11:4*

As I meditated on the meaning of that verse the Spirit whispered to me: "*Don't you see Kim, I want to use this trial to reveal myself to others, but I can't if you don't share it with them from the beginning.*" I followed the Spirit's urging and took the last ten minutes of the meeting to share what I had learned from Todd the night before. As I spoke I tried to make eye contact with each of them. I could tell that they were all as shocked as I had been. After I finished we all sat quietly for what seemed an eternity but then as always this group of people loved me, encouraged me and offered their support for anything our family might need.

After lunch, I met Todd over at the medical center for his appointment with the urologist, Dr.Mering. Before we went in, we stood in the hallway, held hands and prayed together for strength and discernment. Both of us knew that the next hour would be very difficult. We needed God to be at our side encouraging us and guiding our conversation and decisions.

Dr.Mering was very direct and to the point. After examining Todd and looking at the ultrasound, he told us exactly what we did not want to hear but what we were fully expecting; that Todd had a tumor and his left testes needed to be removed as soon as possible. I questioned him about doing a more extensive work up or a consult with oncology first. He shook his head no and said: "Time in crucial right now. First we will take out the testes to get rid of the tumor. We will then biopsy the tumor to see what we are really dealing with. If it does appear to be cancerous we will then get oncology involved." His abrupt answer made me a little uneasy as I had been involved with cases before as a health care professional where the oncologist had wished that the surgeon have done a pre-surgical consult. They felt that the patient's long-term outcome would have been much better if chemotherapy would have been initiated before surgery.

Without further discussion, Dr.Mering left the room to see how soon he could get Todd in for surgery. Todd and I sat and looked at each other with tears welling in our eyes. We were now sure that these were not just a few clouds on the horizon, but instead another fierce storm we would have to face...soon! Silently I looked to God for guidance. I felt entirely inadequate to make this decision about surgery. I was too tired and overwhelmed.

God responded by giving both Todd and I peace with at least agreeing to the surgery until we had a chance to talk to some other colleagues of mine. When Dr.Mering returned and offered a surgical date of the next morning! That was sooner than I was hoping, I wasn't sure I would be able to talk with anyone by the then; but I knew that God's timing was perfect and that I had to follow Him, not the advice of other mortals.

After Todd and I left Dr.Mering's office, we split up to prepare for the next day. Todd went to get his pre-surgical lab work and testing done and I went back to the hospital to see if could find any of the oncologists. I found two of them on the oncology unit and filled them in on our situation. They agreed with the treatment approach outlined by Dr.Mering and said that this was the standard of care for testicular tumors.

At home, Todd and I stopped all discussion of the day's events. We didn't want to scare the kids. Charles funeral was too fresh in their minds. We decided that we would cross that bridge when we needed to. Instead, we allowed God to bear the weight of our burden as we made the most of a family night. After the kids were in bed, we built a fire and lay next to it in each other's arms. We didn't say much, we just enjoyed holding one another. Once again we knew that tomorrow would change our lives forever.

The next morning I called work and asked them to cancel all of my patients. Originally I had planned to work part of the day. However once I read *God Calling* and it was very convicting regarding work on such a day. It said:

### I Make the Opportunities

*Never doubt. Have no fear. Watch the faintest tremor of fear, and stop all work, everything, and rest until you are joyful and strong again.*

*...When Paul said, "I can do all things through Christ which strengthens me" he did not mean that he was to do all things and*

*then rely on Me to find strength. He meant that for all I told him to do he could rely on My supplying the strength.*

*My work in the world has been hindered by work, work, work. Many a tireless, nervous body has driven a spirit. The Spirit should be the master always, and just simply and naturally use the body as need should arise. Rest in Me.*

*Do not seek to work for Me. Never make opportunities. Live with Me and for Me. I do the work and I make the opportunities.*

All my patients could be canceled except one. I agreed to see a new lymphedema patient who was coming from a far distance and could only get transportation that day. The Spirit reassured me that would be Okay; hence I knew that God would work out the timing.

Before leaving for the hospital, Todd and I got the kids off to school together and then called a few people to ask for their prayers that day. We made a conscience decision not to tell our families yet. Frankly, we could not bear to tell them, and we didn't have enough information to do anything but scare them. We called Sue DeGroot and Susie O'Berski as well as Linda and Heather from our church. Each of these conversations increased my peace and confidence in God's plan for the day.

We drove to the hospital in silence, just holding hands and enjoying the beauty and freshness of this spring day. Once we arrived at the hospital we hesitated getting out of the car. We didn't want this time together to end. I had to keep fighting off the clenching fear that was desperately trying to grip my heart. Todd sensed this and prayed with me and for me before we got out of the car and made our way up to outpatient surgery.

As we walked together through this place that was so familiar to me, my workplace, feelings of loneliness gripped me. My journey was not like the journey of my coworkers. I was called to something very different today. Once again my world had stopped while others went on. Today, Todd, my strength, my white knight, was the one having surgery. Today I would sit in the waiting room alone, without him there for support, or Lauren there for distraction. Today, I would have to hear the surgeon's post-op report alone. Silently my soul cried out to Jesus as Satan tortured me with these thoughts of loneliness. I knew this was spiritual warfare. I just couldn't figure out why I was being called into such a battle again so soon? Was this a punishment or a promotion from God?

I pondered these things as I helped Todd get checked in at outpatient surgery. As I pondered and sought God's purpose in this, I was reminded of last Sunday's sermon. It was about spiritual relativism and how it is drowning out the voice of Christianity. The point was that today people can't see the truth and power of Jesus's message because there are so many other messages to cloud the picture. When a Christian tries to share how Jesus is working in their life, the response is: "I'm glad you have found something that works for you. Here is what is working for me." At the end of the sermon, the pastor, challenged us not to speak of our faith, but to live it, especially during a crisis! He commissioned us all to make it impossible for those around us to miss the power of the one true God in our lives!

As I pondered these words, I was challenged: What kind of Christian would I be today? Would I be one of God's knights in His battle against Satan? Would people be able to tell that I had learned how to ride God's rainbow? Would I change someone's journey today because of how they see God working in my life during this crisis? Or would I sit there and pout about the unfairness of my situation and how lonely I felt!

♥

After Todd had changed into a gown and the nurse had finished preparing him for surgery, we sat down and spiritually prepared ourselves for surgery. I read scripture and song lyrics to Todd that I had written in my journal during Tucker's illness. These words which were inspired during a storm of the past, gave us much hope and comfort this morning. As I read, Todd remained very quiet and focused. Later he shared with me his prayer during that time: *"Father, I've told you all of my thoughts and fears. I've asked you for healing and to fill Kim with faith and watch over her. I have nothing left. I am again totally helpless in this situation, and now it's too much for me. Father, I give this to you now...Take it from me and just hold me."* God answered Todd's prayer. He filled Todd with an over powering presence of Himself. That presence didn't leave him; in fact it grew and carried him through the entire day.

♥

I escorted Todd to the operating room. As we parted, visions of saying goodbye to Tucker before his surgery filled my head. I could hardly believe that I was now doing this with Todd. As I walked toward the waiting room, I fought off the feeling of loneliness by holding my bible tight, I knew that only there would I find the reassurance and comfort I longed for. God knew my heart; He knew I would need a friend that day: someone to remind me of His love and His promises. He knew just the Christians to call for that job, Linda and Heather, the two women from our church that I called earlier that morning. I saw Linda sitting in the chair over by the window as soon as I walked in. We caught each other's eye and smiled fondly at one another. I slid into the chair next to her and closed my eyes. My neck was so sore from all the stress of the last two days that I could barely hold my head up. I slouched down into the chair and used the back of it to support my head. We sat there for the next few minutes like that; quietly whispering and praying together. Linda knew that nothing she could say could change how I was feeling at that moment, her presence, and her love to support me was all she could give.

After ten minutes I opened my eyes just enough to see Heather walk in. She sat down on the other side of me and for the next half hour she and Linda took turns reading to me scripture and words of encouragement. At one point, Linda reached across my lap and took Heather's hand as gesture of unity. This was unexpected as Heather and Linda had been struggling in their friendship and hadn't spoken in months. With this I died to self and all my concerns for that day and enjoyed for a few fleeting moments being used as God's tool. My neck still ached so I remained slouched in my chair with my eyes closed. However, the rest of me began to feel light and burden free. I had a peace beyond understanding as I listened to them read. I couldn't focus on their words because I was so caught in the feeling within me. I knew that God was now carrying me just as Todd had asked Him to do this morning.

When I finally opened my eyes it was just after noon. Before surgery the nurses had told me that the procedure would probably take an hour. That meant that Todd should be done by now. Instantly, I slipped out of my peaceful place and back into reality. I started to anticipate Dr.Mering's arrival. Fifteen and then thirty more minutes past without any call from the operating room or sign of Dr.Mering. With each minute, I tried to keep my focus and let God carry me, but too many memories of Tucker's surgery flooded my mind... three hours... four hours... a sacrificed kidney... two more hours!

Heather could see that I was losing my peace and she asked me what I was thinking about. After I admitted my fear she challenged me to start claiming the blessings in my life out loud: "My relationship with Jesus my savior...The Holy Spirit that lives within me...A group of Christian friends to love and support us...Mud walks in the spring with my family...Saturday morning with everyone in in our bed...The snow-covered view from my bedroom window.... The touch of my husband's hand...The giggles of my children...The warmth of a fire warming my toes..."

As I continued to claim my blessings, Dr.Mering walked in and called me into the family conference room. He pulled the door shut and filled me in on surgery details. He said that the procedure had gone well without complication. He had taken the left testes and sent it to pathology. Pathology would determine what kind of tumor it was and if any further treatment would be needed. Dr.Mering then said he would see Todd for follow up in ten days and at that time he would discuss the pathology report with us. Until then, Todd needed to rest and heal and to refrain from any lifting or strenuous activity. Before we parted he told me that Todd would be in recovery for a while so that this would be a good time to go get a "donut or something."

His comment reminded that I also had made a commitment to see a patient at 1 pm. It was then 12:55pm. I giggled within, only God has that kind of timing!

I spent the next two hours with a delightful Christian lady and her husband. It was very therapeutic for me to help them. I could do nothing in the waiting room but wait. Here I could focus my energy on something else and be God's tool. When I saw this lady in follow-up three weeks later it was incredible to see how effective the treatment had been. She looked and moved like a different person. It made me marvel at God's wisdom: He used my gifts to help her, and her need to help me.

After I finished seeing this patient, I hurried back to outpatient surgery to see if Todd had returned from recovery yet. When I walked in his room, he smiled at me and reached out his hand. He looked pale and very sore, but his eyes twinkled. For the next four hours, we talked, held hands and just enjoyed uninterrupted time. We shared our experiences of that morning; mine in the waiting room with Heather and Linda and Todd's in the presence of God as he waited for surgery. Our souls grew closer as we experienced God's love and provision at a deeper level.

♥

The next ten days were long. Todd recuperated slowly. I scrambled trying to be there for Todd, caring for the kids and all the sled dogs as well as keep up the house. I quickly gained a new appreciation for what my husband does throughout the day to keep our house running. There were times when I lost my focus and began having a pity party. During these times I was just wanted to sit down and cry "Why me God... Why does my life have to be so tough?"

I have tried to be faithful so why must I suffer so?" I asked these questions in my heart, but I never really expected an answer. I had to cling to my key memory verses that empower me to rejoice in suffering for it builds perseverance, character and hope. I certainly was growing in these three areas that week.

On Sunday morning, I took the kids to church without Todd. Pastor John preached on the love that God has for each of us. He started the sermon telling the story of a young couple in a hospital room after the wife had just had surgery to remove a tumor from her face. The surgery had left her face partially paralyzed. When she woke from her surgery she was horrified at the disfigurement that had been necessary to save her life, she could no longer even pucker her lips to kiss her husband. When the doctor came in he explained that he removed the entire tumor but unfortunately these losses in function were most likely permanent. Her spouse leaned over and wiped his wife's tear then skewed his own lips so that their lips would still match. He kissed her and then said: "That's OK, I kind of like it!"

As I sat alone in our pew, listening to that story, it was all I could do to keep from falling apart. Memories of Todd and my tender moments at the hospital that week, our love for one another, flooded every ounce of me. My love for Todd was deeper than ever and I feared that he may soon be stolen away from me just like my dad and brother.

In the sermon, Pastor John then went on to describe how God's love for each of us is so much greater than even the love of a spouse. He admitted that there are people that he would give up his life for, but there is no one that he would give up the life of his son for. He wondered how great God's love must be for us that He would give up the life of His son for our salvation. Here again, I nearly had to leave. I pleaded with God from within, "Don't you see what a cup it is that you call me to drink from? First you allow me to go through this trial with Tucker and to live with the uncertainly of his longevity and now you allow this to happen to Todd!"

I almost left the service at that point, but I didn't. It was a good thing, because the last point that John made was the point that God did not want me to miss. He said that God not only loves us but He desires to be loved by us and God's love language is obedience. He calls us to be obedient not only to His commandments but to the little nudges He gives us via the Holy Spirit every day.

As I listened, God whispered to me: *"Kim, be obedient to Me on every nudge I give you now; that is the only way that you can receive the blessings I have for you. It is not that I don't want to bless you and answer your prayers, it is that you can't receive My blessings unless you are obedient."*

I left church challenged and focused. I knew exactly where I had to stay if we were going to overcome this trial. I stayed focused through the first half of my week. I successfully juggled my roles as mom, caregiver, provider and supervisor at the hospital. I did not feel overwhelmed, but rather empowered by the Spirit which dwelled within me.

God continued to put in front of me people and words to encourage me. One incredible gift was the book that I had been reading for the past month. (I bought it three weeks before Todd's diagnosis.) The cover of the book was what caught my eye, it said:

*I don't want to quit...*

*I don't want sympathy...*

*I don't want a miracle...*

*JUST GIVE ME JESUS*

Ironically, this book was written by Anne Graham Lotz, the author of *God's Story*, the book that led me to Noah's trial and taught me to rely on my faith to calm my fearfulness. Once again Anne's words were Divinely put in front of me. *Give Me Jesus* described in detail many of Jesus's experiences through the eyes of the disciple John, and how they relate to why we each need Jesus in our lives. Chapter Ten was titled *"Jesus Makes Suffering Understandable To the Sufferer"*. I started reading it over the weekend after

Todd's surgery. I knew as soon as I read the title, that this chapter would be enlightening, however, I wasn't quite prepared for the first three pages. The words written sent shivers down my spine.

Anne started this chapter telling about the day that her 28-year old son named Jonathon was diagnosed with cancer! She told of her initial anguish yet the unprecedented peace that soon followed. This peace came when she turned to what her spirit knew... that her son had been prayed for everyday of his life...that he was born again...and that he was living God's will. Therefore her spirit knew that this suffering was part of God's plan for Jonathan's life and that it would be for Jonathan's good and God's glory. As I read this I knew the same was true for my husband and this trial. God reminded me as I read: *"You must allow Me to reign, then you will have peace, strength and joy."*

Throughout the rest of the chapter, Anne described John 11, the story of Lazarus death and rising from the dead, and explained how God uses bad things to get out attention and to make out testimony stronger. She challenged the reader to be an eagle and not a turkey. "A turkey reacts to a storm by running into the barn and hoping the storm won't come near it. The eagle on the other hand, leaves the security of the nest and spreads its wings to ride the air currents of the approaching storm, knowing the wind will carry it higher in the sky than it could soar on its own."

I knew that this was my challenge... to soar like an eagle through the winds of this storm. In response, each morning for the rest of the week, I asked God to help me be an eagle.

❤

Mid-week, I attended a dedication of an aquarium from Kim Scott's family and friends to the rehabilitation unit. At the reception I saw Dr. Chen, Tucker's oncologist and my good friend. We were both late getting there and stood in the doorway looking in at the gala and missing our dear friend Kim. After a few minutes I asked her if she had heard from her colleagues my news. She looked at me funny and then said: "No, what news?" I went on and told her about Todd's tumor and surgery. She stood there looking at me in shock. Finally I ended with: "Don't you think that is interesting?" Her response was one of disbelief, she said: "Interesting! I wouldn't call that interesting!" She asked me some more questions and then asked if I would mind if she followed up with Dr.Mering regarding the pathology report. I gave her the permission to do so but also let her know that I did not want the results early. In fact, the only reason I would want her to contact us before our meeting with Dr.Mering the following Monday would be if there was something more we needed to do urgently. She agreed to these conditions and as we parted I thanked her for her concern and help. She smiled and said "I would do anything for you guys!" As I walked away, I knew she meant her words and I thanked God for my sweet friend. She was so much more than a doctor.

♥

The next day, Dr. Chen tried to get a hold of me all morning. I was busy with patients and I did not see that she had paged me until I saw a message to call her lying on my desk. That immediately put me on high guard because I had told her to call me about the pathology report only if there was something urgent that we needed to do. I called her back several times that afternoon but did not reach her until the very end of the day. I was alone in a physician dictation room when she took the call.

She started the conversation by asking me how I was doing. I told her that I had been just fine until I got her message. She laughed nervously and said: "I told them to tell you I was just calling to see how you were!" Then there was a long pause. Finally she continued on saying: "I do have some news that I need to tell you." As she started to talk, I could feel my face becoming flush and the entire room closing in around me.

She said that the pathology report had come back inconclusive. She went on to explain that testicular cancer originates in one of three kinds of cells.

The two most common types had been ruled out in Todd's case. However, his tumor cells were suspicious for the third type called a Seritolli cell tumor. She went on to explain this is a very rare form of testicular cancer and in fact, some Seritolli cell tumors are benign, not cancerous. To get a better read on this she asked the pathologist to send Todd's tumor slides to a specialist at Harvard.

I tried to sound hopeful as I thanked her for intervening and getting the slides sent to Harvard. She encouraged me to stay in the day and not to jump to any conclusions. I tried to do just that as I hung up the phone and finished my paper work, but it was all I could do to put my charges in and get to my car before I burst into tears. I cried almost all the way home. When I walked in the door, I tried to hide my fear but Todd saw right through me. He already knew Dr. Chen's news because I had called and filled him in before I left the hospital. After taking one look at me, he knew that I wasn't handling the news very well. He followed me in the bedroom and held me as I cried in his arms.

As he held me, Todd reminded me of the Divine insight and assurance that he had received on surgery day. I tried to rely on Todd's assurance and strength but I just couldn't fight Satan off that evening. It didn't help that later when I was feeding dogs, one of them got tangled and as I was trying to untangle her, the tie-out pole came around and hit me in the eye. The pole hit me so hard that I lost hold of the dog and my contact fell out. The dog ran off and I fell to the ground. That was the last straw!!! I was so discouraged; I just laid there and sobbed! Then I let God know that I was at the end of my rope. I couldn't take anymore.

When I finished my pity-party I sat there and I considered it all. God challenged me with this thought: *"Do you remember the Israelites and how I lifted them from bondage and parted the Red Sea for them yet they still doubted Me when I tried to lead them into the promised land? Well, Kim you have no more faith then those Israelites. Can't see you see how I parted the Red Sea for your family in Tucker's recovery and now I am calling you into the promise land but you must face opposition to get there. Kim, only your lack of faith will delay your receiving all the blessings I have for you."*

I heard God, but it wasn't until the next morning when I read *God Calling* that I knew what to do about it. It said:

### Kill Self Now

*Self-dethroned-that is the lesson, but in its place put Love for Me, knowledge of Me.*

*Self, not only dethroned, but dead. A dead self is not an imprisoned self. An imprisoned self in more potent to harm. In all training- (in Mine of you, and in yours of others)-let self die.*

*But for each blow to the life of self you must at the same time embrace and hold fast the new life, Life with Me.*

It became clear to me as I read that I was imprisoning myself in my own pity. I was of no use to Him, nor could I receive the blessing He wanted to give me because "self" blinded me. In this state I was right where Satan wanted me... the place he could do the most harm. I recalled what Todd told me about spiritual warfare: "Kim you can either destroy Satan's hold on you for once and for all or you can let him beat you." *God Calling* gave me insight on how to beat Satan. I had to forget about my problem and go out and be God's tool just like I did the day of Todd's surgery.

I prayed that morning for strength to do just that. All the way to work, I remained focused as I listened to my favorite worship songs. At work, I looked for God's will in everything and sought to be His tool. Throughout the day, I could feel my spirit begin to thrive as I reached out to help others.

♥

Early the next week, we were to meet with Dr.Mering to discuss the pathology report. The morning of the appointment, I received some unexpected Divine insight. As usual I started my day with my quiet time of prayer and stretching. During that time, God asked me this question: *"Kim, do you remember February 27, 2000?"* I answered: "Of course I do, that is the day that You had told me to claim as my victory day. You had told me that Tucker's counts would begin to rise on that morning and that would be a sign that our battle with cancer was over. I obeyed you and circled that day on his graph and boldly shared your revelation to me with all who asked. All came to pass as You told me it would." God then responded back: *"That's exactly right! I told you that day that your battle with cancer was over. You assumed that I was only referring to Tucker, but I wasn't. You must believe what Todd told you regarding his health. Kim, Todd does not have cancer, but no human will ever be able to assure you of that, only I can."*

Later that morning, I came upon a piece of scripture that confirmed God's words to me. I was standing in the lobby of the hospital waiting for Todd to pick me up for his appointment. As I stood looking out the window I flipped through my journal. Suddenly, a verse popped out at me that I never remember reading, much less writing down. It immediately grabbed my attention because it was from Exodus. Ever since that day in the dog yard when God pointed out how similar I was to the Israelites in Moses' time, I had been looking to that story for guidance in my actions. The verse is a conversation between Moses and God after they have crossed the Red Sea. Moses was looking for God to guide them into the promise land.

> *Now therefore, I pray if I have found grace in Your sight, show me now Your way, that I may know You and that I may find grace in Your sight.*
>
> *Exodus 33:13*

As I read this verse I said to God: "That is exactly how I feel God. If I have found favor in Your sight, then reveal to me your way so I can do what you want and hence find even greater favor in Your sight. God immediately answered: *"I have revealed to you my way...THIS MORNING! Now when you get in the car tell Todd this story, and don't be surprised when Dr.Mering tells you*

*today that he doesn't have any answers. Then whenever anyone asks you how
Todd is doing? You response will be: "Do you want the Doctor's reports or God's
report?"*

Just as this inspiration drifted out of my mind, Todd pulled up. I jumped in
the truck and I told him about my two Divine inspirations that morning. I told
him what would happen with Dr. Mering and in the future with Dr. Chen. He
listened, smiled and said: "OK let's go see if these inspirations are right."

Dr.Mering's appointment was very short. He looked at Todd's incision and
released him back to all regular activities. He also explained what we already
knew about the pathology report and said that the results from Harvard
were not back yet. He said that he had never seen anything like this tumor in
his twenty-five years. I smiled...I wasn't surprised!

Before we left Dr.Mering's office, we scheduled a follow-up appointment
in ten days. He was confident that the report from Harvard would be in by
then. I wasn't nearly as confident. I knew better than to give God a time
frame. I also knew God had a plan and my job was to tell my story and to be
His tool.

That is just what I did. For the next two days whenever anyone asked me
about Todd and how everything was going, I would ask them if they wanted
to hear the doctor's report or God's report. They would laugh and then usually
say "both?" That response was a ticket to my testimony! I'm sure many heard
more than they were prepared to or wanted to hear. I couldn't stop myself.
God gave me a mission and I was serious about accomplishing His will and
glorifying Him through this trial.

On the third day when I was sitting in the lobby of the rehab unit telling
this story to a Cam Williams, a visiting colleague of mine from a nearby
university, I was interrupted by a phone call from Dr. Chen. After the last
phone conversation I had with her at work, and my response to it, Todd and
I had decided that in the future Dr. Chen was to call Todd at home. Recalling
this strategy, I asked my friend who had taken the message to tell Dr. Chen to

call Todd at home. Both Cam and my friend who had taken the message were amazed that I wasn't going to talk with her. We all knew that she probably had the pathology report from Harvard. I explained that I was confident in God's plan for me but I also know how doctors can inadvertently rob people of their peace. I didn't need that in the middle of my day. Both of them then understood and the message was passed on to Dr. Chen. Her response was one of hesitation and then agreement to call Todd at home. However, Dr. Chen asked if I would return her call when I was ready.

Todd called me a half-hour later. He told me that the pathologist from Harvard agreed that it was a Saritolli-cell tumor. He thinks that it is benign, however he cannot rule out that it is malignant. His recommendation was for meticulous monitoring of the surrounding area with regular CT and bone scans for the next two years. This news filled me with joy. It was just as God said; no human would be able to tell me with confidence that Todd did not have cancer. My only peace would come through my faith in God and His power.

For several weeks after that I believed that this chapter of our lives was over. Todd however was not so sure. He did not tell me, but he really wasn't feeling that good. He was still tired and had a nagging darkness within him. He tried to convince himself that it was just because his body was still healing after surgery. He began praying for Divine wisdom in why he was feeling this way. God answered his prayer at church. During adult Sunday school Todd's study group was given a list of verses to read and expound on. Todd was given the verse James 5: 13-16:

> *Is anyone of you in trouble? He should pray. Is anyone happy? Let him sing songs of praise. Is anyone of you sick? He should call the elders of the church to pray over him and anoint him with oil in the name of the Lord. And the prayer offered in faith will make the sick*

*person well. The Lord will raise him up. If he has sinned he will be forgiven. Therefore, confess your sins to each other pray for each other so that you might he healed. The prayer of a righteous man is powerful and effective.*

Todd silently read the verse but felt very uncomfortable reporting on it in class. He was very private about his health condition and he didn't want to draw attention to himself. He read it out loud and the footnotes written in his bible but did not give his "take" on the verse. He also did not go home and meditate on it but rather forgot about it for time being.

The next weekend, Todd's brother, Jeff, came up from Minneapolis for a visit. Todd was planning on telling Jeff about his illness sometime that weekend. Up until this point we had not shared any of this with our families. We didn't have enough information and really couldn't bear to burden them with worry. On Friday night Jeff and I both fell asleep with the kids. While Todd was waiting for us to wake up, he went into our bedroom and read his bible. His bible literally fell open to that verse in James. He read the chapter and as he read, the words became alive to him and he knew exactly what he needed to do. God revealed to him that he must go before the leaders of the church and ask for healing.

Jeff and I did wake up a half-hour later and Todd shared with Jeff the events of the past month. He then shared with both of us the impact that James 5 had on him as he meditated on it. He now knew he needed to go the prayer meeting this Sunday night and ask for healing.

Todd and I were able to attend the prayer meeting together because Jeff was still here and volunteered to stay with the kids. Ten people including most of the church leadership were there that night. We did not currently have a pastor so Todd jumped right in and brought before the group what was going on with his health and scripture from James. Todd's request for intercessory prayer for healing was as new to this group of believers as it was to Todd; and without a pastor to lead us, we felt a little uneasy about how this should be done. However we were all open minded about how God can and does work, and we knew that God would provide what we needed.

We decided to start by preparing ourselves through thanksgiving and repentance and then allow the Holy Spirit to take over. I had brought Frankincense oil with me and we decided that Walt would anoint Todd with the oil since he was the Chairman of the Board. What happened when we began to pray is very difficult to describe. The Holy Spirit led the entire experience. We became unified in our prayers and the feeling of focus and strength grew within us as we prayed. Walt "knew" when we were ready to anoint Todd and we all joined him by laying our hands on Todd. Our prayers were then answered as Todd experienced healing!

Afterward we were all emotionally and physically drained...except Todd, he was "on fire" with more energy that he can ever remember having. The next day I had to come home from work at midmorning, I felt so horrible. I went right to bed and slept for six hours. Many others who had been in attendance had similar days. We were all wiped out even the next day. Todd, however, finished the painting the ceiling, went for a bike ride and cared for the kids. He felt absolutely great. During the prayer meeting he had felt the darkness leave him and he was filled with a great glowing light. He was now riding on this light with a feeling of unexplainable peace and joy.

♥

After this experience at the prayer meeting, life started to return to "normal" (if there is such a thing for us anymore). The kids finished up their school year, which included Tucker graduating from kindergarten. Tears filled my eyes and I thanked God for His mercy as I watched Tucker perform in the class skits and receive his diploma. I wondered why God had answered our prayers and spared our child. I knew this question had no answer... it is part of the mystery of God that is not for us to know.

Todd was scheduled for this three month follow-up testing and appointment with Dr. Chen on the week on June 11th. That was the same week as
Tucker's diagnosis, my birthday and the annual Relay for Life event. The
Sunday before that appointment, Pastor John was again preaching at our
church. It was "graduation Sunday" and he targeted his message toward
those whom were graduating from school and beginning a new chapter in
their lives. His words hit hard with me, as if the Spirit was telling me to listen
closely.

John's sermon was titled *Breaking All the Rules: Developing a Great
Commission Lifestyle.* His text was from Matthew 28:19-20, Jesus's Great
Commission:

> "All authority in heaven and on earth has been given to me.
> Therefore go and make disciples of all nations, baptizing them in
> the name of the Father and of the Son and of the Holy Spirit and
> teaching them to obey everything I have commanded you. And
> surely I am with you always to the very end of the age."

After John read that scripture he described the spiritual war that we are all
involved in every day. Jesus' commission was both a command and a promise.
We are to go... and He will be with us along with all the authority in heaven
and earth! John then went on and gave an analogy that almost brought tears
to my eyes. He pulled out a baton used in track relay races out of a paper bag.
A baton identical to the ones I had carried throughout my high school and
college career as the anchor of the mile relay team. He asked us what this
was. After we responded correctly, he said that the great commission is kind
of like a relay race. God handed the baton to Jesus. Jesus ran his leg of the
race and now He is handed the baton off to us. Our job is to run for all we are
worth and most importantly "DON'T DROP THE BATON!"

John made four suggestions on how we run that race with the most
success:

1. Have the right focus. Counter the culture of materialism and self-centeredness and take up your cross daily. (Luke 9:23 and Proverbs 14:12)
2. Slow down your pace. Busyness is a sin that often separates us from God. God calls us not to say "yes to all but say yes to the best".
3. Radicalize your faith. Make your life and actions match what you believe.
4. Prioritize your passions: remember people are more important than things!

After the service, I tucked my notes neatly into my journal where I could find them. I knew that the upcoming week had the potential to be very challenging and my soul already knew that something was brewing. I had asked two friends to keep me in prayer and I spent extra time Sunday night in prayer for strength and peace.

Early in the week we celebrated Tucker's victory over cancer. As Todd and I put him to bed that night we praised God for His power and thanked Him for His mercy and for giving us the privilege of raising this special little boy. The next evening we celebrated my 37th birthday quietly as a family along the shores of Lake Superior. As I walked hand and hand with my husband along the pristine beach, I knew that all I ever wanted was right here with me: my God, my spouse and my children. I stayed in the day, just enjoying the touch of Todd's hand and the joy in the kid's play. I tried to forget that the next day we would meet with Dr. Chen and get the results of all of Todd's follow-up tests.

After I finished work the next day, Todd and I met at Dr.Chen's office. I was a little late so Dr.Chen went into to see her next patient first so she could have more time with Todd and I. When the nurse told us that, I immediately went on high guard. Todd reassured me that it was just because she knows that I am a talker. Todd even said as we waited: "When are you going to stop coming to these routine doctor appointments of mine." I told him, "I'm here because I care and I can't wait for these appointments to be routine!" Dr. Chen walked in one minute later and this quickly became anything but a routine doctor appointment.

Dr. Chen started by telling us about the conversation she had with a Dr.Einhorn, the leading expert in testicular cancer from the University of Indiana. She called him after our last appointment because she wasn't comfortable just watching and waiting for any malignancy to develop. Dr.Einhorn recommended that Todd have a surgical resection of his retro-peritoneal lymph nodes as a safety measure to remove any malignant cells that might be present. This surgery would have to be done at the University of Indiana.

Todd and I already knew that Todd was healed and hence we weren't quite sure what to do with that recommendation. We sat there in silence for a moment and then I asked: "Well how did all of Todd's scans look? Were they all negative for malignancy?" Both Todd and I were shocked when Dr. Chen shook her head no. As she began to explain what the bone scan had shown I could feel all the emotions of three years ago begin to fill my soul.

I tried to listen but I couldn't believe that this was happening to me again exactly three years to the date from when we left for Lansing with Tucker! Todd held my hand and gave me a reassuring squeeze as Dr. Chen told us about a large area of increased metabolic activity on Todd's left hip. She said that this could be bone metastasis from the testicular mass, or a sepa-rate distinct bone cancer, or some other benign neoplasm. Todd and I both knew that either of the first two possibilities were bad news. We knew that if the testicular mass was malignant and already in the bone that nothing could be done. We also knew that bone cancer in the head of the femur meant a possible amputation as well as chemotherapy and radiation. We really couldn't believe these results.

After Dr. Chen finished telling us the results she told us that she had already contacted the University of Indiana and they would accept Todd as a patient. She recommended that we go down there for a surgical consult for the lymph node resection and definitive diagnosing of this femoral mass. As she described to me what films and records I would need to pick up and take with us, I shook my head in disbelief. I interrupted her and said, "Do you realize that this is exactly the same thing we were doing three years ago with Tucker?" She looked at me with pity, handed me a Kleenex and said "yes, I know." I responded: "I don't need a Kleenex, I am not devastated, I just perplexed about God's plan in all of this." There was a long pause as we all considered the coincidence of these events and then I added: "If I have learned anything it is to trust God, He has carried us through so much. No matter what, I believe that His plan for us is good...He promises He will never leave us or forsake us. I trust God. We don't really know anything yet, we just need to go where He leads us and see what happens!" Todd and Dr. Chen agreed and we departed cautiously hopeful on what the next week would bring.

All the way home and through dinner I kept my hopeful demeanor. It was Wednesday night, which meant bible study and prayer meeting. I couldn't think of any place I would rather be that night but in God's house; with the people, who have supported us, prayed with us and loved us through this entire ordeal. At the prayer meeting however, I lost my hopefulness. When I was in God's presence I couldn't deny that at this moment I was overwhelmed by today's news and what tomorrow might bring. I was beginning to sink as Peter did when he tried to walk on water because I was seeing the size of the waves not Jesus and His saving power.

Later that evening, after the kids were in bed, Todd finally called his mom and dad and told them what was going on. I wasn't there to support him. I was under a blanket on the couch crying myself to sleep.

The next morning I called my secretary and told her our news. I opted not to go to work, but rather to accompany Todd to the additional scans that Dr.Chen had ordered and to make the arrangements with the University of Indiana. I'm quite sure I was not really any support for Todd that day as my attitude waxed and waned between being fearful and angry (even though I knew that it was wrong) with periodic moments of peace and hope. I was embarrassed but I just couldn't change it.

While Todd was completing his CT scan, I went to my office to make arrangements for the next week. Thankfully no one was around when I first arrived, so I was able to get to the business at hand. I first called Ann Arbor and canceled Tucker's tests and appointments scheduled for the upcoming week. I then got in contact with a social worker at Indiana University Hospital and began learning about that health care system and what we would need to do there. After I had finished making these arrangements, several of my staff members and my boss came into the office. I could hardly speak to them without becoming emotional. My boss, Cathy was very insightful. She said: "I know what this is. This is spiritual warfare! Satan is trying with all his might to shut you up! Don't let him, Kim. We are all here for you and we will do whatever it takes to help you beat him!" I knew she was right. I also knew that no one could take the first step to beating him but ME! I had to stay focused and rely on the Holy Spirit to lead me.

♥

Before I left the office, I gave my "Relay for Life" stuff to another member of the team. Once again that race against cancer was being held the same day that we were beginning our new cancer battle. The memories of three years ago and the coincidences were too overwhelming for me at that point. I didn't even know if I wanted to go. On the way home, we discussed it. I told Todd that I just wasn't sure if could handle seeing all those luminaries of lost loved ones (including Kim and Charles) around that track, or if I could actually get up and deliver my "in remembrance" speech about Kim Scott. Todd reminded that with God's help I could do those things and I would grow from the experience. It was Satan who did not want me there and it was my choice. *I could overcome evil with good* or I could sit home and wallow in my own pity!

I knew that Todd was right. So after a nice run together we packed up our stuff, picked up the kids and went to the relay. I will never regret that decision. We beat Satan up that night! We forgot about our circumstances and allowed the spirit to flow through us. Our team, called "KIMMER"S HOPE" in honor of Kim Scott and Hope Pool, dressed as Hippies and sold tie-die T-shirts and face paintings at the front of our campsite. We supplied a baton (that Tucker and Lauren had painted) to each team. Todd and Tucker walked in the survivor's walk proudly and I gave my "in Remembrance" speech about Kim Scott.

All night our team took turns walking around the track. I walked/ran at three a.m. by the light of the luminaries. As I ran around the track I reflected, prayed and listened. At first, I reminisced about last year's Relay, walking the track with Kim Scott, Dr.Chen and my entire family. What a day of victory that was! Now bags "In Remembrance of Kim" lined the track. Satan tried to bind me with fear about what Todd and/or Tucker's bags would say next year: "In Honor" of or "In Remembrance of". Quickly, I put those fears aside. I knew that no one knows their hour, and to spend life in fear and worry is futile and sinful.

At five a.m., after I passed off the baton and was heading into our tent for a few hours of sleep, Tucker and Lauren jumped out of their tent and asked if they had woken up in time to walk with me. I was very tired but I couldn't say "no" to their sleepy, dirty yet very enthusiastic faces. We walked together for a half-hour, taking time to read many of the bags and talk about what the next week would bring.

Up until that time we had never used the "cancer" word when talking to the kids about Todd's illness. However, Lauren had heard them announce Todd's name as a survivor last night and now she had some questions. As we walked, I gently explained to the kids about "daddy's sickness". Both of the kids accepted my explanation and immediately went on to something else. I was so envious of their faith and trust. I longed for it.

The relay ended the next day with the "Pie in the face" finale. The pies were to be thrown at the team captains who had the most and least money thrown into their "pot" during the relay. The previous night when they had announced the totals, I had the least with only six cents. Thanks to some good friends who were there at that time, I finished with the most money and hence still "received" a pie. Just before noon under the pavilion, in the drizzle, they auctioned off the right to throw the pies. People kept handing Todd dollar bills so that he could up his bid. He eventually won the honor to throw my pie. With much love, he smashed the cream pie in my face and then leaned over and gave me a big smooch so that he could enjoy the pie with me!

As I drove home that afternoon, I pondered all the events of the Relay... how our presence had glorified God. We used the situation that Satan put us in to show others the power of faith. When others who knew our situation watched us they saw that our joy and love were genuine. They saw our faith in action and how we were riding God's rainbow. I smiled as a tear ran down my cheek.

♥

The next day, Sunday, was truly a Sabbath day. Todd had a MRI scheduled for 10am. So instead going to church we all accompanied him into Marquette. The kids and I played outside while Todd had his test and then we all spent the afternoon hiking up Sugarloaf Mountain. When we first started up the mountain there was a split in the trail and a sign that had two arrows, one said "difficult trail" and the other said "easy trail". We all read the signs and then in unison said: "Let's take the difficult one!" A few hundred feet down the difficult trail I contemplated that decision and our triumphant attitude. I looked at Todd and said "Don't we ever take the easy path in life!" We all laughed at that and made up a song about taking the difficult path.

Once at the top of the mountain, we looked out over Lake Superior and the beautiful red rock cliffs dropping into the Lake. There wasn't a cloud in the sky and the brisk fresh air refreshed our souls. After appreciating the view for a few minutes the kids went off and found a place to play while Todd and I found a rocky outcrop to sit down and chat. I rubbed Todd's shoulders as we shared our insight and what we were "hearing" in prayer. An hour later as we walked down the mountain holding hands Todd shared with me how much he needed this today. He needed to know that I wasn't losing my faith...that I would rely on God and trust Him no matter what.

On our way to Indiana, we took the long way and stopped in Iowa first. Todd's mom had volunteered to watch the kids while we were in Indiana; and Todd's dad, Ken, had rearranged his schedule so he could accompany us to Indianapolis and stay at least for the first few days. The kids were very excited to stay with grandma and to have time with their cousins who lived in the area. To them, this seemed like what they always did during summer vacation. Todd and I wished we could feel that way. Despite all the peace that God had instilled into us, going to the clinic in Indiana was scary. We had seen Christians suffer through many trials before and we knew that God's plan here on earth is not always understandable. With these thoughts in my mind and a lump in my throat we left for Indianapolis. As I waved goodbye to the kids, I wondered when I would see them again and how different our world would be by that time.

The trip to Indianapolis was uneventful. We stopped for a lovely dinner and just enjoyed quality time together. It was so infrequent that we had uninterrupted time with just Ken. We caught up on all his latest news and discussed the "God Factor" in all that was presently happening to us. We found our way around Indianapolis including our hotel and the hospital. We all headed to bed immediately after checking in so as to be ready for whatever the next day would bring.

We rose early the next morning. Todd's dad went for a three-mile walk while Todd and I prayed, read God's word, and held each other. I had become so deeply aware over last two months how much I loved Todd, how much his touch meant to me. I savored each minute I had with him that morning.

As part of our morning routine, I read *God Calling to Todd*. Its words were our marching orders for the day. It said:

### Miracles Again.

*Wait to hear My Will and then obey. At all costs obey.*

*Do not fear. I am a wall of protection around you. See this. To see this with the eyes of faith is to cause it to manifest in the material.*

*Remember I long to work miracles, as when on earth I wrought them, but the same condition holds good. I cannot do mighty works because of unbelief.*

*So only in response to your belief can I do miracle-works now.*

After I finished reading I looked over at Todd. He smiled and said that he was praying for a miracle. From the tone of his voice I could tell that he was focused on God and trying not to let Satan overwhelm him with what could happen this day.

When we met up with Ken at the McDonalds next door to our hotel, the first thing he asked was if we had read "*God Calling*". When I smiled and nodded yes! He grinned back and hugged me and said: "That is soooo cool!"

We arrived at University of Indiana Cancer Center in plenty of time, which was good because we had no idea where we were going. As had been the case with the entire trip so far, we didn't need to know where we were going; we just put God in charge and He took care of everything. I drew much strength and peace from His presence as we made our way into the cancer center.

I had no office number nor did I see a directory inside the door so I picked up the telephone at the information desk. I explained to the friendly voice on the other line that I was here with my spouse, Todd Spranger, and we had an appointment with Dr. Steven Williams, Director of the University Of Indiana

Cancer Center. I was amazed when the voice on the other line replied: "Well good morning Mrs. Spranger. We have been expecting you. Dr. Williams has received all of Todd's information from Marquette and his team is upstairs waiting for your arrival! If you just get on the elevator to the left and come up to the second floor his office is the second one to the left."

Once we arrived at Dr. Williams' office, the service continued to be extraordinary. The social worker was waiting there for us. She immediately identified us as the "Sprangers" and took some time to see how we were coping and to find out how she could assist us. Five minutes after we finished meeting with her, we were taken to an exam room and the first resident came in as soon as Todd had changed into a gown.

Over the next half-hour several different doctors came in the room after looking at all of Todd's films and asked him many questions. They all wanted to know how his hip felt...could he move it without pain... and how long had it been bothering him? Todd's reply to all these questions was: "My hip didn't hurt until Dr. Chen told me about the positive bone scan. Now it seems to be hurting more every time someone asks me about it. To me it feels like regular arthritic pain from football. I can still do my biking and jogging without any more pain than usual."

Todd's reply seemed to perplex each one of them. They mentioned some of the additional tests that they might order to figure out what this thing in his hip was. Dr. Chen had mentioned these tests as possibilities so we weren't surprised when they were suggested, however I had a deep peace that Todd wouldn't be doing any of them.

At last Dr. Williams came into the room. Immediately I liked this man. He had big smile on his face and warmth exuded from him. After He introduced himself he looked at Todd and said: "You don't look sick!" Just as enthusiastically, Todd replied "I don't feel sick!" Dr. Williams then went on to explain why Todd had his colleagues so baffled. He said: "Todd you are a very complicated case. The type of tumor you had is very rare. We have only seen seventeen cases of this here ever! Because there are so few cases to compare it to, we can't tell from the histology of the tumor if it is malignant or benign. If it is malignant, we would expect for it to travel up toward your shoulders and back, not over to your femur."

As he talked he examined Todd. When he finished he shook his head and repeated: "Boy you sure look healthy". After a long pause, he added: "Well I don't have any answers for you right now. What I need to do is to take your MRI's, x-rays and bone scan downstairs to our radiologists and get their opinion. If you can be patient, I will return with some answers."

After he left, Todd and I stood and looked at each other speechless. We knew that Satan was playing the game of Russian roulette with us. The gun (cancer) was pointed at Todd...when Dr. Williams returned, we would find out whether it was a bullet (rare spreading cancer), or a blank (a benign tumor).

After a long moment of silence, I asked Todd if he would like me to read to him. I had been reading the book *Intercessory Prayer*, by Dutch Sheets to him as we drove to Iowa. Todd nodded yes, and I began to read. After a few paragraphs, I knew that I wasn't supposed to be reading about the power of intercessory prayer, I was supposed to be doing it. I shut the book and asked Todd if we could pray instead. Again he nodded yes.

We began by thanking God for His ever-present support and guidance over the years with Tucker and Todd's health and the privilege we had to be His followers. We then prayed for Divine wisdom for the doctors regarding this mass in Todd's femur. That they would know that this wasn't cancer. We repeated the truths that He had shared with both us and declared them as truths. We asked Him to fulfill the prophecy that He had foretold to us.

After a while we began to pray separately. As Todd prayed he was filled with an overwhelming peace which calmed all of his fears. He recalled the reassurance that he had received just prior to his surgery that he would not need chemotherapy or radiation to cure his cancer. He recalled the powerful healing he had received at the prayer meeting. By the time he finished praying he was sure that he would not need any more treatment.

With this reassurance Todd stated: "Kimmy, I am bursting with peace and I know that everything is going to be okay." I smiled and hugged him, for my prayer time had brought me to exactly the same peace.

Dr.Williams walked in a few minutes later. As he sat down across the room, he had the most peculiar look on his face. Then instead of giving us the answers he had promised before left. He asked us more questions. Specifically he looked at Todd and said: "What do you think this is?" I could hardly believe his words. Never before had a physician, especially one with this much expertise and prominence, asked Todd or I what we thought about anything medical. Todd replied: "I feel great! I know that I have been healed and although I don't know what that thing is on my bone scan, it isn't cancer."

Dr.Williams smiled and then looked at me waiting for my opinion. First I said: "Do you really want to know what I think?" He nodded yes. So I boldly said: "I'm not in denial, nor am I some desperate woman who cannot handle that my husband might indeed have cancer. God told me that this man does not have cancer and I believe God!" Again Dr.Williams smiled and then replied "I believe you! While I was looking at all of Todd's scans with the radiologists it suddenly crystallized in my head what this wasn't. I don't know what it is, but it is not cancer. I'm so sure that I am not even going to recommend a biopsy of his hip. It is not worth the time or the money."

Todd and I could hardly believe Dr.William's words. We both just stood there with our mouths hanging open. Once again God had saved us from the wrath of Satan and his fiery flame. Never before had we witnessed our prayers being answered in such a direct way. We prayed for Divine wisdom and Dr. Williams received it. The Spirit "crystallized" the wisdom in his head just as we prayed!!!

Dr.Williams then addressed the other reason we were sent to Indiana: the recommended lymph node resection surgery. He told us that it was recommended purely as a preventive measure. It was impossible to know if Todd's tumor was benign or malignant unless the lymph nodes were removed and studied by pathology. If the lymph nodes did contain malignant testicular cancer cells, then that surgery would be the only possible cure. Dr.Williams then went on to explain that this was all only theoretical. Todd's case was so unique and this type of cancer so rare that he had no case study or research to base his recommendation on.

We then discussed the pros and cons of having the surgery and tried to get specifics about the surgery itself: how invasive was it... possible side effects... can any general surgeon perform it... and how long does it take to recover?  Dr.Williams explained that surgery itself was tricky and that the surgeons at this institution had actually developed the least invasive way to do it. Hence he recommended that if we decided to have the surgery that we do it there. Dr. Williams could not answer the rest of our questions, instead he gave us the surgeon's name and contact information and encouraged us to do so before making our decision.

Before Dr.Williams left the room he said that in his report back to Dr Chen he was going to recommend the surgery but he really did not have any strong feelings either way; it was for us to decide. After he left, we hugged each other as our eyes filled with tears. Once again, God had saved us from the Satan's scheme to destroy us.

After a few minutes, Todd went back to the lobby to get his dad. While he was gone I pondered all that had just happened. I was awed by God's presence in my little insignificant life. Why did God show us so much favor?

My thoughts were interrupted by Todd and Ken's return. Todd told his dad all that had happened over the couple of hours. His dad hadn't really understood the reason for and the possible outcomes of this doctor appointment when we went into it. He thought that we were meeting with Dr. Williams primarily to see if Todd should have that second surgery as a precautionary action. Only now did he understand that the bigger question was: Does Todd have metastatic, incurable cancer in his hip? As we filled Ken in, he just kept shaking his head and saying "Thank you Jesus!"

We left the clinic and went out for a celebration lunch. As we ate, we discussed God's favor. We came to the clinic that morning mentally prepared for tests and surgery etc. and a prolonged hospital stay. We left two hours later without even a blood test! We all knew that only Divine intervention could result in what we just experienced. We also knew that the intimacy and closeness to God that we felt could only be experienced after walking through a storm like this with Him! We enjoyed a great lunch and drive back to Iowa complete with folk and blue Grass music and great conversation!

We spent the next several days visiting with our families in Iowa and Wisconsin. We shared our story over and over with different members of our extended family. Each time the story seemed more amazing. I was almost giddy as I told of God's compassion and faithfulness. I wanted to shout from the mountaintops how real God is and how intimately He wants to know and be a part of our lives.

♥

Over the next month we considered the surgery that Dr. Williams spoke of. We prayed together about it but did not discuss our feelings until we each were "sure" of God's will (as to not sway the others opinion). During that time I came upon some excellent guidelines written in the footnotes of my bible (in Jeremiah) about making faith–based decisions. The following are ten questions that one should ask and pray about when faced with a decision:

*1- Have you prayed about it? The Lord's Prayer begins with a petition for His will. Prayer was never intended to be a fourth-down punting situation in which we ask God to bail us out of our hasty decisions. It was intended to be a first down huddle. We aren't supposed to ask God to bless our plans; we are supposed to ask God for His plans!*

*2- Is your decision consistent with the Word of God? What does scripture say about others in this situation? The Bible is alive. Let the two edge sword of God's word speak.*

*3- What direction would make you a positive Christian witness?*

*4- What would glorify the Lord? Are you seeking the glory of man or the glory of God?*

*5- Are you acting responsibly? God doesn't bail us out of our irresponsibility. He will let us suffer the consequences of our sins and irresponsible choices. But when we are faithful in little things, he will put us in charge of greater things.*

*6- Is your decision reasonable? God expects us to think. His guidance may transcend human reasoning, but it never excludes it. God doesn't bypass our mind. We are warned is scripture (Philippians 4: 8,9) not to put our mind in neutral. We are to think and practice what we know to be true.*

*7- Does a realistic opportunity exist? Closed doors are not meant to be knocked down.*

*8- Are unbiased, spiritually sensitive associates in agreement? Take your dilemma to a close unbiased Christian associate and give them permission to ask hard questions and give their honest opinion.*

*9- Do you have a sanctified desire? The joy of the Lord should be our strength so ask yourself: Is this a desire to satisfy a lust of the flesh, or a Spirit-filled desire to see God's kingdom established and people helped.*

*10- Do you have peace about it? This is an inner peace. In the world you will have tribulation, but in Christ we have assurance of overcoming the world. Be sure that the peace of God is guarding your heart and mind regarding the decision that you make.*

These guidelines reinforced our decision not to have the surgery. We both knew what God had revealed to each of us about this trial. To Todd, God revealed before surgery that no more treatment would be needed. To me, God revealed that no one would ever be able to tell me for sure that Todd did not have cancer. I needed to trust Him alone. We knew that God healed Todd at church and if we doubted that and went ahead with the surgery we would not be glorifying God nor would we be living His will for us.

When the surgeon's office first contacted us, Todd allowed them to set a surgery date because we hadn't made our decision yet. The available times became a closed door. The only time they could do the surgery was when we were supposed to be in Ann Arbor for Tucker's follow-up appointments (the appointments we had to cancel to go to Indianapolis the first time). Later, when I talked with the surgeon's secretary I told her that I wanted to know more about this surgery before scheduling it. She told me she would have the surgeon call, but he never did. All these conflicting times and unreturned calls underscored our initially conclusion that it was not God's will for Todd to have lymph node dissection surgery.

Todd and I discussed this one evening on the beach of Lake Superior. It was a beautiful summer evening for a picnic and playing in the sand. After we played tag up and down the water edge with the kids and walked through the water to Little Presque Island, we sat down in the sand and talked while the kids built sandcastles.

We talked about how everything all seemed to direct us toward not having the surgery. We both especially identified with the very last guideline: neither of us had any inner peace about having the surgery. We knew little about it and no one seemed to want to tell us much except that we had to go to Indiana because it was a delicate surgery.

We decided as we watched the sun set over the lake to cancel the current surgery date and take Tucker downstate for his checkup. While down in Lansing we would meet with Mike and Susie (unbiased spiritually-sensitive friends) and seek their wisdom. If they had a different opinion or different insight then we could always schedule the surgery for a later date.

That was the right decision. Our week in Ann Arbor was without flaw. Tucker tolerated all the tests, pokes, prods and waiting like a champ. All of his test results were great and we had great times of fellowship with both the DeGroots and the O'Berskis. One afternoon, Todd and Mike went on a two-hour walk while Susie and I chatted and played with the kids on the trampoline. After hearing our stories, Both Susie and Mike supported our decision not to have the surgery. They even gave us an example in their own family where someone had gone ahead with radiation treatment after God had healed them and in the years since has had many complications because of the radiation. We all agreed that God would not stop blessing us if we decided to have the surgery, however, we might miss other blessings that He had for us and we may suffer consequences of not following Him. He doesn't force us to follow Him but He doesn't control the outcome if we don't.

A few days after we returned home, Todd called the surgeon's office and let them know he had decided not to have the surgery. He called me at work right after he hung up for reassurance. He said: "Every time I pray about this decision, I have much peace about not having the surgery. However, whenever I talk with healthcare people they make me feel like I am crazy. This makes me anxious and causes me to question my decision." I reassured him that few live in close communion with God and hence they cannot understand the "God factor" in decision-making; they can only see solutions that the world can offer. We know that God can heal and we are confident of His healing in this situation, we must not allow other's opinions (especially those who know little about us), sway our decision.

Todd thanked me for my perspective. He hung up the phone and closed the book on that chapter of his life. He was now ready to move forward and receive whatever blessings or opportunities God had planned for him.

# Epilogue:
# *Riding God's Rainbow*

After journeying and journaling through all of this, what is my conclusion? What does it mean to ride God's rainbow? I believe it is a mindset, a way of life that allows you to receive God's favor (blessing).

In the book, *Prayer of Jabez*, Bruce Wilkerson tells the story of a new arriver in Heaven that is getting a tour from St. Peter. The man asks about the huge, mysterious warehouse-type building he sees on one of the side streets. Saint Peter tells him this building is "off-limits", and encourages him to forget he ever noticed it. The man's curiosity is only sparked by St.Peter's reply and he begins to plead for a tour of the mysterious building. Finally St. Peter agrees to take him, but warns him that he will be sorry. In the warehouse there is row after row of boxes wrapped with red ribbons, each with a name on it. The man realizes that he, too, has a box and runs to the "J" section to find his box. Before he opens it, Saint Peter once again discourages him. The man does not listen and hastily opens it. Inside, much to his disappointment, he finds all the blessings that God wanted to bestow on him while he was on earth; blessings that were blocked by fear, doubt, disobedience, pride, self-righteousness or the lack of faith.

I believe that God wants to bless all of us. But often we are the limiting factor on whether He can. I do not believe that God will spare us from tragedy because He knows it is through tragedy that we grow closer to Him and see the favor He has for us. Instead He allows Satan to rule this world and blesses His people as they go through spiritual warfare against Satan. He blesses them with unexplainable peace, joy and hope if they are open to receiving it.

In the years since this story took place we have opened and closed many chapters in our lives. We have experienced life in all of it fullness. Todd was called to be a pastor of our small rural church and he has served this congregation in a mighty way for years. He has not had a re-occurrence of testicular cancer and is still an avid bicyclist.

Tucker is now a mechanical engineer. When he graduated with honors from college, I marveled at all the mercy and favor God has showered on this young man. Tucker has made his faith his own and is now exploring all the ways that God can use him to make this world a better place.

Lauren was blessed with an amazing ability to run. She was cursed with Type 1 diabetes. This blessing and curse truly molded her into who she is today. She won many high school and college running honors including All-American all the while having to manage her blood sugar. She now is a health coach who comes beside people and helps them restore their health though nutrition.

We were blessed with a third child in our mid-forties. It was another boy! We named him Will because truly we knew he was God's Will. His middle name is Isaac which means laughter and that is so appropriate. He brings such joy and laughter to our home.

I too had to deal with the curse of cancer. I was diagnosed with breast cancer at forty eight. It is a whole story of its own but the outcome has been the same; because of God's mercy and favor I have not only overcome the curse but have been able to use it for the good, to help other woman in this situation and point them to Jesus.

Through each of these life chapters I have experienced God's love creating the rainbow. His love is the ultimate of all blessings. When you feel God loving arms around you, you have a light, an energy that is indescribable. To ride the rainbow is to allow God to favor you ...to see where God is working and move toward Him, and to align your will with His and be ready for anything!

♥

I want to conclude with a final story from the days when Tucker was recovering from cancer. This story I think beautifully illustrates what happens when we ride God's rainbow.

After going through Tucker's cancer experience, I was much more aware of and sought out ways to help other families going through this trial in my community. One day a seven-year-old boy was admitted to our rehab unit with a brain tumor after being in a Detroit hospital for ten months. I had read an article about him in the newspaper months before and had been praying for him and an opportunity to provide support to his family. Now literally he was staying in a room two doors down from my office. After he got settled in, I stopped by his room after work and introduced myself to his Mom, Heidi. Heidi had been expecting me as a mutual friend had told her about our situation and that I worked in the hospital.

Heidi and I immediately bonded. Our situations, including our careers in health care, roles as provider in our family, and our son's quick diagnosis and treatment downstate, were so similar. She had endured so much and just wanted some hope that things could get better. I could totally relate to her longings and I did my best to restore her hope and direct her to Jesus.

With her permission, I shared her family's story with Todd and the kids. We all began to pray for them. At dinner each evening, I would update my family on her son's progress and prayer needs.

Things continued this way for a couple of weeks and then one morning in the office I heard that Heidi's insurance company would no longer pay for rehab; hence her son would be discharged soon. My heart ached for Heidi and Al with this news. I remembered when Tucker was first diagnosed and the social worker told me that our insurance was denying Tucker's need for hospitalization, I was devastated. The last thing I needed at that time was a financial concern. I was sure that Al and Heidi must feel the same away.

Suddenly I remembered that we still had money that people had given to us when Tucker was sick. We had used it to pay for expenses when Tucker was receiving treatment and for other needy cases when they had presented themselves, but now it had sat untouched in its own savings account for a while waiting for God to reveal what we were to do with it. I "knew" that it was God's Will for us to give the rest of the money to this boy's family.

I called Todd to see what he thought of the idea. He agreed and volunteered that he and the kids would pick me up from work and then all of us could meet this family and give them the money.

Todd, Tucker and Lauren arrived on the rehab unit around dinnertime. I was supposed to have withdrawn the money during my lunch break, but because of patient care needs, I did not have time to get to the bank. After I explained this to Todd, we decided to just go and meet this little boy and I would give them the card and money the next day.

When we walked in his room, the little boy was in bed, but awake. His dad and brothers were there with him. They were so happy to meet Tucker for they knew all that he had been through. Just seeing him restored their hope. Tucker and Lauren went right up to the boy's bed and tried to interact with him although he wasn't able to speak or communicate with them at all. I was so proud of our kids and the compassion they showed.

When we left, we decided that we wanted to get the money and take it back up there to them as a family. At the bank, we were pleasantly surprised at the amount of money left in the account and without hesitation withdrew all of it in one hundred-dollar bills. We put them in our hand-made card and went back to the hospital. We handed the card to Tucker before we went back in the room. Tucker went up to the bed of this boy, who had now fallen asleep and gave the card to his Dad.

His Dad looked at us not quite sure what to say. We told him that this was not our money, but rather money that had been given to us out of love and concern. We were just passing the blessing on!

This little boy's name was **Noah**! Noah...the person God had given the first rainbow to, with whom we were now sharing a piece of our rainbow!!! We were blessing others as God had blessed us. **We were riding God's Rainbow.**

# Our Family's Journey

Our Wedding picture. Did we have any idea back then what it meant when we said" I do" to "in sickness and in health"!

Hiking trip weekend before our whole world changed!

Lauren carving her pumpkin in the playroom after reverse trick or treating the nurses and patients at Sparrow hospital.

Tucker's fourth birthday. He was looking so good before that big surgery!

Tucker's favorite Christmas present...the 4 wheeler that really had a motor!

The DeGroot Family: Jonathon, Mark, Audrey, Charles and Sue.

Tucker in the middle of the transplant. Two IV poles full of drips and things keeping him alive.

Tucker's senior picture with the boat that he rebuilt!

Lauren's high school senior picture.

The tattered sign that hung first on Todd's back and then in our car for months after Tucker was diagnosed.

The playroom at Sparrow hospital....Our new home over that summer. Todd was such a oood daddy letting the kids play doctor on him!

This is the bookmark we made and handed out as a thank you for all the healing prayers.

The O'Berskis and the Sprangers.... Kindred Spirits!

Our daily companions on this journey: the Bible, God Calling and Tucker's Jesus picture.

Tucker on engraftment day!

**Returning a favor**

Young cancer victim helps raise funds for kid's hospital

Article in the local newspaper about "The Great Ride of Faith"!

Article in a UofM publication about MIBG, a revolutionary treatment for Neuroblastoma where their featured Tucker's recovery.

Noah Michael Wernholm: our Noah that we blessed as we had been blessed!

# About Kim Spranger

Kim Spranger is a wife, a mom, a physical therapist and a God follower. She never aspired to write a book but when God gave her such an amazing story she just had to share it. It took her twenty-two years to finish this book. Mostly because she had to watch the story unravel in order to answer the question: "How does one ride God's rainbow?"

Kim lives in the Upper Peninsula of Michigan with her husband and family. She loves early morning horse rides with her husband and daughter, soccer with her son and dog Molly and playing the hammer dulcimer on the front porch.

Professionally she loves restoring mobility and hope to those with movement limitations. She has been part of the development an amazing new device called the NewGait (www.thenewgait.com) that is now being used by patients and therapists across the country to restore peoples' ability to walk.

You can reach Kim at 906 235-1739 or at Sprangerkim@yahoo.com.

Made in the USA
Monee, IL
02 July 2021

72784556R00154